FRONT OFFICE
OPERATIONS AND MANAGEMENT

For Emma and Ellie

FRONT OFFICE OPERATIONS AND MANAGEMENT

Ahmed Ismail

THOMSON
DELMAR

Australia   Canada   Mexico   Singapore   Spain   United Kingdom   United States

THOMSON

DELMAR

Front Office Operations and Management
Ahmed Ismail

Business Unit Director:
Susan L. Simpfenderfer

Executive Editor:
Marlene McHugh Pratt

Acquisitions Editor:
Joan M. Gill

Developmental Editor:
Andrea Edwards

Editorial Assistant:
Lisa Flatley

Executive Production Manager:
Wendy A. Troeger

Production Manager:
Carolyn Miller

Production Editor:
Joy Kocsis

Technology Project Manager:
James Considine

Executive Marketing Manager:
Donna J. Lewis

Channel Manager:
Wendy E. Mapstone

Cover Image:
© (Pete Turner Inc.) Getty Images/
The Image Bank

Cover Design:
Joy Kocsis

Composition:
Lawrence J. O'Brien

For permission to use material from this text or product, contact us by
Tel   (800) 730-2214
Fax   (800) 730-2215
www.thomsonrights.com

Library of Congress Cataloging-in-Publication Data
Ismail, Ahmed.
    Front office operations and management / Ahmed Ismail.
      p.cm.
    ISBN 0-7668-2343-1
    1. Hotel front desk personnel. 2. Hotel management.
I. Title.

TX911.3.F75.I86 2001
647.94'068—dc21   2001047674

NOTICE TO THE READER

Publisher does not warrant or guarantee any of the products described herein or perform any independent analysis in connection with any of the product information contained herein. Publisher does not assume, and expressly disclaims, any obligation to obtain and include information other than that provided to it by the manufacturer.

The reader is expressly warned to consider and adopt all safety precautions that might be indicated by the activities herein and to avoid all potential hazards. By following the instructions contained herein, the reader willingly assumes all risks in connection with such instructions.

The Publisher makes no representation or warranties of any kind, including but not limited to, the warranties of fitness for particular purpose or merchantability, nor are any such representations implied with respect to the material set forth herein, and the publisher takes no responsibility with respect to such material. The publisher shall not be liable for any special, consequential, or exemplary damages resulting, in whole or part, from the readers' use of, or reliance upon, this material.

Contents

CHAPTER 6   **Front Office Overview** **134**

CHAPTER 7 Room Rate Structure 169

CHAPTER 13   Measuring Hotel Performance 308

CHAPTER 14   Guest Service 319

Preface

INTRODUCTION

This text introduces concepts of organization, communication, ethics, and policy within a hotel. The primary focus is the front office, housekeeping, reservations, and night audit departments. Other departments are discussed to provide an understanding of how these departments relate to the front office and how they operate to enhance the guest experience. An introduction of basic analyses, techniques, and trends both in policy and technology will be reviewed as they relate to management and the guest. This text is intended to give students a "real world" perspective of the hotel industry. *Front Office Operations and Management* balances the need to see where hotels have been, and where they are going.

WHY THIS TEXT?

As an instructor, and hotel industry veteran, I felt the need to write a text on the front office that portrayed the nature and operation of hotels as they exist today, a text that revealed the inner workings of a hotel in a way that both promoted learning and interest in the reader. This text prepares the student for what to expect in the current and future hotel market. The Property Management System has changed the way hotels operate, therefore this text devotes extensive time to this technology. Because the hotel industry will always be about and for people, this text devotes chapters to both the hotel guest and hotel employee. The arrival chronology is discussed from arrival to departure. Additional chapters feature analysis of the physical makeup of hotels, yield management, and operational techniques. Performance measurements and analysis of what makes a truly successful hotel are discussed in detail.

SPECIAL FEATURES

This text is organized logically so that each chapter builds on the previous one. Considerable effort was made to ensure that *Front Office Operations and Management* was presented in a way that promotes learning and discussion. Several unique features are incorporated to provide learning tools that encourage thinking "outside the box." These features include:

- *"Industry Perspectives."* Industry professionals wrote this feature element. They reinforce concepts and introduce new points of view. Cutting-edge trends in the industry are discussed.

- *"About My Job."* This feature, written by actual employees, relates real-life viewpoints on various job roles.

- *"Internet Resources."* This feature gives students Web sites to research topics covered, either on their own time or as class projects. Numerous opportunities are presented to incorporate the Internet into class discussion.

- Numerous case studies, exercises, and critical thinking discussion questions end each chapter. In addition, all chapters have ample review questions.

- Dozens of photos, charts, and graphs illustrate and reinforce concepts throughout the text.

INTERNET DISCLAIMER

The author and Delmar affirm that the Web site URLs referenced herein were accurate at the time of printing. However, due to the fluid nature of the Internet, we cannot guarantee their accuracy for the life of the edition.

INSTRUCTOR'S GUIDE

The Instructor's Guide gives educators state-of-the-art tools to teach with, in keeping with the timely nature of the text. The features of the guide include:

- Answers/talking points to discussion questions and exercises
- Suggestions for additional exercises, lecture topics, guest speakers, and hotel tours
- Answers to end of chapter review questions.
- A test bank of additional questions (with answers) for each chapter, as well as completed sample tests and quizzes.

Acknowledgments

The author wishes to thank the professionals who gave of their time, expertise, and knowledge in the planning and writing of this textbook.

Sarah Suggs
KSL Resorts

Jill Reyes
Corporate Meeting Services

Jamie Doyle
Indianapolis Marriott North

Pete VanOverwalle
Westin Indianapolis

Rick Shuffitt
Adams Mark Hotels

Wendy Hensley
Crowne Plaza Union Station

Douglas Reddington
BSA Design

Dominic Russo
Omni Hotels and Resorts

Thomas Roth
Indianapolis Marriott Downtown

Jeff Beck
Columbia Sussex Hotels

Glenda Arnold
Indianapolis Marriott North

Kathy Bannasch
Embassy Suites Hotels

John Pohl
Lexington Convention and Visitors Bureau

Carol McCormack
Omni Severin Hotel

Linda Brothers, Ph.D.
IUPUI

Ted Stumpf
Omni Los Angeles Hotel

Malcolm Jennings
Hyatt Hotels and Resorts

Thomas Errigo
Marriott Hotels and Resorts

Stacia Howard
Seattle Marriott Sea-Tac

Erik Olsen
VingCard

Mecheal Johnson
Execu/Tech Systems

Clark Williams
TPE Research

Jason Bean

Richard Haberman

Michelle Quick

Lori Harris

Jeff March

Darlyne Freedman

Stephany Brush

Kristin Wunrow

Penny Woodruff

Jackie Schult

Delmar and the author also wish to express their thanks to the content reviewers. Their input and expertise added greatly to this text.

Patrick Beach
William Rainey Harper College
Palatine, Illinois

Robert McMullin
East Stroudsburg University
East Stroudsburg, Pennsylvania

Maria McConnell
Lorain County Community College
Elyria, Ohio

David Hanson
Idaho State University
Pocatello, Idaho

Deanne Williams
Bethune-Cookman College
Daytona Beach, Florida

Tim Hill
Central Oregon Community College
Bend, Oregon

For additional hospitality and travel marketing resources, visit our Web site at <**http://www.Hospitality-Tourism.delmar.com**>.

About the Author

Ahmed Ismail is an acknowledged authority in the hospitality industry. Currently serving as a university instructor and working in the meetings industry, he received his Bachelor of Arts in international management from Gustavus Adolphus College in St. Peter, Minnesota. His professional experience spans many years in hotel operations, sales, catering, and marketing with the Marriott, Hyatt, and Renaissance Corporations. He is currently considered a pioneer in the field of meeting consolidation technology. He is a sought after speaker and has received numerous awards for leadership and innovation. He is also the author of *Hotel Sales and Operations* and *Catering Sales and Convention Services* (Delmar/Thomson Learning).

Hotels—
Past and Present

OBJECTIVES

After reading this chapter, you should understand:

- The historical origins of the lodging industry
- The various relationships between lodging ownership and management
- The three keys to a hotel's success
- The importance of room sales

INTRODUCTION

The hospitality industry is a fascinating and ever-changing field. This area of study can be very rewarding. Many concepts and innovations developed by the hotel industry have found their way to other fields. The student of hospitality gains insight into the intricacies of management, customer service, accounting, leadership skills, and food/beverage operations to name but a few. Hotels, due to the many disparate disciplines functioning under one roof, have been referred to as "miniconglomerates." Indeed, the successful hotel manager is easily able to change industries, as the many skills learned in a hotel can be applied elsewhere.

HISTORICAL PERSPECTIVE

In order to fully comprehend the intricacies of the modern hotel, it is important to look at its origins. The history of lodging can be traced back to the civilizations of Sumaria and ancient Egypt.[1] Indeed, the need for a place to stay away from home is as old as the first nomadic traveler.

Trading between cultures created the need for groups of people to travel often great distances. Along these trade routes, certain stopping points became favored out of necessity. An oasis in the desert or a mountain pass in winter became logical places for trading caravans to rest. Areas where different trading routes intersected also became favored stopping points. These **junction points** often grew into trading centers. Many junction points eventually evolved into cities.

Along trade and caravan routes without junction points, a different type of stopover location evolved. When traveling over vast distances, people were limited by their mode of transportation and the supplies they could carry. A **journey segment** is the maximum reasonable distance traveled in one day along these routes using the transportation of the day. The length of a journey segment by camel or horse was significantly longer than the journey segment on foot. At these journey segments, lodging facilities became a need. They were called relay houses in China, khans in Persia, and tabernas in Rome.[2] Whatever they were called, these earliest lodging facilities began a tradition of hospitality that endures today.

> *"A good traveler has no fixed plans, and is not intent on arriving."*
>
> –Lao Tzu

As the history of lodging unfolded, innovations began to emerge. At some point, innkeepers began to incorporate food and beverage service in their operations. This led to a change in the way people traveled. No longer did people have to carry enough supplies for an entire overland journey. They simply needed enough to get them from one journey point to another. Another development was the Roman network of roads that crisscrossed Europe and parts of Asia and Africa. These roads provided fast and safe routes for travelers, which created new junction points and journey segments. The industrial revolution of the mid-1700s created new modes of transportation that further changed the way people traveled.[3]

As the evolution of lodging continued, new facilities began to emerge as an option for travelers. The wealthy and landed aristocracy of the world began to view the many spare rooms in their castles and estates as sources of revenue. Generating money in this fashion assisted them in maintaining these expensive holdings. The best examples of this can be traced back to the English and colonial inns of the 1700s.[4] Each fulfilled the need for housing of travelers by renting spare rooms. The significant difference between the two was that colonial inns offered rooms to anyone who could afford to pay, whereas English inns were most often reserved for the aristocracy. Indeed, the word *hotel* is the Anglicized version of the French *hôtel garni*, which translates into "large, furnished mansion."[5]

Another difference between the two was that English inns rented out individual sleeping rooms, whereas colonial inns regularly offered large rooms with several beds inside. This meant that English inns could offer private guest rooms, whereas colonial inns were better suited for communal accommodations. Monasteries also provided accommodations similar to the colonial inns, albeit in a typically more spartan environment.

The first lodging facility that can be directly considered a precursor of the modern hotel was the City Hotel built in New York in 1794.[6] It is a significant milestone in the evolution of lodging because its sole purpose was to house guests. All the previous inns were homes first, and lodging facilities second. City Hotel's 73 rooms made it quite large for its time.

The emergence of railroads and later the automobile played large roles in lodging's history because both dramatically increased the lengths of journey segments for a traveler. For overland travel, the endurance of animals always limited the length of journey segments.

In 1829, Tremont House was built in Boston.[7] This property was another milestone in the early evolution of hotels. By the standards of the day, it was considered the first five-star hotel. Highly trained staff, French Cuisine, and luxuriously appointed rooms combined to give guests the finest hotel experience available ever to that point. Amenities the Tremont House offered, such as in-room water pitchers and free soap, were considered revolutionary.

From the mid-nineteenth century to the early twentieth century, the railroad became the dominant form of overland travel in America. As the country expanded westward, the railroads brought people and supplies from the east. New junction points emerged along these railroad lines. These junction points eventually evolved into cities like Chicago and St. Louis. All along these railroad lines, the various junction points served as trading centers that needed lodging facilities.

At about this same time, in the established cities in the east, the lodging industry began its modern evolution. In 1908, Ellsworth Statler opened what many believe to be the first "modern" hotel, the Buffalo Statler.[8] It is considered to be the precursor of the modern hotel because of the many innovations Mr. Statler incorporated into his product. These innovations, considered commonplace today, were revolutionary at the time. In addition to setting the first real standards for cleanliness and guest comfort, these innovations included:

- Fire doors

- Installation of light switches inside the door so that guests could enter a lighted room

- Private bathrooms
- Key holes placed directly above doorknobs for easy access
- Circulating hot and cold water in each room
- Full-length mirrors
- Morning newspaper

"Necessity is the mother of invention."

—Popular Adage

The Statler Hotel Company went on to achieve great success. Until the 1950s the Statler Hotel Company was a major force in the industry. It is ironic that one of Mr. Statler's two contemporaries would end up buying his company. The famous names of Mr. Statler's contemporaries are Hilton and Marriott. It was Conrad Hilton who would eventually buy the company of his former rival.

In 1919, Conrad Hilton purchased his first hotel, The Mobley, in Cisco Texas.[9] In 1925, he built the first hotel to carry the Hilton name in Dallas. In 1938, Conrad Hilton opened his first hotel outside of Texas, the Sir Francis Drake in San Francisco. By 1943, Hilton had properties from coast to coast. In 1945, as World War II ended, Hilton purchased what was the largest hotel of its time, The Stevens, and renamed it the Chicago Hilton and Towers. In 1949, Hilton leased one of the most famous hotels of all time founded by the legendary William Waldorf Astor, the Waldorf-Astoria. Hilton would later buy the hotel outright.

In 1954, Hilton purchased the Statler Hotel Company in what was then the largest real estate transaction to date. Throughout the 1950s and 1960s, Hilton expanded domestically and internationally. In 1979, the founder, Conrad Hilton, died. His son, Barron Hilton became president and continues to run the company today.

The other contemporary of Mr. Statler's who played a pivotal role in the modern hotel industry is J. Willard Marriott. Mr. Marriott began as a restaurateur in Washington, D.C., in 1927.[10] The Hot Shoppes restaurants owned by Marriott became popular drive-ins. In 1937, Marriott, exhibiting his trademark sense of innovation, offered the first ever in-flight food service to airlines servicing the old Hoover Airfield in Washington. Eastern Air Transport served Marriott's first in-flight meal, which consisted of a choice of a ham and cheese or chicken sandwich, coleslaw or salad, a cupcake, and an apple.[11] Expanding on the name recognition of his restaurants, Marriott opened his first hotel, called Twin Bridges, in 1957. Marriott's experience in food service gave his hotel restaurants a reputation for quality that added to the appeal of the hotel. Throughout the 1950s and 1960s, Marriott expanded its restaurant and hotel operations. In 1972, J. W. Marriott, Jr., succeeded his father as chief executive officer. In the 1980s, Marriott divested itself of much of its food service holdings, positioning itself as a lodging and contract services company. Today, Marriott is a widely recognized name with several hotel brands under management (see Figure 1-1).

FIGURE 1-1

Marriott hotel exterior
(Courtesy Indianapolis Marriott North Hotel)

At about the same time as Conrad Hilton and J. W. Marriott were expanding their empires, the U.S. government embarked on a massive expansion of the nation's highway system. Linking both coasts with direct superhighways again affected the nature of lodging. People began to drive long distances for vacations or to visit friends and family.

One man, Kemmons Wilson, became frustrated with the locations and varied quality of hotels on one such family driving trip.[12] He created the Holiday Inn concept to provide a clean, low-priced room for families like his. The first Holiday Inn was opened in Memphis in 1952.[13] Mr. Wilson saw the need to expand this concept throughout the nation at various junction points and journey segments. He incorporated the theory of **brand loyalty** to his chain of hotels. Brand loyalty is defined as the institutionalized preferences of a consumer for a product or service based on a brand name or logo. Soon, people knew exactly what to expect at a Holiday Inn, and would seek them out. Often, people would drive out of their way to find the nearest Holiday Inn. Mr. Wilson coined the popular phrase "The best surprise is no surprise." This philosophy of consistency has lead many to credit Kemmons Wilson as the founder of the modern hotel chain. Mr. Wilson is widely considered to be the first hotelier to put two beds in one hotel room. Mr. Howard Johnson, a contemporary of Mr. Wilson, is said to have followed the same business model in the creation of his hotels. Today, the Holiday Inn brand is part of the Six Continents Hotel Group.

MARKETPLACE CONSISTENCY

The McDonald's restaurant chain is perhaps one of the most successful examples of a corporation creating brand loyalty through consistency. A consumer knows that a cheeseburger purchased in Boston will taste the same as one purchased in Seattle. If the consumer enjoys that cheeseburger, brand loyalty will cause the consumer to choose McDonald's again, especially when he or she has no other familiar choices.

Another major name in the modern hotel industry also began in the 1950s, Hyatt Hotels. In 1957, Chicago-based Jay Pritzker purchased the Hyatt House hotel located near Los Angeles International Airport.[14] Hyatt Hotels became the brand name, and the Pritzker family continued building small hotels. In 1967, Hyatt opened the world's first atrium hotel, the Hyatt Regency Atlanta. This marked a turning point for Hyatt, and the industry as a whole, as the 21 story Hyatt Regency Atlanta was a hotel that celebrated open spaces. Most hotel architects of the time worked hard to eliminate extra space. Hyatt itself began developing larger, more luxurious hotels and stopped developing smaller hotels. Today, Hyatt remains privately held by the Pritzker family, but is a leader in the hotel and resort industry.

During the 1960s and 1970s, another milestone emerged. Smaller, non-chain hotels watched as the major chains began to dominate the marketplace. Companies like Hilton, Marriott, Hyatt, and others quickly achieved success due to their brand awareness. In response, these smaller hotels realized that they needed to band together to pool their resources. These hotels found that by combining their individually small advertising budgets into one large one, they could create awareness on their own. These **referral organizations** emerged as an alternative to chain affiliation.[15] The best known referral organization today is Best Western.

The 1980s marked another milestone in the evolution of the modern hotel. The limited service hotel concept was introduced. Pioneers in this type of hotel included Ray Schultz, who developed Hampton Inns. Detailed explanation of the limited hotel concept is addressed in another chapter. The proliferation of the limited service brands such as Econolodge, Motel 6, and Red Roof heralded a new era of inexpensive, quality lodging.

Only innovation and imagination limit the future of hotels. New concepts are introduced regularly. Future texts will herald the pioneers of underwater hotels or the first hotel in space. The World Wide Web, and its ability to connect people instantly, is already being considered for its application into hotel design. This limitless future is best reflected in the old hotel adage: "Dreamers Wanted."

LODGING MANAGEMENT ASSOCIATION

The present state of the hotel industry is as broad as it ever was in the past. Variations in design, structure, and operation are immense. In studying the modern hotel and how it operates, it is important to understand its basic management structure and how that structure is related to a hotel's ownership arrangement. This relationship between ownership and management is defined as a hotel's **lodging management association**. This association classifies a hotel at the foundational level. There are five basic lodging management associations: owner-operated, owner-managed, independent, franchised, and management contract.

Owner-operated hotels are historically understood to have been the first type of lodging management association. As was reviewed earlier, the earliest lodgings were offered out of people's homes. A hotel that is run by an owner and the owner's family is considered owner-operated. The currently popular bed and breakfast hotel is considered owner-operated because the owner cooks the meals, cleans the rooms, and performs all such tasks.

Commonly referred to as "mom and pop" hotels, owner-operated facilities are limited by the size of the owner's family.

Owner-managed hotels are those where the owner has hired additional (nonfamily) personnel to help run the property. These hotels can be large or small. The overall management remains with the owner, but day-to-day operations can be in other hands. Many of the hotel chains we see today began with a single owner-managed property. From that first hotel, they grew using different management associations. Therefore, current owner-managed hotels cannot be affiliated with a chain, as that would alter its management association.

Independent hotels are also not chain affiliated. In these hotels, the owner has no role in management or day-to-day operations. An independent group of managers are responsible to the owner for the hotel's performance. This is a more common affiliation than the previous two. In situations where a hotel is owned by a group of investors, an independently managed hotel eliminates any potential conflict of interest.

Franchised hotels are independently owned hotels that affiliate themselves with a chain. In a franchise agreement, the owner (franchisee) pays a franchise fee to the chain (franchiser) in exchange for the rights to use their name. In addition to the name, the chain provides standard operating procedures and other guidelines on administration so that a consistent level of quality and service is maintained. The franchise hotel also benefits from national marketing campaigns (utilizing television, print, and radio media) that might be too cost prohibitive for an individual hotel to undertake. Another benefit of franchising is access to a **central reservations system (CRS)**. A central reservations system provides the consumer with an avenue to locate a hotel of choice in a certain location. Using an easy-to-find toll free number (such as 1-800-hotels-1) or Web site (such as <http://www.hyatt.com>), the CRS can generate significant demand for a hotel through brand loyalty. The chain itself is able to broaden its exposure in the marketplace without incurring the extra costs of ownership through franchising.

A concern with franchising for some chains can be the lack of control at each hotel. With franchising, there are limited corporate mandates on operational procedures and quality levels. The franchisee has some freedom to operate independently. To address this, most franchise agreements have minimum standards of quality and service written in them. A franchise hotel that fails to meet these levels can be in danger of losing the right to use the franchiser's name. The use of a chain's name, logo, and signage is often referred to as "flying a flag." When a hotel changes its association from one chain to another, it is said to have been reflagged.

The cost of a new franchise differs greatly from chain to chain. Prospective owners must decide if the development and operational costs of their chain of choice will suit their needs. Building a new franchise hotel or converting an existing hotel into a new brand (reflagging) will require an initial investment and on-going payments. Depending on the chain, these costs can range into the hundreds of thousands of dollars per room.[16] Some of the costs involved in operating a franchised hotel are:

- Construction cost per room
- Application fees
- Franchise fees (also called royalties)
- Marketing fees
- Reservation fees

Some owners who choose the franchise association do not want to be involved in the operation of the hotel itself. In these cases, the owner can leave the running of the hotel up to a **franchise company**. A franchise company will act as an agent on behalf of the owner and implement the franchise agreement between the owner (franchisee) and the hotel chain (franchiser). Some franchise companies have become very adept at running hotels under the flag of a certain chain. Organizations such as White Lodging, Interstate, and Columbia Sussex are examples of successful franchise companies. Their expertise and experience at franchising hotels for a specific chain make their services attractive to owners looking to franchise from that particular chain.

Hotels that operate under a **management contract** arrangement are the most common in the marketplace today. A hotel under management contract is similar to a franchise in that it is supplied with standard operating procedures as well as quality and service level targets. However, these hotels differ in that they are actually operated by the company that supplied those standards. Remember, a franchise hotel can choose its own management.

The hotel chains offer most management contract agreements. Companies such as Hilton, Marriott, and others offer management contracts in addition to offering franchise agreements. Not to be confused with a franchise company, which is actually a third party in the association, the company offering the management contract is directly associated with the organization supplying the operational standards and guidelines.

The management contract association extends many of the same benefits to owners that franchising does. In addition to the name brand, CRS, and marketing efforts, the owner benefits from managers trained and supervised by the management company itself. Because these companies administer so many hotels under this association, they bring a wealth of experience to the operation at all levels. The management fee is often greater than the franchise fee from the same chain for this reason. With this association, the owner retains less control, as the management companies require higher levels of autonomy. In exchange for this autonomy, performance expectations may be higher (see Figure 1-2).

It should be noted here that hotel chains can be involved in the ownership of a hotel. The ownership and operation of a hotel are not mutually exclusive. Depending on the organization's goals and corporate structure,

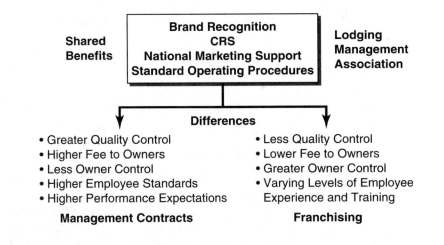

FIGURE **1-2**

Franchise versus
Management Contract

ownership of hotels can simplify their operation. As was seen in the owner-operated and owner-managed associations, there are some benefits to owning the hotel you operate: greater autonomy, freedom, and the like.

However, corporate owned hotels are not as common as they once were. It was discovered that ownership can expose an organization to potentially volatile market factors, such as real estate fluctuations and interest rates. Stock prices would be affected by these market conditions. Stock prices could be depressed for reasons other than hotel performance. An analysis of an organization's **core competencies** will reveal their strengths and weaknesses. Many hotel companies realized that their core competency was in running hotels, not owning them.

In an effort to address this issue, hotel companies began to reorganize. The Marriott organization is one example. They split into two different entities. The first new organization, called Host Marriott, was created to handle the ownership of the hotels and all their respective physical assets (i.e., buildings, equipment, land, etc.). The other, now called Marriott International, was focused solely on growing the management contract and franchise segments of their business. Indeed today, Marriott International operates the management contract of several hotels owned by Host Marriott. As other chains came to the same conclusions regarding core competencies, they too reorganized.

Hotel companies are not the only ones who offer management contracts to owners. **Nonaffiliated management companies** are organizations with no tie to a chain, but who also offer hotel management and operational expertise in much the same way a chain would (see Figure 1-3). Some owners prefer these types of arrangements because they allow for greater flexibility in operation. An owner seeking to retain a unique hotel identity may choose not to be aligned with any chain. This situation is common with independent hotels. The nonaffiliated management company typically cannot offer much in

Lodging Management Associations

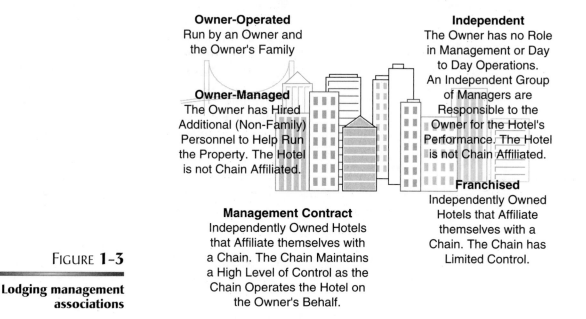

Owner-Operated
Run by an Owner and
the Owner's Family

Owner-Managed
The Owner has Hired
Additional (Non-Family)
Personnel to Help Run
the Property. The Hotel
is not Chain Affiliated.

Management Contract
Independently Owned Hotels
that Affiliate themselves with
a Chain. The Chain Maintains
a High Level of Control as the
Chain Operates the Hotel on
the Owner's Behalf.

Independent
The Owner has no Role
in Management or Day
to Day Operations.
An Independent Group
of Managers are
Responsible to the
Owner for the Hotel's
Performance. The Hotel
is not Chain Affiliated.

Franchised
Independently Owned
Hotels that Affiliate
themselves with a
Chain. The Chain has
Limited Control.

FIGURE 1-3

Lodging management
associations

terms of national marketing or CRS support. However, these nonaffiliated management companies can be very flexible in operations and more effective at implementing change than the larger chains. The lack of a model to base expectations on often allows for more freedom.

REVENUE SOURCES

In the hospitality industry, as in any other industry, a successful and profitable operation is the ultimate goal. Hotel owners, managers, and employees all play a role in achieving this goal. What exactly is meant by success in hospitality? A successful hotel has maximized all its revenue sources to the best of their potential.

A **revenue source** is the result of a product or service a hotel makes available to guests for a price. The size and scope of these sources can differ greatly from hotel to hotel. The majority of hotels utilize three main revenue sources:

1. Sleeping rooms
2. Meeting/function space
3. Outlets/ancillary revenue sources

Sleeping Rooms

A **sleeping room** is traditionally the main product of any hotel. A hotel's primary purpose is to provide accommodations. A sleeping room is defined as one of these accommodation units. The price of each of these units is called the **room rate**. Therefore, the room rates collected from all the utilized, or occupied, sleeping rooms are a significant revenue source. **Occupancy** is the measurement of how many rooms are sold each night versus how many rooms the hotel has available to sell. This measurement is viewed by the industry as one of the most important to overall hotel performance.

Meeting/Function Space

In addition to the sales of sleeping rooms, many hotels incorporate the revenue source of non-sleeping room sales. Different from sleeping rooms, meeting rooms—or function rooms, as they are also referred to—are utilized for any type of **group function** (see Figure 1-4). A group function can be a meeting, meal, dance, exposition, or any other gathering of more than one person.

FIGURE **1-4**

Meeting space (Courtesy Omni Severin Hotel)

In addition, a group function must have at least 10 sleeping rooms per night associated with it. The revenue sources from meeting/function space come from:

a. Selling the space for a specified period. These function rooms are not sold as much as they are rented. The proceeds from the renting of these rooms is called room rental.

b. Providing the food and beverage service in these rooms. This revenue is called banquet or catering revenue.

Outlets/Ancillary Revenue Sources

An **outlet** is defined as a food and beverage point of sale. Restaurants, bars, lounges, room service, and other outlets can provide a hotel with significant revenue sources (see Figure 1-5). **Ancillary** revenue sources are revenue sources outside of sleeping rooms or food/beverage.

An ancillary revenue source can be a hotel's business center, golf course, tennis center, audio/visual services, or gift shop. Other ancillary revenue sources include products/services available inside the guest room that are sold at a profit. These include in-room movies, minibars, and telephone service.

FIGURE **1-5**

Outlets *(Courtesy Omni Severin Hotel)*

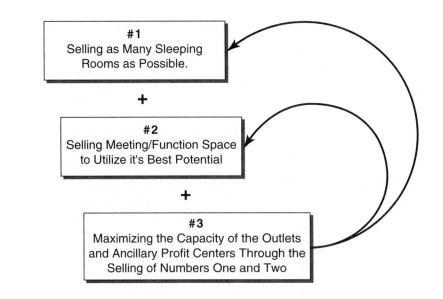

FIGURE **1-6**

Successful hotel equation

The revenues from outlets and ancillary revenue sources are generally tied to the number of guests in the hotel. Therefore, the ability to fill the sleeping and meeting rooms will lead to better outlet/ancillary performance.

The measurement of what a successful hotel entails is illustrated in Figure 1-6.

The selling of the three main revenue sources in a hotel will dictate its success. It is the room sales effort that fills the sleeping rooms on a nightly basis. The catering sales effort endeavors to fill the meeting space. The combination of the two translates into sales in the outlets and ancillary revenue sources. This three-sided relationship can be viewed as a hotel's successful sales triangle (see Figure 1-7).

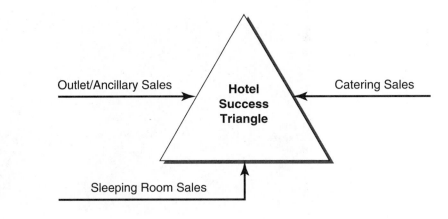

FIGURE **1-7**

Hotel success triangle

In hospitality, the financial health of a hotel is measured by the strength of the three components of the success triangle. The base of any triangle needs to be able to support the other two sides. Room sales, by definition, endeavor to fill the sleeping rooms in a hotel. A fully occupied hotel dictates the total hotel's financial health.

Profit Margin

The hotel sleeping room is the most profitable portion of all the products and services sold in any given hotel because of the profit margin. **Profit margin** is determined by comparing the sales revenue versus the costs incurred in providing a service or product. There are no concrete rules that dictate what a hotel's profit margin should be. Hotels differ widely, so their respective margins will do so as well. To fully understand why the sale of rooms is so vital, one must conduct an analysis of the cost of a sleeping room sale.

Room Cost

In **room cost** analysis, one must look at what it costs the hotel to keep a room up and running in relation to what that room is sold for to the average guest. The actual cost of providing a clean, comfortable room differs from market to market and from hotel to hotel. The basic components that make up room cost at most hotels are illustrated in Figure 1-8.

In combination, these may seem like potentially imposing costs, but in reality, they make up a small portion of the hotel room rate. Again, the actual numbers may vary, but in most markets, the cost of preparing and maintaining rooms for sale to guests will range from $20.00 to $50.00 per night.

Room Cost Components

H/L/P	Labor	Overhead
Heat Light	Housekeeping Engineering (Internal Structure Maintenance) Grounds Maintenance	Debt Service of Owners Marketing (Local Effort)
Power	(Land Surrounding Building).	Management Costs (Including Applicable Franchise or Management Contact Fees) Taxes Corporate Obligations

FIGURE **1-8**

Room cost

The following example relates this analysis to a fictional hotel.

Assume that ABC Hotel sells a room for an average of $150.00 a night. The costs incurred by the hotel in preparing each room for sale may be:

Heat	$3.00
Light	$2.00
Power	$2.00
Housekeeping	$9.00
Engineering/Grounds	$5.00
Debt service of owners	$ .50
Marketing	$2.25
Management costs	$2.75
Corporate obligations	$2.00
Taxes, etc.	$2.50
Total:	**$31.00**

Compare this actual cost to the price sold (room rate) and the room cost can be determined:

$$\text{Room Cost} = \frac{\text{Actual Cost}}{\text{Room Rate}}$$

$$= \frac{\$\ 31.00}{\$150.00}$$

$$= 21.0\%$$

Room Rate – Room Cost = Profit

The difference between costs incurred and the sale price makes up the profit margin. In order for profit margin analysis to be best understood, it is helpful to compare it to the cost of other products sold in a hotel. As was shown in the success triangle analysis, food sales in catering and the outlets can be a large revenue source. Therefore, a look at food cost may be useful in comparison to room cost. A common misconception in the hospitality industry is to consider food sales as profitable as room sales. This is not the case, as the following review of food cost reveals.

Food Cost

The difference between the profit margins of food and room sales is at the heart of why room sales are so important. As we know, to determine profit margin, one must first determine the costs incurred in providing the item.

Food cost is defined as the cost of a particular food item in relation to the price for which it is sold. This cost is often measured as a percentage. The simplest way of understanding this is that the food cost percentage is the percentage of the profit taken up by the actual cost of the item. Simply, divide the purchase price of an item by the menu price and you have the food cost percentage. The following equation is what you use to determine the cost:

$$\text{Food Cost} = \text{Purchase Price}/\text{Menu Price}$$

For example:

Item	Purchase Price (cost of meal)	Menu Price	Food Cost
Steak	$5.95/ea.	$22.00	27.0%
Chicken	$3.95/ea.	$17.95	22.0%
Caesar Salad	$1.99/ea.	$ 9.95	20.0%

(The prices and costs shown here are strictly for demonstration. These prices include labor, overhead, and other fixed costs. They also include the total cost of the meal including starch, vegetable, and beverage if applicable. The respective food costs reflected the hotel's cost in relation to the menu price.)

Hotel food and beverage operations are measured often in how well their food costs are controlled in relation to profits. A high food cost could be the result of a hotel not charging enough money for the menu items. Other reasons for high food costs include waste, large meal portions, spoilage, and pilferage. A very low food cost could mean that the hotel is overcharging for the menu items in question. The actual measurement of too low or too high depends in large part on the management philosophy of the property and the market in which it is competing. For example, some hotels offer free breakfasts to all guests. This would result in very high food cost because no profit is being made on this service. However, these same hotels view this service as a valuable amenity to attract guests, so the high food cost would be acceptable. For the sake of analysis, food cost percentages in lodging operations between 30% and 50% are fairly common.

At first glance, one might assume that the percentages of cost between food and rooms are fairly similar, which they are. Compare these figures with the average room rates in the country and you will see that the sleeping room has a much higher profit margin than does food. In the analysis of percentages of cost, the amount not taken up by the cost of the item equals the profit.

Some in the industry prefer to view profit margin differently. The contribution margin of a sale item (food, sleeping room, etc.) would not include fixed costs (such as heat/light/power, labor, etc.) in the calculation of profit. Therefore, the contribution of the item for sale should be factored in before pure profit can be calculated. However, most disregard the contribution margin analysis in lieu of profit margin. If fixed costs are considered up front, as they are in the profit margin, it would save the extra step of analyzing them after determining contribution margin.

If, as in our examples, the amount of the cost of a room or food is 20% to 40%, then the profit is the remainder, which is 80% to 60%. Let's look at a comparison of profit margins:

Item	Purchase Price	Menu Price	Profit Margin
Steak	$5.95/ea.	$22.00	$16.05
Chicken	$3.95/ea.	$17.95	$14.00
Caesar Salad	$1.99/ea.	$ 9.95	$ 7.96

	Room Cost	Room Rate	Profit Margin
Sleeping Room	$30.00	$150.00	$120.00

Extending this analysis further, assume that this hotel has 400 sleeping rooms. If each room generates a profit margin of $120.00, the total sleeping room profit on any given sold out night will be $48,000.00. The food/beverage outlets would have to sell 2,991 steak dinners or 6,030 Caesar salads to make up the profit margin difference. This illustrates how room revenue can be more profitable than food and beverage revenue.

Opportunity Cost

The preceding profit margin analysis demonstrated the importance of sleeping room sales in a hotel. That profitability is only beneficial when the rooms are sold. Sleeping rooms at a hotel are considered a perishable commodity. Each night, when a room goes unsold, the hotel loses that opportunity to ever sell it again. A hotel cannot regain that opportunity. This is called **opportunity cost**.

Unlike a manufacturer of widgets, for example, who can make as many widgets as they wish and store them in inventory until they are sold, a hotel's inventory expires on a nightly basis. A hotel has only 365 (days in the year) multiplied by its number of sleeping rooms available for sale in a year. This is again where room sales differ from food sales. Catering sales and food/beverage sales in the outlets have two advantages:

1. Food sales can be ordered based on projected demand (upcoming group meal functions, projected occupancy, etc.).

2. Unprepared food can be stored, if not sold, for future sale. Of course the amount of time a food item can be stored will depend on many factors. Even if that storage time is only one day, it has an opportunity to be resold.

The "Empty Room Theory" states that once a room goes unoccupied, it is gone forever.

If we refer back to the example used in determining room cost and profit margin:

(ABC Hotel has 400 sleeping rooms)

	Room Cost	Room Rate	Profit Margin
Sleeping Room	$30.00	$150.00	$120.00

The daily maximum room profit potential is: **$48,000**   **($120 × 400)**
Weekly: **$336,000**
Monthly: **$1,400,000**
Yearly: *$17,520,000*

$17,520,000 is the maximum potential room profit that ABC Hotel could make in a year. Each unoccupied room, in essence, subtracts from that number. It is understandable why hotel owners and managers focus so much effort on occupancy.

Captive Audience Quotient

A hotel cannot have significant outlet/ancillary traffic or groups that contribute to the catering revenue portion of the success triangle without occupied rooms. Beyond the profit and opportunity cost differences, occupied rooms provide a captive audience.

A **captive audience** in hospitality is defined as guests who are staying at the hotel and will, for convenience and lack of other options, utilize the outlets in the hotel. A captive guest will eat in the restaurant, use the business center, and be part of or host a meeting at the facility as a function of this quotient.

The captive audience quotient applies to both outlet/ancillary sales and catering sales. The captive audience guest is already there at the hotel. Freestanding restaurants must attract their patrons to the facility before any sale can be made. This is where the separation between relying on local traffic and a captive audience is most apparent.

A guest staying at a hotel is more likely, for convenience and other reasons, to choose some outlet of the hotel (if it offers such services) at least once. The appeal of room service and specialty on-site restaurants may be one of the buying decisions that drive a guest to choose a particular hotel. Golf courses and other recreational facilities can be of such stature that the guest chooses the hotel for that very purpose.

The catering traffic at a hotel benefits by the same captive audience quotient. Group related catering is measured by its contribution to the overall catering effort, which is reviewed next.

The **group catering contribution** is defined as the catering business acquired by a hotel that has all, or a major portion of, the attendees staying at the hotel itself. A local seminar may have few sleeping rooms associated with it, so it is not group related. A major corporate convention may have all the attendees staying at the hotel. All the functions that result from this group (breakfasts, lunches, dinners, receptions, etc.) become group related catering functions (see Figure 1-9). The group related functions contribute to greater catering revenue.

The group catering contribution has a direct impact on the catering operation of a hotel. Periods of lower group occupancy in a hotel invariably result in weaker catering performance. Lower group-occupancy levels dictate lower levels of the group catering contribution. Non-group occupancy has no tangible effect on catering revenue.

FIGURE **1-9**

Group catering (*Courtesy Indianapolis Marriott North Hotel*)

An argument can be made that a hotel can have a significant portion of its business derived from local traffic—enough local traffic so as to significantly impact both the outlet/ancillary and catering parts of the success triangle. This rare situation may result in a hotel filling its meeting space with non–group-related functions. In that instance, the hotel has precluded any group business from booking because most groups have functions tied to their sleeping rooms. With groups, most properties find it difficult to fill all their sleeping rooms. Of course, having empty sleeping rooms means that the profit margins of room sales will go unrealized.

INDUSTRY PERSPECTIVE

Usage of Function Space

Jamie Doyle
Director of Sales and Marketing
The Marriott Indianapolis North

Meeting facilities and hotels are unique in that they have only one opportunity to maximize revenue. Meeting space and function rooms not sold on a given day can never be sold again. From a hotel perspective, maximizing space so that every possible dollar made is crucial. This is especially important in the relationship between meeting space and sleeping rooms. Because groups almost always need function space in conjunction with their sleeping rooms, a hotel wanting to sell sleeping rooms needs to have space available. From a meeting planner's perspective, securing a venue that meets every space need exactly is not always easy. In some cases, creativity is needed to meet both objectives.

If traditional function space is at a premium, one might look at nontraditional options. Nontraditional function space can include outdoor courtyards, gardens on the grounds, pool areas, lobby/foyer areas, sections of a restaurant, and even tented parking lots. If both the facility and planner are flexible, an urgent space need can almost always be met.

Another way of maximizing function space is to make it dual-purpose. Most groups typically use one room for their meeting, and another for their meal functions. Groups that can, as we say in the industry, "meet and eat" in the same room allow for that room to serve a dual purpose. That, in turn, frees up another room to sell.

Overall, being creative to meet customers' needs shows that a hotel has the customers' best interests in mind (see Figure 1-10). Going above and beyond for customers creates loyalty, which as we all know is worth its weight in gold.

FIGURE **1-10**

Unique function space
*(Courtesy Crowne Plaza
Union Station Hotel)*

NOTES

1. Montgomery, R., and Strick, S. (1995). *Meetings, Conventions and Expositions*. New York: Van Nostrand Reinhold.

2. Vallen, G., and Vallen, J. (1996). *Check-in Check-out*. Chicago: Richard D. Irwin.

3. Montgomery and Strick.

4. Deveau, L., et al (1996). *Front Office Management and Operations*. Saddle River, NJ: Prentice Hall.

5. Vallen and Vallen.

6. Vallen and Vallen. *Ibid.*

7. <http://www.schonwalder.org>

8. Deveau, et al.

9. <http://www.hilton.com/corporate/press/milestone.html>

10. <http://www.marriott.com/milestone.asp>

11. O'Brien, R. (1977). *The J. Willard Marriott Story*. Salt Lake City: Desert Book Company.

12. Deveau, et al.

13. <http://www.sixcontinentshotels.com>

14. <http://www.hyatt.com/explore_hyatt/press_releases/cback.html>

15. <http://www.schonwalder.org>

16. *Hotel and Motel Management, 216,* 9 (May 21, 2001), Advanstar Publications.

CHAPTER ONE **REVIEW**

KEY TERMS

junction points
journey segment
brand loyalty
referral organizations
lodging management association
owner-operated
owner-managed
independent
franchised
central reservations system (CRS)
franchise company
management contract
core competencies
nonaffiliated management
   companies

revenue source
sleeping room
room rate
occupancy
group function
outlets/ancillaries
profit margin
room cost
food cost
opportunity cost
captive audience
group catering contribution

REVIEW QUESTIONS

1. Explain the similarity and difference between English and Colonial Inns.
2. List and explain the five different types of lodging management associations.
3. Explain opportunity cost and its impact on hotel room sales.
4. What are some of the innovations of the Buffalo Statler Hotel that made it the precursor of the "modern" hotel?
5. Explain the differences and shared benefits of franchising versus management contract affiliations.
6. Name three in-room ancillary revenue sources for a hotel.
7. What is the Empty Room Theory?
8. Who coined the phrase "The best surprise is no surprise"? What did he mean by it?
9. What innovation in hotel design did the Pritzker family implement?
10. What is a referral organization? What do they offer?

Discussion Questions/Exercises

1. Compare the hotel industry to the airline industry. In what ways are they similar and in what ways are they different? Do the airlines face a similar expiration of product? What factors could go into "airline seat cost"?

2. What were some of the major trade routes in Europe and Asia? Determine three major cities that grew out of those junction points. Research the current hotel market in those cities and find a historic hotel in each. Bring your findings back to class and discuss.

CASE STUDY

Food Cost

The hotel restaurant in a city property is in the process of developing new menus. The chef is excellent at creating exciting culinary options. However, the pricing of the menu items needs to be analyzed. The property owner will not allow a food cost in excess of 25%. Determine the minimum menu price for each item.

Menu Item	Cost of Ingredients	Minimum Menu Price
Stuffed Quail Eggs	$5.13	
Tomato Balsamic Salad	$1.02	
Pecan Crusted Trout	$6.78	
Vegetable Medley	$ .83	
Individual Sourdough Baguette	$ .98	
Chocolate Torte	$2.21	

1. What is the total cost of this meal?

2. What is the minimum menu price to maintain a food cost of 25% for this meal?

3. What other factors would you consider when determining the menu price for this meal?

CASE STUDY   Chain Histories

In this chapter, the histories of Hilton, Marriott, Holiday Inn, and Hyatt were briefly discussed. Choose a different hotel chain and obtain any printed materials you can about their beginnings and history. Answer the following questions:

1. What is the name of the hotel chain you selected?
2. When was the hotel chain established?
3. What was the name of the first hotel in the chain?
4. Where was it located?
5. Who was the person or persons who started the chain?
6. How many hotels are now in this chain?
7. How long has this chain been in operation?
8. What types of hotels does this chain operate?
9. Where is the corporate office for this chain located? Has it changed locations?
10. Have there been any mergers or acquisitions within this chain?
11. Does this chain have more than one brand in its repertoire?
12. What unique thing did you learn about this chain that you did not know before?
13. Why did you choose this chain?
14. Describe the hotel in this chain that you would most like to visit.
15. Would you like to work for this hotel chain? Why or why not?
16. Is this chain publicly traded? If so, what is the current stock price?
17. What is the stock price history during the past 12 months?
18. What factors have been involved in any fluctuations over the past three years?
19. What is the current focus of this chain?
20. What percentage of this chain's properties are corporate owned?

INTERNET RESOURCES
Hotel Web Site Home Pages

The hotel industry of today is made up of numerous brands. The Internet provides an easy way to learn more about each of them and how they helped shape the history of the industry. The following list highlights several different hotel chain Web sites and the affiliated brands of each. Choose a site and look for specific pages with relevant titles (such as "About Us," "Our History," or "Press Releases").

CHAIN NAME	WEB SITE	AFFILIATED BRANDS
Accor	<http://www.accorhotel.com/>	Accor
	<http://www.sofitel.com/>	Sofitel
	<http://www.novotel.com/>	Novotel
	<http://www.mercure.com/>	Mercure
	<http://www.ibishotel.com/>	Ibis
	<http://www.etaphotel.com/>	Etap
	<http://www.hotelformule1.com/>	Formule1
	<http://www.motel6.com/>	Motel 6
	<http://www.redroof.com/>	Red Roof Inns
	<http://www.coralia.com/coralia/gb/index.html>	Coralia
Adam's Mark	<http://www.adamsmark.com/>	Adam's Mark
Amerisuites	<http://www.amerisuites.com/>	Amerisuites
ANA	<http://www.ananet.or.jp/anahotels/e/>	ANA
Aston	<http://www.aston-hotels.com/>	Aston
Best Western	<http://www.bestwestern.com/>	Best Western
Cendant	<http://www.cendant.com/>	Cendant
	<http://www.super8.com/ctg/cgi-bin/Super8#>	Super 8
	<http://www.knightsinn.com/ctg/cgi-bin/KnightsInn>	Knights Inn
	<http://www.hojo.com/ctg/cgi-bin/HowardJohnson>	Howard Johnson
	<http://www.villager.com/ctg/cgi-bin/Villager>	Villager
	<http://www.ramada.com/ctg/cgi-bin/Ramada>	Ramada
	<http://www.travelodge.com/ctg/cgi-bin/Travelodge>	Travelodge
Choice	<http://www.choicehotels.com/>	Clarion, Comfort, Econo Lodge, Mainstay Suites, Quality, Rodeway, Sleep
Dorint	<http://www.dorinthotels.com/>	Dorint
Drury	<http://www.druryinn.com/>	Drury
Elegant Resorts	<http://www.elegantresorts.com/>	Individually Branded
Fairmont	<http://www.fairmont.com/>	Fairmont
	<http://www.cphotels.com/cp.asp?loc=corp>	Canadian Pacific, Princess

Hotel Web Site Home Pages *(continued)*

CHAIN NAME	WEB SITE	AFFILIATED BRANDS
Fiesta Americana	<http://www.fiestaamericana.com/>	Fiesta Americana, Caesar Park
Four Seasons	<http://www.fourseasons.com/index.html>	Four Seasons
Golden Tulip	<http://www.goldentulip.com/>	Golden Tulip, Barbizon, Tulip Inn
Harrah's	<http://www.harrahs.com/home/home.html>	Harrah's, Rio
Hilton	<http://www.hilton.com/> <http://www.hilton.com/doubletree/index.html> <http://www.hilton.com/conradinternational/index.html> <http://www.embassy-suites.com/> <http://www.homewood-suites.com/> <http://www.hampton-inn.com/> <http://www.redlion.com/> <http://www.hilton.com/hiltongardeninn/index.html>	Hilton Doubletree Conrad International Embassy Suites Homewood Suites Hampton Inn Red Lion Hilton Garden Inn
Hyatt	<http://www.hyatt.com/>	Hyatt Regency, Park Hyatt, Grand Hyatt
Jameson	<http://www.jamesoninns.com/> <http://www.signature-inns.com/index.html>	Jameson Signature
Le Meridian	<http://www.lemeridien-hotels.com/> <http://www.forte-hotels.com/> <http://www.heritage-hotels.com/> <http://www.posthouse-hotels.com/>	Le Meridian Forte Heritage Posthouse
Loews	<http://www.loewshotels.com/>	Loews
Mandarin Oriental	<http://www.mandarin-oriental.com/>	Mandarin Oriental
Manhattan East Suite Hotels	<http://www.mesuite.com/>	Individually Branded
Marriott	<http://www.marriott.com/> <http://www.renaissancehotels.com/> <http://www.courtyard.com/> <http://www.residenceinn.com/> <http://www.fairfieldinn.com/> <http://www.towneplacesuites.com/js/Default.asp> <http://www.springhillsuites.com/js/Default.asp>	Marriott Renaissance Courtyard Residence Inn Fairfield Inn Towne Place Suites Spring Hill Suites New World
Metropolitan	<http://www.methotels.com/>	Metropolitan

(continued)

Hotel Web Site Home Pages *(continued)*

Chain Name	Web Site	Affiliated Brands
Nikko	<http://www.nikkohotels.com/>	Nikko, JAL
Noble House	<http://www.noblehousehotels.com/>	Individually Branded
Omega	<http://www.omegaresorts.com/omega_info/index.html>	Individually Branded
Omni	<http://www.omnihotels.com/>	Omni
Outrigger	<http://www.outrigger.com/>	Outrigger
Park Place	<http://www.parkplace.com/>	Bally's, Caesar's, Grand
Radisson	<http://www.radisson.com/RAD/RadissonHome/0,2509,,00.html>	Radisson
Red Carnation	<http://www.redcarnationhotels.com/>	Red Carnation
Regal	<http://www.regalhotel.com/main.html> <http://www.millennium-hotels.com/>	Regal Millennium
Ritz Carlton	<http://www.ritzcarlton.com/>	Ritz Carlton
Rosewood	<http://www.rosewoodhotels.com/>	Individually Branded
Royal	<http://www.royalhotels.com/>	Royal
Sholodge	<http://www.shoneysinn.com/> <http://www.sumnersuites.com/>	Shoney's Sumner Suites
Sierra Suites	<http://www.sierrasuites.com/>	Sierra Suites
Six Continents	<http://www.sixcontinentshotels.com/sixcontinentshotels> <http://www.interconti.com/> <http://www.sixcontinentshotels.com/crowneplaza> <http://www.sixcontinentshotels.com/holiday-inn> <http://www.sixcontinentshotels.com/hiexpress> <http://www.sixcontinentshotels.com/staybridge>	Six Continents Inter-Continental Crowne Plaza Holiday Inn Holiday Inn Express Staybridge Suites
Sonesta	<http://www.sonesta.com/sonesta/sonweb2.nsf>	Sonesta
SRS	<http://www.srs-worldhotels.com/>	SRS, Steigenberger, Pan Pacific
Station	<http://www.stationcasinos.com/home/default.asp>	Station
Starwood	<http://www.starwoodhotels.com/> <http://www.westin.com/main.taf> <http://www.sheraton.com/main.taf> <http://www.fourpoints.com/main.taf> <http://www.stregis.com/> <http://www.luxurycollection.com/main.taf> <http://www.whotels.com/>	Starwood Westin Sheraton Four Points St. Regis Luxury Collection "W"
Summit	<http://www.summithotels.com/>	Individually Branded

Hotel Web Site Home Pages *(concluded)*

CHAIN NAME	WEB SITE	AFFILIATED BRANDS
Super Clubs	<http://www.superclubs.com/>	Breezes, Grand Lido
Swissotel	<http://www.swissotel.com/index.html>	Swissotel
Thistle	<http://www.thistlehotels.com/>	Thistle
Trump	<http://www.trump.com/>	Trump
U.S. Franchise Systems	<http://www.usfsi.com/> <http://www.microtelinn.com/> <http://www.hawthorn.com/> <http://www.bestinn.com/>	Microtel Hawthorne Best
Walt Disney World Resorts	<http://asp.disney.go.com/disneyworld/db/seetheworld/resorts/index.asp>	Individually Branded
Warwick	<http://www.warwickhotels.com/>	Warwick
Wyndham	<http://www.wyndham.com/default.cfm> <http://www.summerfieldsuites.com/>	Wyndham Summerfield Suites

For additional hospitality and travel marketing resources, visit our Web site at **<http://www.Hospitality-Tourism.delmar.com>**.

Hotel Classifications

OBJECTIVES

After reading this chapter, you should understand:

- How hotels are classified by size, location, and product type
- Hotel rating systems

INTRODUCTION

Learning the history and evolution of the hotel, as was reviewed in the previous chapter, is the best way to begin the analysis of the industry as it is today. The hotel pioneers discussed set the groundwork for many of the designs, services, and amenities considered commonplace today. This chapter builds on that history by identifying the criteria by which hotels are classified. Identifying hotels by standard criteria allows for comparison and further understanding. Establishing a single criterion that could sufficiently identify all the hotels in the world today would be impossible. Therefore, the generally accepted criteria for identifying hotels are based on three separate measurements. Those are hotel size, location, and product type.

HOTEL SIZES

Modern hotels come in myriad sizes and shapes. It is difficult to compare or understand the differences in hotels without establishing a standard size classification for the industry. While the understanding within the industry is to classify hotels based on their number of sleeping rooms, the specific breakdowns will differ. Many in the industry use the following to determine a hotel's size based on its number of rooms.

Classification	Number of Sleeping Rooms
Small	1 to 150
Medium	151 to 400
Large	401 to 1,500
Mega	1,501 and over

As a general rule, management salaries increase as the number of guest rooms increase. A larger hotel will theoretically be harder to manage (due to a larger staff, more outlets, and a greater amount of meeting space), therefore a manager of a mega-size hotel will probably make more in salary than a comparable manager of a medium-size hotel. Larger hotel sizes will also necessitate a greater number of specialized management positions. A small-size hotel may have one front office manager to oversee all front office employees. A large-size hotel may have a front office manager as well, but reporting to him or her may be the following: one or two assistant front office managers, several front desk managers, valet manager, concierge manager, PBX manager, bell captain, parking garage manager, numerous supervisors, and so on.

HOTEL LOCATION CLASSIFICATIONS

The location of a hotel is also important to its success. As in many other industries, the old adage "location, location, location" applies. Being cognizant of a hotel's surroundings provides the means to effectively market a hotel to the community. Hotel **location types** are classified by physical positioning in relation to the customers in the area and to their tangible locale. The four main hotel location types are downtown, resort, airport, and suburban. The following looks at each location type and the corresponding traditional business mix.

Downtown

Downtown location types apply to hotels located in dense urban areas. This doesn't necessarily mean the city center, but most often does. Hotels that have large clusters of corporate structures or office parks surrounding them can be considered downtown location types regardless of exactly where in the city they are located.

Traditionally, downtown hotels are located in the center of a city's business district, the "heart" of the corporate structure in any given city, if you will. These areas will often include a convention center.

A **convention center** is a locally funded, or privately owned structure that caters to large groups and conventions for meetings of all kinds. These centers will have their own staff of salespeople who sell their facility to various market segments. The size and capacity of a convention center may allow it to provide its own food and beverage service, or it may rely on outside providers.

Many times, in classifying the location type of a hotel near a convention center, the term convention hotel is used. The difference between downtown or convention hotels, if they are both located near the city's convention center, is based on whether they cater to business related to the convention center or not. Those hotels located in dense urban areas or office parks without a convention center cannot be classified as convention hotels.

Resort

Resort location types can be classified as such only if they fulfill one of two main criteria.

1. A resort can be located near some sort of **special attraction** that attracts guests for a reason other than the hotel itself. An ocean, natural wonder, mountain, amusement park, or golf course can be that attraction. Warm weather areas with plenty of sun can be a special attraction. Attractions and their interest to people will vary from person to person. Special attractions can be as varied as the city or country where the hotel is located. The Grand Wailea in Figure 2-1 is a classic example.

2. Hotels that create their own special attraction can also be considered resorts. Health spas, private golf and/or tennis facilities, expansive pool areas, and other unique **signature attractions** created by the hotel itself allow for the resort location classification. The signature attraction is defined as an event, activity, or facility that is identified with a specific hotel. The golf course at the Doral in Figure 2-2 is an example of a signature attraction.

These resort hotels can be located anywhere. They can often boast of signature attractions that provide perceived value to the **receptive customer**. A

FIGURE **2-1**

Grand Wailea outdoors
(Courtesy KSL Resorts)

FIGURE **2-2**

Doral golf course
(Courtesy KSL Resorts)

receptive customer is one who is more likely to be interested in a product or service than the general population due to personal interest or need. Receptive customers may feel that they received a special return for their money if they perceive a value in the product or service they purchased over and above what the general population may perceive.

In the resort environment, this value can be derived from recreational skill enhancement (some resorts offer "schools" that teach golf, tennis, skiing, and other sports). Perceived value can also come from partaking in other signature attractions like celebrity health/beauty salons and unique restaurants. The consumer will in many of these cases be willing to spend more money than he or she normally would because of the perceived value of the product or service.

The resort classification should only apply to hotels that fit these criteria. There are a few hotels in the marketplace who use the term "resort" in their name to, in effect, trick the customer into believing that they offer some sort of special attraction. These types of hotels employ what's called the deceptive location classification. This practice most often occurs in the resort location type.

Resorts built near special attractions that are not their own may be at the mercy of the attraction's **seasonality**. Seasonality is the term used to define the time of year when a special attraction is open or at its peak level. Terms also used to describe seasonality are "in season" and "off-season." Most attractions like amusement parks and ski slopes are open during a fixed time during the year. Other attractions like a beach are open all year but are at their peak during temperate weather months. Desert golf resorts are not in as high a demand during the hot summer months as during the more pleasant winters. The seasonality of these resorts dictates their demand level.

Airport

The airport hotel location type is perhaps the easiest to identify. Most major airports in the world have one or more hotels located very close by. It can be said that the special attraction of an airport hotel is the airport itself. The airport provides a steady stream of travelers coming to and from the city at almost all hours.

Airport hotels commonly provide complimentary shuttle service to and from the airport to make it convenient for the traveler. The hours of operation in the restaurants, lounges, and other facilities may be longer than at other location types in order to accommodate those travelers dealing with changes in time zones and jet lag. Multilingual staff members are common at airport hotels in major gateway cities to assist international travelers.

Gateway cities are traditionally those located in an area that makes them the first practical stop for an international flight coming into a country.

In the United States, Seattle, San Francisco, and Los Angeles are considered gateway cities for Asia and the Far East. New York, Boston, and Washington, D.C., are gateways to Europe and beyond. Miami is a convenient U.S. gateway city to South America. It should be noted that current improvements in airplane technology are allowing for longer direct flights from cities not commonly considered gateways. Chicago, Minneapolis, and Atlanta are good examples of new gateway cities that have emerged due to these airplane innovations.

Suburban

The suburban location type is perhaps the most common. **Suburban** hotels are generally considered to be those that do not fit into the other three location types. Given that criterion, it can be said that most hotels in the world are actually suburban location types. These hotels are not located in the downtown area or near airports. They have no special attractions to qualify them as resorts. They are common on major roadways and near small office complexes. A large company headquarters or manufacturing site will often warrant a small or medium-size suburban hotel with its own demand. The Marriott Indianapolis North pictured in Figure 2-3 is an example of a suburban hotel.

FIGURE **2-3**

Marriott North at night
(Courtesy Indianapolis Marriott North Hotel)

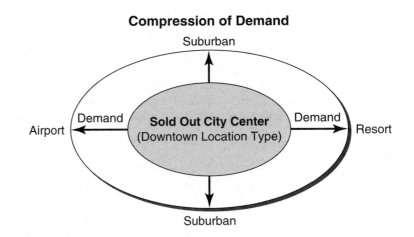

Compression of Demand

FIGURE **2-4**

Compression of demand

Suburban hotels often thrive in environments where the **compression of demand** in the city lessens the importance of a hotel's location type. Compression of demand is the theory that the need for hotel rooms in a city or geographical region will remain static and fairly constant in spite of what the occupancy level is (see Figure 2-4). In effect, if one part of an area is sold out, the demand for rooms will compress in such a way as to drive those looking for rooms elsewhere. This compression often occurs first with downtown and convention hotels. A citywide convention may take up all the rooms in the downtown area, while the normal or average demand for transient and other group rooms remains fixed. These people have no where to go but outward from the downtown area. This compression leads to increased occupancy for the hotels not normally affected by the demand in the downtown area.

HOTEL PRODUCT TYPES

In hotel classification, location types provide half of the equation. Hotel product types will help complete the picture needed to fully analyze any hotel. The service levels they provide as well as their target market define hotel **product types**.

Service Level

This analysis of product types first entails understanding exactly what is meant by service level. A hotel's **service level** is measured by the amount of actual and perceived consideration a guest can reasonably expect to receive. This is based on the hotel's reputation as well as by comparison with other product types.

Consumers of all products experience different levels of service. A favorite restaurant may make you feel special by using your name in a greeting, or by reserving your favorite table. The grocery store that special orders something for you is providing a higher service level than the one that doesn't. You may know by reputation where to go in your area for the best auto mechanic or barber. In many cases, you may pay more for the product you feel gives you more in return. However, service level is not necessarily tied to increased cost. A consumer perceives a value in receiving quality service.

In the hotel industry, the differences in service levels is often (but not always) tied to incremental increases in cost. Figure 2-5 looks at the most common service-level classifications and contemporary examples of brands in the market today.

The examples in Figure 2-5 are listed in two columns, full service and limited service, with the mid-market examples straddling both sides. The definitions of full versus limited service exemplify the differences in service level we have been discussing.

Full-service hotels, by definition, provide their guests with services, amenities, and facilities that they want or need to complete a total hotel experience. To varying degrees, these services can include, but are not limited to:

- Restaurant(s) on site serving breakfast, lunch, and dinner
- Room service
- Meeting space (sales and catering staff on site)
- Business center
- Health club/recreation facilities (see Figure 2-6)
- Bellstaff/Doorstaff

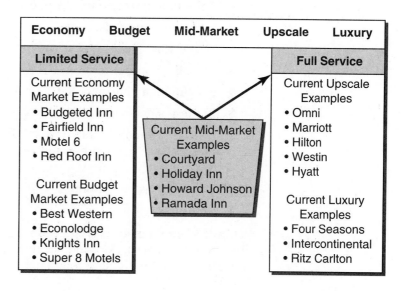

FIGURE **2-5**

Service level

FIGURE **2-6**

Health club *(Courtesy Indianapolis Marriott North Hotel)*

- Gift shop
- Complimentary services like bed turndown and newspaper delivery
- Lounge(s)/entertainment
- Suites, upgraded rooms
- Concierge lounge and services
- Executive or "business class" floors
- Express/video checkout ability
- In-room amenities such as: minibars, voice mail, data ports with Internet access, work areas, oversize beds, sitting areas, toiletries, in-room movies
- Security/loss prevention
- Shuttle services

Limited service hotels typically do not offer the above services. The most notable differences are lack of food or beverage outlets and no meeting space on site. They do offer a quality room and a good night's sleep for a fair price.

FIGURE **2-7**

Cost versus product relationship

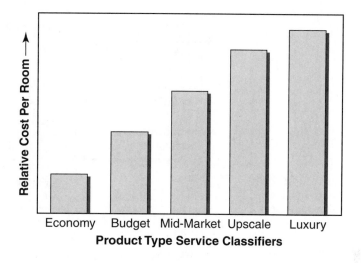

The **mid-market** service level was listed as being a combination of both the limited- and full-service hotel classification because these hotels can vary from one place to another. In one location, one may find a full-service mid-market brand hotel; in another, the same brand may be of limited service.

As was stated earlier, the price versus service relationship is not universal. In most markets, the increasing service level will be tied to an increased price (room rate). Differences will occur from location to location. The price versus service comparison must be made within the same market. The prices of a luxury hotel of the same brand may differ from, say, New York to Tulsa. The local market factors such as competition, operating costs, and availability will skew these comparative numbers.

Figure 2-7 illustrates the generic price versus service relationship in relation to the different product types. (Please note: The differences in price are not universal. The price relationships within the same markets could mirror Figure 2-7, but anomalies may occur. Factors such as real estate costs, labor costs, and others can affect these relationships.)

Target Market

Service levels are helpful in understanding half of the product type. The other component of that knowledge is the target market. A **target market** is a (combination of) market segment(s) the hotel wants to penetrate. The target market can be inherently tied to a product type or specifically designated by a marketer as a new focus.

In the modern hotel market there are vastly different target markets available. These markets contribute to each hotel's available business mix. The

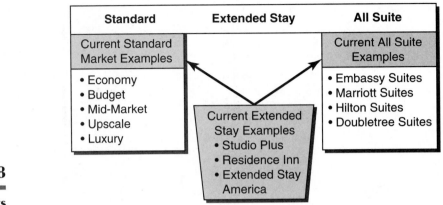

Figure **2-8**

Target markets

target market is comprised of those consumers wanting a different type of hotel room. The physical differences in the room itself—that is, product and service level—reflect the differences in the intended target markets. Today, those target markets can be summarized as in Figure 2-8.

Notice that the standard market examples listed in Figure 2-8 do not list specific hotels. In fact, the standard target markets are comprised of the very same segments that made up the classifications of service-level product types. The standard target market itself does not differentiate between service level and product types. Guests who are looking for a traditional hotel room (albeit with varying degrees of service) comprise the standard target market. The target markets that are looking for a different room product type are the ones that will differ from the standard. The physical differences in the hotels set them apart. These differences become apparent when looking at the target markets that comprise those seeking different room types from the standard—namely, extended stay and all suite markets.

Extended stay hotels provide their guests with services, amenities, and facilities that they want or need to facilitate a long-term stay in one location. To varying degrees, these services/facilities can include, but are not limited to:

- Stove and/or microwave
- Refrigerator
- Dishes and kitchenware
- Limited housekeeping services (not every day)
- Grocery shopping service and, occasionally, business services
- Limited recreation facilities

Often, the room rate at an extended stay hotel is based on the length of the guest's stay. The more nights a guest stays at a hotel, the fewer rooms it must attempt to sell each night. That can be desirable if the hotel can fill with many multiple-night guests. Therefore, most extended stay hotels reduce the room rate in relation to longer guest stays. A guest can rent a room by the day, week, or month.

The extended stay hotel target market is one of the fastest growing in the industry today. They have become popular choices for individuals relocating between jobs. Business travelers on extended assignments may find that extended stay hotels feel more like home. The cost of an extended stay room is often less than that of all suite hotels. They rarely have on-site food and beverage outlets, but they are often built in locations that have nearby restaurant options.

The **all suite** hotel, on the other hand, is targeted to the consumer looking for a hotel experience rivaling the suites in upscale and luxury hotels. The appeal of a suite can be attractive to more consumers. These all suites can have:

- Two or more rooms per suite
- Varying service level
- Limited on-site food and beverage facilities
- Complimentary receptions and breakfasts for all guests

The staffing levels at all suite hotels are generally leaner than those at upscale or luxury properties. Breakfast inclusive rates appeal to many. The reduced staff levels enable the rates at all suites to be more affordable than the suite rates at upscale or luxury hotels.

In hotel marketing there is a need to define precisely the many variations that can occur within the three main target markets (standard/extended stay/all suite). The more specific the target market, the better a marketer can apply resources to reach the intended consumer. These variations are no more than combinations of service and product types. Combined target markets are called **hybrid markets**. Hybrid market classifications allow the marketer to determine specific market segments within and amongst the main three market segments. The combinations among those markets create numerous possible hybrid target markets. Hybrid markets are generally more defined and narrower in scope because they focus on a smaller, more specific mix of customers. The standard target market, which comprises all the service product levels, provides the starting point for analysis of hybrid markets.

The price relationships for hybrids will mirror Figure 2-9, with the economy and budget hybrids being on the lower end and the upscale and luxury being on the upper end.

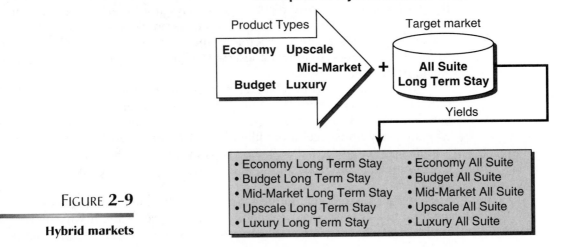

Examples of Hybrid Market Formations

Product Types

Economy Upscale

Mid-Market **+** Target market

Budget Luxury

All Suite
Long Term Stay

Yields

- Economy Long Term Stay
- Budget Long Term Stay
- Mid-Market Long Term Stay
- Upscale Long Term Stay
- Luxury Long Term Stay
- Economy All Suite
- Budget All Suite
- Mid-Market All Suite
- Upscale All Suite
- Luxury All Suite

Figure **2-9**

Hybrid markets

INDEPENDENT HOTEL RATINGS

Understanding the standard service level of a hotel will give guests a very good idea of what to expect during their stay. The industry recognizes other classifications for the level of quality and service at hotels. These ratings are useful in further defining the service level at a particular hotel.

In many foreign countries, the government plays a role in the service classification of their hotels. A star system is primarily used to denote the level of quality and service, with one star being the lowest and five stars being the highest level. International travelers can be reasonably confident about what to expect by using these stars as a guide. However, the criteria by which each hotel is judged may vary from country to country.

In the United States, the government does not play any role in classifying hotels. This is left up to independent organizations. Magazines, associations, and other special interest groups issue ratings based on their own criteria. In much the same way as carmakers tout their industry awards, hotels that are awarded high ratings will be sure to do the same thing. Some independent ratings organizations incorporate ratings for food and beverage, others for the quality and scope of the service and amenities. Still others issue judgments on a hotel's or resort's ancillary offerings. The most recognized ratings are the star system of Mobil and the diamond of the American Automobile Association. The highest awarded level in each of these is 5. There are very few hotels in North America that are awarded these distinctions. Each organization rates tens of thousands of hotels/resorts annually, but the top level is awarded to less than fifty properties.[1] A sampling of these independent organizations is shown here:

Rating Organization	Award Issued
American Automobile Association	Diamonds (1 to 5)
Mobil	Stars (1 to 5)
Meetings & Conventions Magazine	Gold Key Award, Gold Key Hall of Fame, Gold Platter Award, Gold Tee Award
Successful Meetings Magazine	Pinnacle Award, Pinnacle Hall of Fame, Ace Award
Corporate Meetings & Incentives	Paragon Award, Golden Links Award
Insurance Conference Planner	Premium Circle Award
Medical Meetings	Merit & Distinction Award
Association Meetings	Inner Circle Award
Meeting News	Planner's Choice Award
Golf Magazine	Gold Medal
Fodors	Recommendation
JD Power and Associates	Guest Value, Satisfaction and Service
Condé Nast Traveler	Gold List
Malcolm Baldridge	Quality Award
Zagat	Survey Ranking
Gourmet Magazine	Survey Ranking

NOTES

1. Vallen, G., and Vallen, J. 1996. *Check-in Check-out.* Chicago: Richard D. Irwin.

CHAPTER TWO **REVIEW**

Key Terms

location types
convention center
special attraction
signature attractions
receptive customer
seasonality
gateway cities
suburban
compression of demand

product types
service level
full service
limited service
mid-market
target market
extended stay
all suite
hybrid markets

Review Questions

1. List the four hotel size classifications and their corresponding room number ranges.

2. What is the difference between the downtown and convention location types?

3. What differentiates a full-service hotel from a limited-service hotel?

4. Why is a signature or special attraction important to the resort location classification?

5. How do receptive customers perceive value in a resort setting?

6. What effect does seasonality have on a hotel?

7. Name the major East and West Coast gateway cities and the markets they serve. What city serves as a traditional gateway to Latin America?

8. Explain the theory of compression of demand.

9. List at least 10 services/amenities identified with the full-service hotel.

10. Explain the principle behind target market analysis.

Discussion Questions/Exercises

1. In your area, find and list a hotel that fits into each of the location classifications. Be sure to note the criteria that you used to make these determinations (e.g., signature attractions). Are there any hotels you found that you could not reasonably classify? Did you find any hotels that employ the deceptive location classification?

2. What events or activities that occur in a downtown area could affect compression of demand? Can compression work in the other direction? What role can the local Convention/Tourist Bureau play in managing compression of demand? Given the cyclical nature of supply and demand, how many times would significant compression occur before construction of a new hotel would be justified?

Hotel Types

As was the case throughout history, the practice of establishing hotels as areas of rest in relation to journey segments and junction points is in practice today—for example, roadside motels along stretches of highway, bed and breakfast inns in areas of grand nature, high rise hotels in city centers. List three external factors that would affect the success and profitability of each property in this example:

Roadside Motel:

1.

2.

3.

Bed and Breakfast Inn:

1.

2.

3.

High Rise Hotel:

1.

2.

3.

Did you find any factors that applied to more than one type of property? Why or why not?

(continued)

CASE STUDY

Hotel Types *(concluded)*

Choose two of the three examples. Find a hotel that fits each description in your state. Call the properties and ask the following questions:

1. What is the rack rate for a "standard" room?
2. What is included in this rate?
3. What amenities are offered at this property?
4. Are rates different on the weekend? Higher or lower?
5. What other hotels are in the area?

Compare and contrast the two properties you selected.

The Hotel Guest

OBJECTIVES

After reading this chapter, you should understand:

- Room sales differentiation between group and transient
- How guests can make a hotel reservation via different avenues
- How group and transient business is categorized by market segment

INTRODUCTION

The very reason hotels exist is to provide service to people. Fulfilling a need, whether it is a room for the night, or a meal, or an activity, a hotel is there to serve people. It is important to understand the nature of the hotel customer. The guest at any hotel can be from any walk of life. We now know how to classify hotels. Hotels themselves have, over time, developed their own unique way of classifying and categorizing their guests. By understanding who these guests are, and what their characteristics are, a hotel can better serve them.

ROOM SALES DIFFERENTIATION

The first chapter touched briefly on the nature of groups and their impact on a hotel's performance. The group catering contribution plays an important role in food and beverage revenue, and also impacts the sleeping room sales portion of the hotel success triangle.

Occupancy, as was reviewed earlier, is the measurement of room sales versus available rooms. The rooms that are sold fall into two types or categories: group and transient. The combination of group and transient rooms makes up the hotel's occupancy.

Group Rooms

Group rooms originate from reservations that are made to bring more than one guest into the hotel. A reservation is a booking made by a travel agent, some other intermediary, or the guest for one or more nights at a hotel. An **intermediary** is the person or entity that acts as a liaison between a guest and the hotel. Intermediaries are also referred to as third parties. Group rooms involve a series of bookings that correspond to specific functions. These functions can be conventions, meetings, or other events held at the hotel or nearby. Most hotels consider bookings of 10 or more rooms per night a group booking.

The purpose of the group room sales effort is to seek these group bookings and bring them to the hotel. A relatively recent development in the evolution of the hospitality industry, group sales is counted upon to fill a certain number of hotel rooms per night. The **group base** is the measurement of how many group rooms are "on the books" on a given night. The groups reserving this base are contractually obligated to arrive on a certain day and to fill a specific number of rooms. Therefore, a hotel can look to future group bookings as a good indication of upcoming occupancy levels.

Groups, because they can be booked far in advance, are sought after. The group sales team may reduce the room rate offered to a group in exchange for the group's contribution to the hotel's overall base of rooms. The specific tools used in booking groups are too detailed to address here, but it is important to note that group rooms are often offered at lower rates. This distinction is important when reviewing transient rooms, which is next.

Transient Rooms

Transient rooms are rooms that originate from individual reservations. Business and pleasure guests who stay at the hotel for reasons unrelated to functions being held there generally fill transient rooms. Transient rooms are non-group rooms. Transient rooms differ from group rooms in that there is no way to predict when these guests will arrive. Individual reservations are made at the guests' discretion, so predicting their level on any given night is difficult. Determining the most likely levels of transient demand entails looking at historical data. In the transient sales arena, the individual booking cycle dictates the historical transient demand levels. The **individual booking cycle** is the time between when an individual reservation is made and when that reservation is due to arrive. The booking cycle can be anywhere from a few days to a few months. The transient demand is low outside the traditional booking cycle and increases drastically within it. Whereas the group base can be reserved far in advance, the individual booking cycle can be more short term. **Walk-in reservations**, which are made by guests arriving unannounced at a hotel looking for rooms, cannot be measured as part of the booking cycle because they are difficult to predict. However, walk-ins can play a major role in the transient demand at certain hotels, which is why they are important to understand.

A sample relationship between group and transient rooms at a fictitious downtown hotel is illustrated in Figure 3-1.

This illustration is not meant to reflect a universal relationship. The group and transient makeup of a hotel depends on many factors. Location type, service level, target market, size, and other factors will alter the group versus transient makeup. The room sales effort for both group and transient rooms endeavors to fill up the hotel each night. Because the levels of group rooms are known in advance, the transient effort knows exactly how many rooms it needs to sell per night. In-depth analysis of this process is addressed later in the reservations chapter.

FIGURE **3-1**

Group versus transient rooms

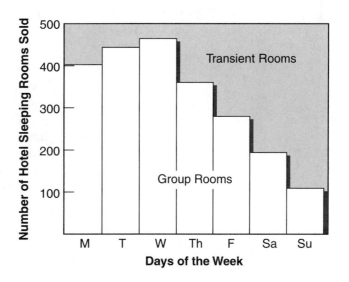

Transient Reservation Avenues

Any given hotel that wishes to minimize the opportunity costs associated with transient sleeping room sales will incorporate as many **reservation avenues** for the guest to utilize as possible. A reservation avenue is defined as a means by which a guest is able to make a reservation at a hotel.

Hotels incorporate as many reservation avenues as possible. The greater the access guests have to a specific hotel, the more likely they are to book. The most common reservation avenues are:

- GDS system (global distribution system)
- CRS (central reservation system)
- Direct travel agent or travel management company contact
- Direct guest contact

The Global Distribution System (GDS) is a network of travel and hospitality entities that communicate via an integrated computer system. The most common networks are called: Apollo, Sabre, Worldspan, and SystemOne. These GDS computer networks were originally developed by airlines to link their availability to travel agents. The ease of access enabled travel agents to directly book flights. Now, through various fee arrangements, hotels and car rental companies also link their individual products to the GDS systems. Any intermediary can now book an entire itinerary for a traveler using the GDS system.

A central reservations system, as reviewed earlier, provides the consumer with an avenue to locate a hotel of choice in a certain location. Using an easy-to-find toll free number (such as 1-800-hotels-1) or Web site (such as <http://www.hyatt.com>), the CRS can generate significant demand for a hotel through brand loyalty.

Within the transient reservations process, travel agents and travel management companies act as intermediaries. These intermediaries make money in one of two ways:

1. They may charge a flat **management fee**. Intermediaries acting on a large company's behalf typically make their money this way. Many large organizations now utilize travel management companies to arrange all their travel needs. This volume purchasing arrangement often entitles the organization to discounts with certain suppliers. The travel management company manages these relationships, which allows the organization to focus on its core competency.

2. They are paid a **commission**. A commission (usually 10 percent of the rate for hotels) is paid to travel agents by hotels, airlines, and other travel-related suppliers to induce further bookings. Intermediaries booking travel for individuals or small organizations most commonly utilize this.

It should be noted that travel agent commissions have come under fire recently, primarily by airlines. Airlines have instituted caps on the commission paid to travel agents. Though most hotels continue to offer the traditional 10 percent commission on the room rate, that could change if the industry faces an economic downturn.

Larger organizations often prefer to use the management fee method because there is no direct benefit to their intermediary for using any specific supplier. The absence of direct remuneration eliminates any conflict of interest.

Direct guest contact is another reservation avenue. The guests themselves can make reservations via phone, fax, or Internet. As the Internet grows in popularity, its use as a reservation avenue grows as well. Most hotel chains offer a direct booking capability on their home pages. A recent study predicts that reservations made on the Internet will triple by 2005.[1] Other Internet sites also offer a variety of travel related services. See the end of this chapter for a sample listing of Internet sites offering these services.

All these reservation avenues are illustrated in Figure 3-2.

Understanding the nature of group and transient rooms is very important. How group and transient rooms reach the hotel (reservation avenues) and their general impact on rates is crucial to further understanding. In order to fully exploit the benefits of group and transient rooms, it is important to understand their characteristics. How are these rooms classified? That is best understood by examining market segments.

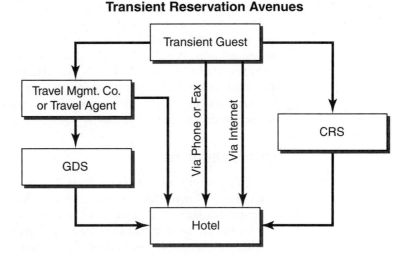

Transient Reservation Avenues

FIGURE **3-2**

Transient reservation avenues

MARKET SEGMENTATION

Group and transient rooms make up the demand for hotel rooms. This business mix can be further analyzed. A **market segment** is a portion or segment of the actual or potential business mix at any given hotel. Grouping this business pool into segments with similar characteristics is called market segmentation. Market segments can be grouped in many different ways. Market segment characteristics may differ from one hotel to another due to local market factors. In various combinations, all hotel business can be classified into one or more market segments. Both group and transient rooms have their own distinct market segments. The main group market segments are corporate, association, and SMERF. The main transient market segments are business and pleasure.

Group Market Segments

Corporate Segment

The corporate market segment consists of for-profit companies. The corporate market segment may have more money to spend than nonprofit or business segments. As a result, corporate business is often more concerned with content than with cost. This market segment frequently pays higher rates than others to ensure quality programs.

Association Segment

Associations are, by their nature, groupings of individuals or companies that share common purposes or goals. In a way, associations are a market segment within a market segment. Individuals can band together in association to share ideas, hobbies, beliefs, or any number of things. Companies can band together in association for research, educational, political, or public relations reasons. This market segment may be more cost-conscious than the corporate segment, because its members often pay for services out of their own pockets. Associations can have very large memberships and require large facilities.

Other Segment

Most hotels' group market segments that do not fall easily into the previous two categories fall into this "other" category. Also called the primary market, this segment consists of groups that have characteristics that set them apart from the corporate or association category. This separation does not diminish the quality or impact of this segment but rather affords it the attention it deserves.

The other market segment has five primary components: **social, military, educational, religious,** and **fraternal (SMERF).**

Primary Component	Market
Social	Weddings, Proms, Fund Raisers, Bar/Bas Mitzvahs
Military	Reunions, Award Ceremonies
Educational	Continuing Education, Certification Classes, Training
Religious	Revivals, Enlightenment Gatherings
Fraternal	Fraternities, Sororities

These components meet for reunions, bonding, continuing education, or any number of reasons. The SMERF components, which can be large or small, tend to look for lower rates than the corporate or association segments.

Group markets can be analyzed more deeply to separate the potential business pool into even more defined and/or diverse subsegments, including:

Corporate	Association	Other
Manufacturing	Local	SMERF
Construction	State	Tour/Travel
Distribution	Regional	Cultural
Retail	National	Sports
Publishing	International	Seminars
Health		Government
Insurance		
Media		

Transient Market Segments

Business Segment

The guest who stays at a hotel primarily because of its location in relation to another organization is called a **business transient** guest. The general term "business" can mean anything, but these guests have a primary purpose other than relaxation and recreation. The business guest makes his/her hotel choices based on many things, but one of the most common is called guest brand loyalty. As was reviewed earlier, brand loyalty is defined as the institutional preferences of a consumer for a product or service based solely on a brand name or logo. Many hotel chains have implemented programs to increase this loyalty. These are called guest loyalty programs, and they offer various incentives to the guest based on the frequency of their stays in a similar fashion to airline frequent flier programs.

These programs offer repeat guests earned points that can be redeemed for some type of reward. These rewards can include free room nights, vacation packages, and other such perks. Most programs grade customers based on volume usage. Those at top volume are often entitled to lower rates, upgrades, and other amenities. Some business transient guests become so loyal to a hotel chain's program that they may pay higher rates or stay at a lesser-quality facility to earn points. Many of the larger chains offer incentive tie-ins with airlines and car rental loyalty programs so that a business guest may earn points in multiple programs during one stay. Credit card companies also offer perks for guests to stay at certain chains from time to time.

Pleasure Segment

The **pleasure transient** guest stays at a hotel because of its proximity to an attraction and/or because of a signature attraction in the hotel itself. In the previous analysis of resorts, it was shown that an attraction can be an ocean, natural wonder, mountain, amusement park, a museum, or something else that attracts people but is not associated with the hotel itself. A signature attraction is an event, activity, or facility identified with a specific hotel.

The similarity between the pleasure-transient guest market and the characteristics that make up the resort location type are unique. It is because of these shared characteristics that the pleasure guest makes up a significant portion of the transient demand at resorts. The lagoon complex at the Doral, shown in Figure 3-3, is an example of a signature attraction that appeals to the pleasure guests.

FIGURE **3-3**

Doral lagoon complex
(Courtesy KSL Resorts)

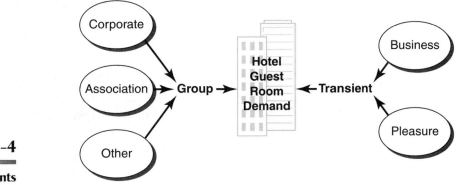

FIGURE 3-4

Market segments

Resorts may cater to individuals, couples, or families, which often translates into higher weekend demand and weaker weekday traffic. Family resorts may cater to their market by offering activities for children and more affordable rates. The term "family friendly" is often used in describing these resorts.

Figure 3-4 illustrates how both group- and transient-market segments come together to make up guest room demand.

NOTES

1. *Hotel & Motel Management, 216,* 11 (June 18, 2001), Advanstar Publications.

CHAPTER THREE **REVIEW**

KEY TERMS

group rooms
intermediary
group base
transient rooms
individual booking cycle
walk-in reservations
reservation avenues

management fee
commission
market segment
SMERF
business transient
pleasure transient

REVIEW QUESTIONS

1. Sleeping rooms are differentiated by classification into what two categories?
2. Market segmentation consists of what?

3. How do the goals or motivations of the transient business guest differ from those of the pleasure guest?

4. What are the two entities commonly referred to as intermediaries for transient reservations?

5. What five components make up the SMERF market segment?

6. Name some common corporate market subsegments.

7. Explain the unique relationship resorts and transient pleasure guests share.

8. How do guest loyalty programs impact brand awareness?

9. List the most common reservation avenues.

10. Define the individual booking cycle and its impact on a hotel.

DISCUSSION QUESTIONS/EXERCISES

1. Guest loyalty programs are typically the most expensive portions of a hotel chain's marketing budget. Are they worth it? In what ways could hotels create brand awareness and guest loyalty?

2. What effect would the reduction or elimination of hotel commission payments have on the industry? In other industries, such as the airline industry, the effect to passengers has been minimal due oligarchic factors. What is an oligarchy? Would the limited number of suppliers in a given hotel market have the same effect? Of course travel agents did not appreciate this reduction in airline commissions. What effect could the reduction of hotel commissions have on the travel agent industry?

3. Contact a hotel located in the downtown area of a city. Speak with the Director of Sales to determine their group/transient mix of business. Of the group business, determine what the primary segment is for them. Give five reasons you believe they focus on this segment.

4. Contact a suburban hotel located in the same city. Speak with the Director of Sales to determine their group/transient mix of business. Of the group business, determine what the primary segment is for them. Give five reasons you believe they focus on this segment. Compare and contrast the two properties. Are these competing hotels? Are their markets the same or different? Why?

Market Segmentation

"The Golden Bay Star Hotel"

This case study is an opportunity for a classroom to analyze the market segmentation situation of a fictional hotel. It has been organized in such a way as to stimulate discussion. In order to get the most out of this case, the participants need a thorough understanding of the first two chapters of this text. (*Note:* This case study is a work of fiction. The names, locations, and situations are products of the author's imagination. Any resemblance to actual persons, events, or organizations is purely coincidental.)

BACKGROUND

Hotel Name: Golden Bay Star Hotel
Product Type: Luxury
Location Type: Downtown—San Francisco, CA
Size: Medium (400 rooms)
Business Mix: Corporate Transient and Group

SITUATION

The Golden Bay Star Hotel was developed by a group of investors in the late 1970s to be the premier luxury property of its type in the Bay Area. The location in downtown was chosen for its proximity to the financial district and art gallery community.

In its early years of operation, the Golden Bay Star enjoyed modest success. But the ownership felt that better performance was possible. They decided that name recognition was what they lacked. By 1982 the ownership decided to affiliate the hotel with a national luxury management company. The hotel and management company signed an agreement that was renewable every five years.

For the next few years, the Star (as it is called) experienced record revenue performance. The boom in the financial markets was reflected in strong transient and group demand at high rates. The art market was experiencing strong interest from individual and institutional inventors from across the world. Auctions and other meetings were traditionally held at the Star. All parties involved were satisfied with the arrangement.

By the late 1980s, accelerated hotel construction in the vicinity of the hotel began to manifest itself. Properties of all product types and sizes began to pop up all around the Star. Newly developed hotel concepts (the extended stay and all suite) started to vie for the traditional business of the Star.

(continued)

Market Segmentation *(continued)*

After several years of declining performance, the hotel owners began to get nervous. They needed to know why they were in this situation and how it would be remedied. The ownership sent a representative, Tom Anderson, to the hotel to monitor the situation. Tom met with the hotel's general manager, Shelly Burns. Shelly had been at the hotel for 10 years. She had been on board for the period of exceptional performance, so naturally as the leader, she had been lauded. She was not used to being in the position of having to explain poor performance.

Shelly Burns was a "hands on" general manager. She involved herself in all aspects of operations and sales. She was so involved in sales and marketing, she saw no need for a change. They had never needed to advertise, and the sales office seemed to run itself. After all, she could make those decisions if need be, so why incur the extra salary costs?

The senior sales person at the Star, Frank Nevins, had been on staff since the opening of the property. He had long enjoyed a healthy relationship with the local financial community. His contacts were renowned, and he spent a great deal of time cultivating those relationships.

Tom asked Shelly to take a good look at the current state of the hotel. He needed to report back to the owners and wanted a solid plan from the hotel as to how it would improve performance. The owners were in the fifth year of their current management contract and needed to act quickly. He gave her one week to come up with a plan.

DISCUSSION

If you were Shelly, what would you do? This case presented background on a fictional hotel, but these situations occur every day. As a group, or as assigned, develop a plan for the Star. What factors should you take into consideration?

Points to Consider

- **The hotel's age**—a hotel new in the late 1970s is not new now. Does that matter?
- **Its location**—the Bay Area was in a downward business cycle. Is that cause for alarm? Shouldn't trends be anticipated?
- **Management contract**—could the management company be to blame?
- **Target markets**—what are the pros and cons of relying exclusively on two market segments?

Market Segmentation *(concluded)*

- **Ownership**—accountability to the owners only when a hotel performs poorly is common. What can be done to improve the relationship?
- **Competition**—how is supply and demand affected? What impact do the new hotel product types have on the Star?
- **Management style**—is it reasonable for a hotel general manager to be involved in sales and marketing? When is new leadership most needed—when the hotel performs well, or poorly?
- **Sales direction**—Frank Nevins spent a lot of time cultivating a slumping market. Was that the best use of his time? How might he better direct his sales efforts?
- **Advertising**—what kinds of advertising, if any, could be incorporated into the new plan?

Use these points as a guide to developing your own plan. Share the results with others and see what different ideas you all can come up with.

Theoretical Buying Decision

Question: "What can motivate a consumer to choose one option over another?"

Background: A consumer has an empty tank of gas. He or she is equidistant from two gas stations. One is on the left, the other is on the right (Figure 3-5A). Assume that they are both equally accessible.

What makes the driver choose the gas station on the right (Station B) over the gas station on the left (Station A) (Figure 3-5B)? Is it a whim, or is there an underlying goal? What makes the consumer choose between two similar options?

This driver chose Station B for a reason, even if that reason is not readily apparent. The driver may not even be aware of that reason. The motivation or goal of this driver may have included one or more of the following:

- **Value**—the price for gas at Station B may have been lower than Station A.
- **Quality**—the driver may have wanted the performance enhancing additives of Station B's gas.
- **Service**—Station B attendants may wipe windows or pump gas for the driver.

(continued)

CASE STUDY **Theoretical Buying Decision** *(concluded)*

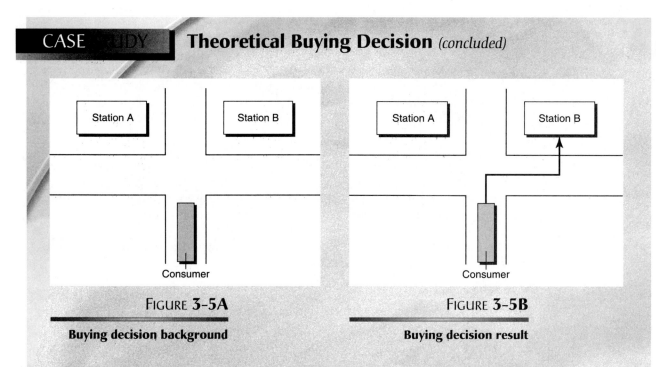

FIGURE **3-5A**

Buying decision background

FIGURE **3-5B**

Buying decision result

- **Reputation**—word of mouth or other forms of advertising may have triggered the driver's decision.
- **Other factors**—the driver may have sought out the convenience store in Station B, he or she may have known the owner, he or she may have gone there for years out of habit, he or she may have chosen it because it was brightly lit or closer to home or any number of other reasons.

The preceding goals or motivators may have triggered the buying decision in the driver, or something else may have. The point of this case study is to prompt thought into what drives a buying decision.

Hotel guests undergo similar processes when deciding on a hotel. What could some of the goals be in the hotel buying decision?

INTERNET RESOURCES
World Wide Web Travel Sites

Most of the following Web sites offer a full range of booking options that include hotel, air, and car. Some serve as third-party wholesalers who buy hotel rooms in bulk and then offer them on their Web sites for resale to consumers. Others simply search out the Internet for best available prices and fares.

<http://www.travelocity.com>
<http://www.expedia.com>
<http://www.priceline.com>
<http://www.travelnow.com/usa/?cid=3462>
<http://www.travelweb.com>
<http://www.sundaynews.com>
<http://www.usahotelguide.com>
<http://www.funtastiktravel.com/AmericaHotels.html>
<http://dir.travelzoo.com/Lodging.asp?intCategory=21>
<http://www.skyauction.com>
<http://www.lodging.com>
<http://www.traveleader.com>
<http://www.hoteltravelnetwork.com>
<http://www.11thhourvacations.com>
<http://www.travelguys.net>
<http://www.hotelreservation.com>
<http://www.hoteldiscount.com>
<http://www.travelscape.com>
<http://www.hotel-accommodations.com>
<http://www.hotelbook.com>
<http://www.travelhero.com>
<http://www.hotelreservations.org>
<http://www.quikbook.com>

For additional hospitality and travel marketing resources, visit our Web site at <http://www.Hospitality-Tourism.delmar.com>.

The Guest Room

OBJECTIVES

After reading this chapter, you should understand:

- How hotel guest rooms are laid out and categorized
- How to determine a guest room's status
- The impact of the Americans with Disabilities Act
- The differences in key control systems

INTRODUCTION

Hotels try to create a guest room that invokes a feeling of home in the occupant. The layout of the bathrooms, beds, and other features are carefully planned. Each area of the room mirrors a room in a home (i.e., bedroom, bathroom, office, etc.). Many hotels make a sizable investment in the design of rooms. They do this with the understanding that an appealing room invites a return visit.

The sleeping room is understood to be the main product for sale at any hotel. The importance of the sleeping room is evident when looking at opportunity cost. As has been reviewed, each hotel has a limit on the number of sleeping rooms it can sell. Therefore, hotel owners and managers continually strive to maintain a high level of quality in each of their sleeping rooms. Renovations and repairs are an ongoing process in all hotels. Those hotels that do not maintain their guest rooms suffer in the long run.

CATEGORIZING THE GUEST ROOM

The hotel guest room comes in myriad sizes and shapes. Hotels of differing product types (service level and target market) each have differing standards for the look and composition of their guest rooms. Location types can affect the look of a guest room as well. Continuing analysis of hotel guests' needs and wants have shaped guest rooms over time. Today, the modern guest room is created to meet a guest's room preferences. **Room preferences** are defined as the individual guest's choice of room type, configuration, and designation.

Room Types

Room types are based on the intended number of occupants. The standard room type is understood to be based on one occupant. This is called **single occupancy** (see Figure 4-1). The single room type has one bed. Typically, in North America, these beds are of queen size or larger. In Europe and Asia, it is common to find smaller beds equivalent to the twin or full size.

FIGURE **4–1**

Single occupancy
(Courtesy Indianapolis Marriott North Hotel)

FIGURE **4-2**

Double occupancy
*(Courtesy Omni Severin
Hotel)*

However, these room types set the foundation for specific room rates covered later. Although not universal, single occupancy room rates will often be lower than those with two people in a room, or **double occupancy** room rates (see Figure 4-2). In some cases, hotels will combine the two and offer a single/double occupancy rate.

Room types intended for three occupants are **triple occupancy**, and **quad occupancy** house four guests. It is rare for a standard room to house more than four people. Figure 4-3 illustrates these room types in architectural drawing format.

Room Configurations

Whereas room types look at the occupancy makeup of a guest room, room configurations look beyond the number of people. Room configurations characterize the physical makeup of the guest room. In essence, room configurations look at differences in guest rooms within a particular hotel. How hotels differentiate between room configurations is one important aspect of how they determine sleeping room rates. For the sake of this discussion, the following configuration analysis applies only to the standard target market. An examination of the all suite and extended stay markets will follow.

King Room

Double/Double Room

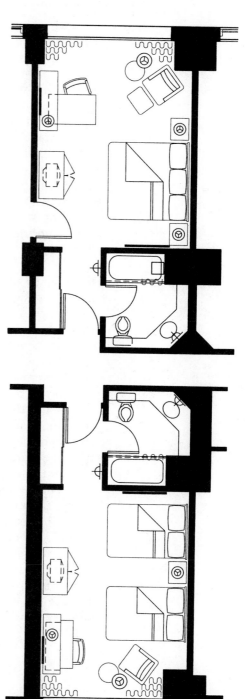

FIGURE **4-3**

Room layouts *(Courtesy Indianapolis Marriott Downtown Hotel)*

The ability to offer guests incrementally nicer configurations, called **upgrades**, allows the hotel increased room revenue. Upgrades do not always go hand in hand with a higher rate though. Upgrades are offered to VIPs or regular, loyal guests. Disgruntled or unhappy guests can receive upgraded rooms as a sign of good faith by hotel management. Upgrades to nicer room configurations are often part of group agreements as well.

It must be noted that room configurations only identify the room itself. Configurations must not be confused with what the hotel considers an added value. Hotels that designate rooms with a particularly nice view, balcony, or other amenity as added value may indeed charge more for those rooms. However, the room itself remains the same. The configuration does not change with the amenity alone.

The **standard configuration** is defined as the room configuration that makes up the majority of the sleeping rooms at a particular hotel. Because hotel chains and other affiliations differ in how they design their sleeping rooms, the standard configuration needs to be hotel specific. This is analogous to shopping for a new car. One can go into a dealership and look at varying levels of options on the same make of car. The standard configuration can be thought of as that car's base model (without options). Some hotels refer to their standard configuration as the **run of house (ROH)**. The run-of-house rooms are understood to be the greatest number of available rooms.

It is becoming increasingly rare for hotels to refer to their sleeping rooms as "standard." Hospitality marketing executives have begun a trend to refer to the standard configuration rooms as "deluxe" or "superior." The thought behind this trend is that consumers may perceive added value in these names, resulting in a greater willingness to pay higher rates. The truth is, many consumers realize the intent after staying in the room. If there is nothing that justifies the standard room being labeled differently, then it should remain as a standard configuration.

The next level up from the standard configuration is the enhanced guest room. The **enhanced configuration** is understood to include more amenities and/or services than the standard configuration. The enhanced configuration is sometimes called a "concierge" or "business level" room. Most major hotel chains and franchise companies offer some type of enhanced guest room. The enhanced configuration carries a higher room rate than the standard. These rooms include everything the standard rooms do (whatever that may be) plus additional amenities and/or services. The added amenities and services may include:

- Upgraded soft goods (drapery, bedspreads, robes, etc.)

- Upgraded hard goods (nicer/larger work areas, larger beds)

- Upgraded amenities (bath soaps, mouthwash, lotions, etc.)

- Items targeted to the business traveler (additional phones with long cords or cordless phones, additional phone lines for laptop computers, in-room fax machines, Internet access, coffee makers, access to copiers and printers, discounted dry cleaning and shoe shine, etc.)

- Access to a private lounge (typically offering complimentary continental breakfast in the morning and hors d'oeuvres in the evening)

The final room configuration is called the suite. The **suite configuration** involves a larger room (in terms of square footage) than the standard configuration (see Figure 4-4). Contrary to popular belief, not all suite configurations include greater levels of service or more amenities than the standard. By definition, the suite must only be larger than the standard. However, most reputable hotels offer the same services and amenities to suites that they offer to the enhanced configuration.

The suites themselves may be ranked within the hotel itself. Varying the size of suites allows the hotel to charge an ever-higher rate for the bigger rooms. Suites are identified by their size in relation to the standard configuration. The

FIGURE **4–4**

Suite configuration
(Courtesy Indianapolis Marriott North Hotel)

names may differ from hotel to hotel, but the following is an example of how the suite names change respective to the room size:

- "Jr." Suite—the smallest room in the suite configuration. It is often marginally larger than the standard room.

- Corner Suite—a suite that is located in the corner of the hotel building itself. This suite often takes up the same area that two standard rooms would (see Figure 4-5).

- "Bi-level" Suite—also takes up more square footage than standard rooms. Instead of taking the horizontal square footage of the corner suite, they take up the vertical area of two rooms. These suites span two floors or more to create very high ceilings.

- Hospitality Suite—intended to be more than a sleeping room. Hospitality suites (or "hospos" as they are often called) are intended to

FIGURE **4-5**

Corner suite *(Courtesy Indianapolis Marriott North Hotel)*

entertain groups of people. They may include a kitchen and/or bar area. Large tables make them conducive for small group meals or meetings. The rooms themselves may take up the square footage of three or more standard rooms. Often, a standard room opens to the hospitality suite to serve as the sleeping portion of the suite. Called **connecting rooms**, these rooms have doors that lock for privacy, but can be opened up to give the suite even more area. Most hotels also offer some standard configuration rooms that can connect to one another. Those rooms are useful for families.

● Presidential Suite—sometimes called the "Chairman's Suite" or the "Royal Suite." This suite is understood to be the best room in the hotel. It must be the largest room and typically has all the best amenities and services the hotel can offer. It will always carry the highest rack room rate in the hotel as well, but this suite is a very effective upgrade. Hence, it is rare to charge full price for this suite. This suite can be a very good incentive for large group bookings when offered complimentary or as an upgrade to the group for their VIPs.

Figure 4-6 and Figure 4-7 illustrate even more variations on the suite.

Room configurations remain constant amongst all hotel target markets. At first glance, the configurations for all suite and extended stay hotels may seem to differ from those of the standard target market. In fact, room configurations do not assume any universal starting point. The standard configuration is the category of guest room that is the most prevalent at a specific hotel. Therefore, if the most prevalent configuration is a two-room suite, then that suite is considered the standard configuration. All suite hotels in fact do have enhanced configurations and in many cases larger suites as well. Of course, the amenities of continental breakfast and evening hors d'oeuvres that many hotels in the standard target market offer for enhanced rooms do not apply as that is a standard offering in the all suite target market. All suite hotels do offer corner rooms and varying levels of large suites that they consider upgrades. The term suite is misleading in these cases as these upgrades are "suite upgrades of suites."

The extended stay target market uses the same philosophy. Perhaps the majority of sleeping rooms at an extended stay hotel are small studio apartments, or "efficiency" rooms (see Figure 4-8, page 72). The hotel in these cases would consider those rooms the standard configuration. Any larger room upgrades would fall into either the enhanced or suite category.

Room configurations are not limited to standard, enhanced, or suite. A relatively new development in the industry has been to develop rooms that are ADA (Americans with Disabilities Act) compliant. This configuration, called disabled access, includes rooms that are equipped to make the overnight

Marriott Suite

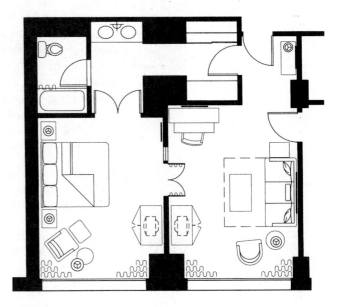

Hospitality Suite

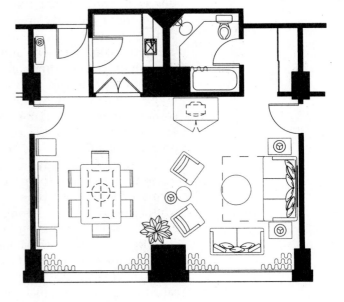

FIGURE **4-6**

Other suites *(Courtesy Indianapolis Marriott Downtown Hotel)*

Luxury Suite

Presidential Suite

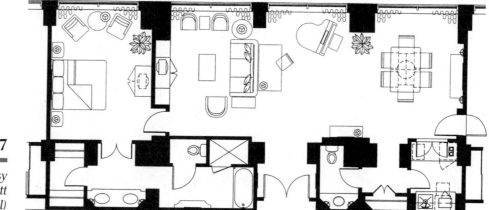

FIGURE **4-7**

Other suites 2 *(Courtesy Indianapolis Marriott Downtown Hotel)*

FIGURE 4-8

All suite *(Courtesy Embassy Suites)*

stay of the disabled guest more pleasant. The **disabled access configuration** may include the following in the room:

- Raised beds
- Wider doorways (threshold of less than 0.5″)
- Telecommunication Devices for the Deaf (TDD)
- Voice activated digital dialing
- Clocks with larger and brighter numbers
- Lowered peepholes in the door
- Closed Caption televisions
- Elevated toilets
- Bathrooms equipped with metal handrails
- Roll-in showers (minimum of 36″ × 60″)
- Visual alert smoke detectors, door knocks, telephones. and alarm clocks

New hotels must be built with a portion of their rooms ADA compliant. Older hotels are converting existing configurations into disabled access. The ADA applies to the entire hotel, not just sleeping rooms. Meeting space, entrances, and common areas must all be ADA compliant. Public telephones and water fountains must be lowered. Elevators should close slower in order to allow the disabled time to enter. Most of the front desk configurations in older hotels are far too high for those in wheelchairs; they must be lowered. Main hotel entrances must have some form of automatic opening mechanism. Hotels must make an effort to ensure that ample parking is reserved for the disabled near the entrances and that all curbs have cuts for wheelchair access as well.

Room Designations

The final remaining identifier for room categories is the room designation. The **room designation** simply identifies whether it is a smoking or nonsmoking room. In the early 1980s, hotels began to convert a portion of their sleeping rooms to permanently nonsmoking rooms. These rooms are regularly deep cleaned, filters on vents changed, and the air purified. In the beginning of this trend, nonsmoking guests were even willing to pay a higher rate for these rooms.

Since the advent of nonsmoking rooms, hotels have begun to designate more and more sleeping rooms as nonsmoking. It is common to find entire floors of hotel sleeping rooms designated as nonsmoking. Today, most hotels have a minimum of 50 percent of their sleeping rooms designated as non-smoking. In some markets that figure is as high as 75 to 80 percent. A few new hotels have even begun to experiment with entirely smoke-free guest rooms.

The combination of room type, configuration, and designation all come together to create the specific room a hotel guest may seek. The guest's room preference, if met, will play a major role in overall satisfaction. Figure 4-9 illustrates how room preferences come together.

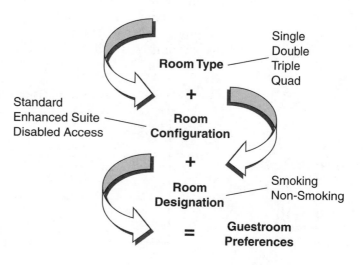

FIGURE **4-9**

Room preferences

Room Numbering

Assigning guest rooms a number is the identification method hotels have used for most of history. The way each hotel assigns its numbers is fairly straightforward. Each floor designates the first portion of the room number, the rest of the room number is sequentially assigned on that floor. All rooms on the third floor begin with a 3, and so on. Typically, the odd numbers are on one side of the floor, the even numbers on the other side. The actual assignment of the first floor is relative to the location of the front desk and lobby. Some hotels have built their lobbies above ground level. If the lobby is on the third floor, then the guest rooms will begin on the fourth floor, and so on. Whatever pattern is begun with the initial guest room floor, it is carried on throughout the remainder of the floors. This is to assist the hotel personnel in recognizing individual room locations by the number alone.

For example, a resort may number all the guest rooms facing the ocean with low even numbers starting on the north side of the building. As the room numbers progress down the hall they may finish with high even numbers on the south side. Bellstand personnel, room service, housekeepers, and others can find the room easier when they know exactly where it should be based on the number (see Figure 4-10).

In North America, as in parts of Europe, the 13th floor is omitted in the room count, even if the hotel has 13 or more floors. Due to the superstition of the number 13 being unlucky, hotels will number their floors 11, 12, 14, 15. The same can be said of individual rooms on a floor. Many hotels skip room number 13 altogether. Parts of Asia feel the same way about the number 4. Hotels in Asia may omit 4 as Western hotels omit 13.

Figure 4-11 and Figure 4-12 present hotel blueprints that, even though the actual room numbers had not been assigned at the time these were made, are useful in gaining a clearer picture on how guest rooms are initially laid out.

This foundation of understanding the guest room is very important to the front office. Few hotels build every room in exactly the same way. The hotel that minimizes the differences in rooms limits the number of people it

Sequential Room Numbering

101	103	105	107	109
1st Floor Guest Room Corridor				
102	104	106	108	110

Figure **4-10**

Room numbers

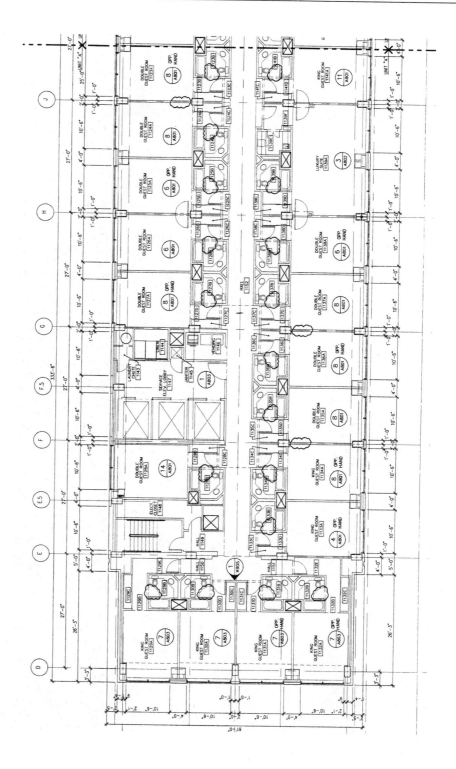

FIGURE **4-11**

Blueprints *(Courtesy Indianapolis Marriott Downtown Hotel)*

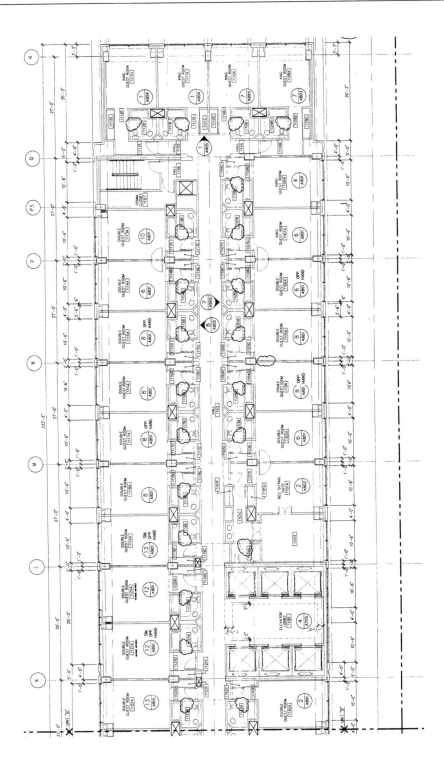

FIGURE **4-12**

Blueprints 2 *(Courtesy Indianapolis Marriott Downtown Hotel)*

will appeal to. Car manufacturers, for example, make several models of cars. If everyone wanted the same car, these manufacturers would not need to diversify their product lines. Hotel guest rooms can be viewed in the same way.

> *"A doctor can bury his mistakes but an architect can only advise his clients to plant vines."*
>
> —Frank Lloyd Wright

Room Status Reconciliation

The review of guest rooms was important to conduct before introducing the next section. Hotels monitor each and every guest room very closely. They are in business to sell rooms, and that includes each room type, configuration, and designation. The most important aspect of this monitoring process is discerning what guest rooms are available for sale and when. This is to avoid the obvious embarrassment of checking two guests into the same room, as well as to maximize room revenue by selling every room as soon as it becomes available. The hotel industry assigns a status to every guest room. Reconciling the guest room status is the way a hotel is able to manage availability.

Room status reconciliation is defined as ensuring that rooms are properly designated by their current status, and assigned a new status as it changes. Both housekeeping and the front desk maintain room status. Each coordinates with the other to make sure that rooms are assigned, cleaned, and assigned again to maximize room revenue, while avoiding a miss-assignment. Room status categories/designations are grouped by the guest room's **state of occupancy**, **state of cleanliness**, and **state of exception**. The most commonly used room status codes are Occupied, Vacant, Dirty, Clean, Ready, and Out of Order.

State of Occupancy

- Occupied—applies to a room that has been assigned to a guest and that guest has checked in
- Vacant—the guest has checked out of the room
- Ready—room is available for new occupancy

State of Cleanliness

- Dirty—room has not been cleaned by housekeeping
- Clean—room has been cleaned but not yet verified as clean

State of Exception

● Out of Order—room was removed from inventory for a specific reason (e.g., repairs or renovation)

The room status can be thought of as the "life cycle" of a guest room. Describing the status of a guest room requires determining its "readiness" for new occupancy. Therefore, a hotel must know its current state of occupancy and cleanliness. When determining a room's state of occupancy and state of cleanliness, a room status code is assigned. A **room status code** combines both occupancy and cleanliness information.

Room Status Codes

Status Code	Meaning
Vacant/Ready	Available for sale. A "V/R" room status is the only status a room can be sold in.
Vacant/Clean	Cleaned room, not yet inspected. All sleeping rooms are cleaned by a housekeeper and then inspected by a supervisor or manager to ensure it is ready for sale. These inspectors then change the code from "V/C" to "V/R."
Vacant/Maintenance	A "V/M" room has been taken out of inventory for some reason. This is the code assigned to out-of-order rooms.
Vacant/Dirty	Guest checked out, not serviced by housekeeping yet. "V/D" codes take top priority in housekeeping, as they must be readied for resale.
Occupied/Dirty	Guest currently occupies the room, the night has passed, but room has not yet been serviced by housekeeping.
Occupied/Clean	Guest currently occupies the room, and room has been serviced by housekeeping. Typically, there is no inspection for rooms cleaned during the length of an individual guest's stay. The expectation is that all rooms are cleaned well, but an occupied room is generally easier to clean than one from which the guest has checked out.

Figure **4-13**

Room status cycle

The life cycle of a guest room as reflected in these status codes is illustrated in Figure 4-13.

Chapter 11 focuses on housekeeping, where the room status plays an important role in day-to-day operations.

GUEST ROOM MAKEUP

Most North American hotels have their guest rooms configured basically the same. The product for sale is a place to sleep, so all guest rooms have a bed of some kind. The other universal items in a guest room are phone, television, and a bath. European hotels do not always include a private bath. Beyond these basic items, hotels differ greatly. The guest room makeup often dictates the hotel's service level and target market. A hotel is given industry ratings (stars and diamonds) based in part on the makeup of their guest rooms. Service classifications (luxury versus budget or economy) are also based in part on the guest room and what is inside it. Though these industry classifications place a higher emphasis on service levels, the physical room product is also important.

Because of the vast differences in the industry, it would not be practical to list every item that can go into a guest room. Bed sizes differ, often between queen and king for single occupancy, to double or twin for double occupancy. Furniture and other case goods differ widely. The year a hotel was built may dictate the square footage of each standard configuration room. Older hotels tend to have smaller rooms.

Consumers have a basic understanding as to what they are purchasing when they seek a hotel room. Unless they are seeking a facility for more than just the room (as is the case with resorts that have a signature attraction) or due to a group or convention meeting at the facility, the product is basically the same. It is the amenities and services they receive with the guest room that often distinguishes one hotel from another. National hotel chains spend millions of dollars a year trying to distinguish their product from that of their competitors. "Our beds are softer," "our TVs are larger," or "kids eat free" are some ways hotels try to create interest in their product. Consumers make their buying choices based on many reasons, but assuming that their guest room preference is met, why they make that decision is the subject of much debate.

The universal items create the starting point for guest room makeup (see Figure 4-14). The standard configuration of every hotel room, though differing amongst hotels, always contains the universal items. Again, the standard configuration for one hotel may be very different from another. The following items may be included in a hotel's standard configuration:

- In-room workstations (i.e., desk, lamp, chairs, etc.)
- Pull out sofa beds or Murphy beds. A **Murphy bed** is a bed that is stored in the wall of the room and pulled out when needed.

FIGURE **4-14**

Guest room makeup
(Courtesy Indianapolis Marriott North Hotel)

- One or more nightstands beside the bed(s)
- Vanity areas in or next to the bathroom
- Coffeemakers
- Irons and ironing boards
- In-room safes
- Closet(s)
- Dresser(s)
- "Blackout drapes," which are a second set of drapery that darken the room for sleep
- Clock radio or alarm
- Hotel collateral (i.e., room service menus, hotel facility summary, safety information, chain brochures, etc.)

- Selection of local phone directories and activity guidebooks

- Phones with a message light to indicate a waiting message. Most hotels now offer in-room voicemail in addition to written messages taken by PBX.

- Several chains offer retrieval of written messages on a closed-circuit TV channel. These in-room TV offerings also incorporate other services such as account review, summary of available hotel services, a listing of meetings taking place at the hotel (called a **readerboard**), and other services.

- The in-room television usually offers a selection of movies available for viewing at the guest's leisure. VCRs and DVD players are sometimes connected to the TV, or available for rental on request.

- Video games may also be available.

- Data ports are becoming universal in-room offerings as the use of laptop computers increases for business travelers.

- Glasses and ice bucket

- An in-room "honor bar" is offered at many hotels of the mid-market service level or higher. This bar is stocked with snacks and beverages that are charged to the guest based upon consumption.

- Many hotels will deliver complimentary newspapers to the room each morning.

In addition to these offerings, many hotels keep less frequently requested or needed items on hand. In an effort to please as many guests as possible these hotels may provide the following at little or no additional cost:

- An extra, portable bed (sometimes called a "roll away" cot) can be brought into a room when the existing number of beds (one or two) does not suffice.

- A small refrigerator may be brought into a room for a guest's use. Often they are needed to store food for special dietary needs and infants. Some medicines may need to be refrigerated as well.

- A bed board may be available at some hotels to make a mattress firmer and offer greater back support.

- Feather down pillows may be requested. Those hotels that stock each guest room with feather pillows as a standard will offer foam pillows to those guests with allergies to down.

- Cribs are often available as well.

KEY CONTROL SYSTEMS

One of the most important features of a guest room is the lock on the door. Guest security is very important, and hotels have been cognizant of that fact for years. **Key control systems** are used to ensure guest safety by changing the access to a guest room between guests.

In the past, key control systems were limited to basic metal keys. These were easily lost and costly to replace (see Figure 4-15).

Key control systems eventually evolved into systems that were easier to replace called key cards. These plastic keys resembled a playing card and were filled with small holes on one end that the door lock could read when inserted. Although an improvement over metal keys, they had to be replaced as well. Another drawback to key cards was that they had the room name printed on it. This posed a security risk for those guests who misplaced keys during their stay.

Modern hotels today use computer-controlled key control systems. A credit card–type card is assigned a special code when activated by the front desk. This key is preprogrammed with a guest's arrival and departure information as well as specific guest room information. These cards will only work for the duration of the guest's stay and only in a specific room (see Figure 4-16).

Upon departure, these cards can be reprogrammed for a new guest and new room. If lost, the information can be erased easily. Another benefit to these keys is that no guest room number is printed on them, therefore lost keys pose no security risk.

As technology advances, so does the evolution of key control systems. New key card systems are being developed with embedded memory chips and multipurpose microprocessors (see Figure 4-17). These advancements over the more traditional magnetic stripe allow hotels to better manage their key control systems. Efficiencies are gained in improving security, while also reducing the need to change door locks as often.

FIGURE **4-15**

Key access (*Courtesy VingCard*)

FIGURE **4-16**

Key cards *(Courtesy VingCard)*

FIGURE **4-17**

Key programming *(Courtesy VingCard)*

The Role of Architecture in Hospitality

Douglas Reddington, AIA
Principal, BSA Design

The basic definition of architecture is "the practice of building design and its resulting products."[1] Architecture is the combining of art and science to create buildings and space for people. More than this, architecture has a profound effect on society as a whole. The majority of people spend most of their lives in the built environment we call architecture. The physiological effect of good or bad architecture can be significant and long lasting. "Architecture is a social art"[2] on permanent display to the public. Architecture, unlike two- or three-dimensional art, is experienced by the participant, not simply observed. Because architecture resides in the public realm, architects bear a burden of responsibility when designing buildings not only for their client but also for the common good of society. This principle is very evident in the hotel industry.

Architecture in its simplest and primary role provides for our security, provides structure around us, and protects us from the elements (rain, snow, heat, vermin, etc.). Beyond these basic requirements, architecture can define who we are and what we stand for. Armed with a proper design solution, a building can project virtually any image. This can be a powerful tool for the hotel owners who want to define who they are and display these facts to the public. The selection of the proper architect for a hotel project can make the difference in a successful building project. For more information, visit the American Institute of Architects at <http://www.aiaaccess.com>.

The location of a hotel relative to the traveler and his/her place in their journey has been reviewed in this text. Therefore, it has been established that location is a critical issue. Given that a particular location may have several competitors, what will differentiate one hotel from the next? Architecture plays a major role in differentiating one hotel from the next. Name recognition and branding play a major role, but architecture itself is a part of the branding process. Combining the hotel's physical structure with the landscaping surrounding it comprises a hotel's architectural style.

INDUSTRY PERSPECTIVE
(continued)

Hotels will always be remembered for their architectural style. Everything a guest does from the minute they arrive on the hotel grounds and step into the building is affected by the architecture. This architecture is intended to provide for a guest's needs and comfort. In addition, the design and layout of a hotel creates perceptions early in a guest's stay. This is true at the most basic level. For example, if the rest rooms are placed directly in front of a hotel's main entry, then the rest rooms become the guest's first impression of the hotel's interior. The lobby requires rest rooms to provide for the guest's needs, but the layout and design of these rest rooms could be poor. There is no amount of extra service a hotel could provide to undo this negative first impression.

Architecture defines everything in the built hotel environment from the basic creature comforts of a guest room to the ambience of the grand lobby (see Figure 4-18). The physical form can subtly direct guests through the main entry and on to the front desk. The architecture should be able to do this without the use of signage and without being so forward as to be intrusive. The basic requirements of the hotel must be properly designed and the hotel's values adequately reflected for the architecture to be successful.

The architectural style can be so defining as to help attract business itself. Examples of this would be the Swan and Dolphin hotels on the Disney property in Orlando. Obviously, the entire

(continued)

FIGURE **4-18**

Grand Wailea lobby
(Courtesy KSL Resorts)

Disney facility is designed to attract crowds, but arguably the Swan and Dolphin are even more popular than the other hotels competing with them on the Disney campus. The bold architecture and exaggerated features, such as the swan and dolphin structures mounted on top of the buildings and the bold triangular shape of the Dolphin hotel, create an attraction within the Disney attraction itself.

Disney accomplished this by hiring architect Michael Graves. Mr. Graves is a world famous architect responsible for designing many famous works. Through his use of reinterpreted architectural icons such as "columns, pediments, and arches,"[3] Mr. Graves is credited with developing the style known as postmodern. "His buildings often combine whimsy and sophistication. Michael Graves was, perhaps, at his most playful when he designed the Dolphin and Swan hotels for Walt Disney Resort in Florida."[4] For more information on these works, visit <http://www.michaelgraves.com>.

Throughout history, hotel developers have recognized the value of architecture by enlisting the services of top-notch architects to design their buildings. For instance, American architect Frank Lloyd Wright was commissioned to design the Imperial Hotel in Tokyo in 1923. He also collaborated on the design of the Arizona Biltmore, which was opened in 1929 and was known as "the jewel of the desert."[5] The Arizona Biltmore survives today as a premier destination resort (see Figure 4-19).

FIGURE 4-19

Arizona Biltmore outdoors *(Courtesy KSL Resorts)*

Today, the use of high-end architectural design is still common. An example of this is the recent development of the Jumeirah Beach Resort in the Persian Gulf emirate of Dubai.[6]

The Jumeirah Beach Resort was designed as a destination resort and features the Burj al Arab (Tower of Arabs) hotel and the Jumeirah Beach Hotel. The resort was designed by W. S. Atkins Consultants of Surrey, United Kingdom for the Chicago Beach Resort LLC, Dubai, United Arab Emirates. The resort features two signature hotels and a water park. The Burj al Arab is a 1,053-foot-tall tower designed in the shape of a sail with a stunning 600-foot atrium and constructed 1,300 feet offshore on a man-made island. This makes it the tallest hotel in the world and can be seen from miles around. The Jumeirah Beach Hotel has a serpentine plan with a sleek profile designed to resemble a breaking wave. The weather in this region of the world can be inhospitable with occasional sandstorms and temperatures that can reach 130°F. Clearly the attraction here isn't the location, but the bold and striking architecture. For more information and pictures, visit <www.architecturemag.com>.

In contrast to these very high priced hotels, entrepreneurs have developed a competitive solution. Development of smaller hotels, or renovation and restoration of existing structures, has paved the way for a new design style. They are referred to as "boutique hotels" and are created for the "design hungry travelers who can't afford top of the line."[7] The Avalon Hotel in Beverly Hills, the Hotel Burnham in Chicago, and the Hotel Le Germain in Montreal are examples of these new boutique hotels. Their recipe for success is the combination of an older building redesigned into a unique, one of a kind, trendy hotel.[8] Boutique hotel designs are not limited to renovations. Chains like Hyatt have developed brands that are built as boutiques from the ground up. Several of the Park Hyatt hotels exemplify this design.

An example of renovating an older design into a boutique hotel can be seen with the Avalon Hotel. The Avalon was a circa-1950s hotel in need of repair. This hotel had a colorful history as the sometime home of Marilyn Monroe and the occasional location of the *I Love Lucy* show. In its redesign, the architects kept the basic boomerang building concept but updated the image to target today's fashion and entertainment industries. They turned

(continued)

INDUSTRY PERSPECTIVE
(concluded)

this run-down building into an up-to-the-minute retro-chic hangout. Terrazzo floors and 1950s-style furniture was added to the overall retro feel of the architecture. The guest room strategy was to create rooms that feel like apartments. They were also equipped with all the modern technology needed by today's wired professionals.[9] Again, in this example, the architectural design becomes the differentiation between this hotel and its competition. For more information, visit <http://www.architecturalrecord.com>.

In conclusion, architects have a responsibility in all of their design solutions to society as a whole. These designs are on public display for the life of the building. Their building solutions can be a reflection of the culture itself. Architecture can be used to create successful hotels in all markets. Hotel design plays a significant role in the hotel business. Properly used, the power of architecture can be used to create a statement that will be a draw to customers.

NOTES

1. "Architecture," Microsoft Encarta 98 Encyclopedia, 1993–1997 Microsoft Corp.
2. *Ibid.*
3. Craven, J. "Architecture," <http://architecture.about.com/arts/architecture/library/bld-graves.htp>.
4. *Ibid.*
5. <http://www.arizonabiltmore.com/hist.html>
6. McBride, E. "Burj al Arab," *Architecture Magazine* (August 2000).
7. Pearson, C. A. "The Second Wave," *Architectural Record Magazine* (February 2000).
8. *Ibid.*
9. *Ibid.*

CHAPTER FOUR **REVIEW**

KEY TERMS

room preferences
room types
single occupancy
double occupancy
triple occupancy
quad occupancy
upgrades
standard configuration
run of house (ROH)
enhanced configuration
suite configuration

connecting rooms
disabled access configuration
room designation
room status reconciliation
state of occupancy
state of cleanliness
state of exception
room status code
Murphy bed
readerboard
key control systems

REVIEW QUESTIONS

1. Why are guest room configurations hotel specific?

2. What is an enhanced configuration?

3. What might be included in a disabled access guest room?

4. What does "V/R" stand for?

5. Do all-suite hotels have a standard configuration? Explain.

6. Describe the room status life cycle.

7. Why is room status reconciliation so important?

8. Explain what an upgrade is and how hotels use them.

9. List four of the common added amenities/services offered in the enhanced configuration.

10. How does a "bi-level" suite differ from a hospitality suite?

DISCUSSION QUESTIONS/EXERCISES

1. Via the Internet, or directly from a hotel, obtain floor plans of three different room types for a property. Answer the following questions:

   a. What is the name of the property you selected?

   b. Where is it located?

   c. What is each room type called at this hotel?

   d. What is the rack rate for each room type?

   e. What is the incremental difference between the rooms?

   f. What differs between each type?

g. If added services and amenities are provided, what are they?

h. If each of these items were purchased separately, what would the cost be?

i. Does the incremental difference cover these costs?

j. Is it more than or less than purchasing them ala Carte?

k. Which is the better deal for the guest?

Now, call the hotel's reservation department. How well does the reservationist "sell" the various room types? Are all the services and amenities explained accurately? How would you rate your level of understanding the differences between room types and room rates?

2. Contact the reservations department of a city hotel. Inquire about the services they provide a disabled guest. Answer the following questions:

a. What items are available in disabled access guest rooms?

b. What items are available to be placed into the room upon request?

c. How many disabled access guest rooms do they have?

d. How many total guest rooms does this property have?

e. How are these rooms sold?

f. Are they "hard blocked" from time of reservation, or assigned the day of arrival by the front desk?

g. What would happen if the hotel were in a sold-out situation?

h. Is this hotel in compliance with the ADA?

i. What about the exterior access and meeting space access? What provisions are there in the public spaces of the hotel?

j. What is the name, address, and phone of the property you contacted?

k. What was the name of the person with whom you spoke? Was he/she knowledgeable about the details of the disabled access guest rooms, services, and policies?

If you were a disabled guest, would you be satisfied staying at this property? Why or why not?

SPECIAL FEATURE: NEW HOTEL CONSTRUCTION

The planning and design of a new hotel is a very interesting process. At the start, it is nothing more than an artist's conception. When completed, it becomes an exciting new place to work and serve guests. This section illustrates the evolution of the Indianapolis Marriott Downtown, from conception to final construction in photos covering each stage (see Figure 4-20 through Figure 4-25).

FIGURE **4-20**

Artist's conception
*(Courtesy Indianapolis
Marriott Downtown Hotel)*

FIGURE **4-21**

Laying the foundation
*(Courtesy Indianapolis
Marriott Downtown Hotel)*

FIGURE **4-22**

Walls go up *(Courtesy Indianapolis Marriott Downtown Hotel)*

FIGURE **4-23**

Roof started *(Courtesy Indianapolis Marriott Downtown Hotel)*

FIGURE **4-24**

Meeting space/Entry
*(Courtesy Indianapolis
Marriott Downtown Hotel)*

FIGURE **4-25**

Ready for business
*(Courtesy Indianapolis
Marriott Downtown Hotel)*

INTERNET RESOURCES
Hotel Design Web Sites

The Internet offers a variety of resources for hotel designers, builders, and architects. Owners can shop for products and services. Designers often share ideas and practices in various forums and chat rooms. In addition to the following sites, the American Architectural Association's home page provides numerous links.

<http://www.hotel-decor.com/>

<http://www.objekt.co.uk/design.htm>

<http://www.amerailsys.com/>

<http://www.hotelplans.com>

For additional hospitality and travel marketing resources, visit our Web site at <http://www.Hospitality-Tourism.delmar.com>.

Hotel Organization

OBJECTIVES

After reading this chapter, you should understand:

- The organizational makeup of a large hotel
- The differences between functional areas
- The responsibilities of a number of different job descriptions

INTRODUCTION

For any group, an organizational chart outlines the positions and responsibilities of each team member. Not unlike a team roster, which identifies the position each team member will take on the field, the organizational chart aids in identifying and directing the management team. Learning how a hotel organizational chart is laid out is important to understanding the different departments a hotel may have and how those departments work together. Hotel departments work together every day, each relying on the other to do their part in delivering a product they all can be proud of. The preceding chapters offered an overview of hotels in general. This chapter highlights hotel departments and how they interact with each other. Because this text focuses on the front office, a greater amount of detail is provided on its organizational structure.

HOTEL ORGANIZATION

The staffing and deployment within hotels can differ from property to property. Many factors go into determining the organizational makeup of a hotel. At the most basic level, a hotel will be staffed based on the following criteria:

- A hotel's size classification
- A hotel's location type
- A hotel's product type (service level and target market)

If one was to strictly look at the management organization of a hotel, each of the above would play a role in dictating who and how many did what. How each of these criteria affects the organization also depends on the hotel's lodging management association and the mandates, if any, placed upon it by a management company or hotel chain.

A small owner-operated hotel would obviously need fewer managers than a mega-size hotel operating under a management contract. A resort, simply by the nature of its facilities and services, would need more management personnel than an airport hotel of the same size. A limited-service hotel does not have the need for restaurant or kitchen help because they do not typically offer that amenity.

Given the variety of ways a hotel could deploy its staff using these organizational criteria, a standard example that covers all would be difficult. It would be most useful to select a hotel profile that illustrates the most widely used organizational deployment structure. Therefore, later in this chapter an in-depth analysis of the organizational deployment of an example hotel will be conducted.

FUNCTIONAL DEPARTMENTS

Most full-service hotels have six main functional departments. Each of these departments will exist, in one form or another, regardless of location type or product type. It is when the other organizational criteria are considered that the problem of defining the size and scope of these departments arises. Before looking at the organizational hotel example, an overview of these functional departments is warranted.

Functional Departments
- Rooms Division
- Food and Beverage
- Accounting
- Human Resources
- Engineering
- Sales/Marketing and Catering

A variety of responsibilities and duties exist within each department. All these departments rely on each other to provide the best product. Understanding each department is vital to understanding the hotel as a whole.

Rooms Division

Within a hotel, perhaps no area is as vital and in some cases as visible as the rooms division. The rooms division is the "nerve center" for most of a hotel's operations. It is, after all, the area most responsible for the main hotel product, the sleeping room. This is evident in the hotel industry maxim: "Everything Begins with the Rooms Division."

The rooms division of a hotel is an image easily conjured up in the mind of most people. They know what happens at the front desk (on the surface, at least) (see Figure 5-1). Most people understand what a bellperson does. People

FIGURE **5-1**

Lobby/Omni *(Courtesy Omni Severin Hotel)*

understand the basic premise of housekeeping, and so on. Even if the actual titles differ, such as "greeter" for a bellperson, or "room attendant" for a housekeeper, their functions are fairly universal. What goes on behind the scenes in the rooms division is what most people do not know.

The rooms division is a functional area within the hotel that includes the front office, housekeeping, reservations, night audit, and loss prevention/security departments. The size and scope of these areas may differ from one hotel to another depending on the hotel size and product type. The management philosophy of the hotel may also affect the organizational structure of the rooms division.

This section first provides a general overview of the rooms division. It concludes with an analysis of other hotel departments. Successive chapters deal with other rooms division departments—namely, housekeeping, reservations, and night audit.

Front Office

Within the rooms division, lies the front office. The front office is comprised of two main areas: (1) front desk, and (2) uniform services. Each of these areas performs unique roles. They report directly to the front office manager.

Front Desk. Being one of the first (and often last) points of contact with a hotel guest, the front desk plays a big role in the hotel. The front desk manages the in/out flow of guests on a daily basis. The front desk is often called the "hub" or "command center" of the rooms division because so much information is funneled through it. The front desk is the logical point of contact for the dissemination of information for guests and other hotel employees.

Uniform Services. Uniform services encompass the areas within the front office other than the front desk. Sometimes referred to as guest services, the areas within uniform services include:

- Bellstand
- PBX
- Valet parking/Garage
- Shuttle driver
- Concierge
- Doorpersons

The name derives from the fact that each of these employees used to wear a uniform of some sort. The garage and valet parking groups manage guests' automobiles. The bellstaff assists guests to and from their rooms. The concierge tends to special guest needs of any sort. The private branch exchange or PBX manages communications into and out of the hotel.

Confusion may arise in identifying this department because today it is uncommon to find PBX, for example, in uniform, as they never actually greet a guest in person. Also, although housekeepers wear uniforms, they are not considered uniform services in this definition.

Housekeeping

The housekeeping department is considered a vital part of the rooms division. Though not generally considered a part of the front office, housekeeping works directly with the front desk to ensure that the main products of the hotel (guest rooms) are ready for sale. Their main tasks are to clean and prepare guest rooms and to maintain the cleanliness of hotel common areas, such as the lobby. **Common areas** within a hotel are spaces where most, if not all, guests may walk through. The hotel lobby, entry, main rest rooms, foyer, and meeting pre-function areas are all considered common areas.

In conjunction with the front desk, housekeeping must determine what rooms are to be cleaned, what rooms are available, and what rooms are occupied. This monitoring of the available product, the room inventory, ensures that there is no opportunity cost incurred in empty rooms. Within the housekeeping department, certain individuals may be responsible for washing sheets and linens. This can be a very large operation for a mega hotel.

Reservations

The reservations department strives to book individual reservations in conjunction with group sales to maximize room revenue. The reservations department is also referred to as transient room sales. It could be argued that reservations actually have the first contact with most guests in that they communicate with them before they actually arrive. This would generally apply to transient reservations. It is for that reason that reservations is located in the front office

THE UNIQUE ROLE OF RESERVATIONS

It must be noted here that the reservations department is unique in that it is part of two functional areas. Though generally considered part of the rooms division, the transient sales effort must be coordinated with the group sales effort in order to maximize room revenue. But, because the reservations department deals extensively with guests, it is often located in the front office area. The reservations department will usually have a direct reporting structure to the sales functional area and a "dotted line" reporting structure to the front office area.

area and has an indirect reporting structure to it. (Again, further analysis of reservations comes later in this text.)

Night Audit

The **night audit** team reconciles the hotel's daily financial transactions and other activities for reporting purposes. Due to the twenty-four-hour nature of hotel operations, this department conducts its duties at night, when hotels are generally less busy. The staffing of the night audit group is commonly small in comparison to other rooms division departments. The team is led by the night audit manager and is supported by anywhere from two to five night auditors. This department assumes some front office duties, such as management of the front desk, at night. Therefore, the night audit team will have a "dotted line" reporting structure to the rooms division manager in addition to their direct reporting to the accounting department.

Loss Prevention/Security

The loss prevention department can be very important to a hotel. The main priority of loss prevention is the safety and security of all hotel guests and employees. Members of the loss prevention staff patrol the hotel common areas and guest room hallways. The **director of loss prevention** must ensure that all accidents and guest complaints are handled professionally and thoroughly. Large hotels in crime prone areas may hire off-duty police officers to enhance their loss prevention capability. In many hotels, loss prevention also serves as a shipping and receiving department.

The loss prevention team may be one of the smallest of the rooms division (often one or two people), but their responsibilities are quite large. The size of this team can grow as hotel operations warrant. For example, a large or mega-size hotel casino may have a substantial loss prevention team on hand to ensure safety and deter theft. Loss prevention can also work to limit future hotel liability by facilitating continuous employee safety and awareness programs. (Guest and employee security issues are addressed in Chapter 10.)

As has been reviewed, the rooms division area is perhaps the largest and most visible of all hotel departments. The front desk and uniform services have the highest amount of guest contact within the hotel. Reservations, night audit, and housekeeping play vital roles "behind the scenes." A very good way to understand the functions of the rooms division departments is to examine the role each plays in the arrival and registration of hotel guests. The process of a guest arrival and registration is summarized in a sequential format called the arrival chronology addressed in the next chapter. However, with this basic understanding of the rooms division, one can begin an analysis of other hotel departments.

Food and Beverage

As we have come to understand, only full-service hotels will have this functional department. The size of this department will vary greatly based on the food and beverage outlets available at a particular hotel. The responsibilities of the food and beverage department are:

- Kitchen(s)
- Restaurant(s)
- Lounge/Bar(s)
- Room service

The food and beverage functional department has minimal interaction with other departments. Some hotels do not have integrated computer systems (called property management systems) to track guest charges throughout the hotel. In those cases, members of the food/beverage team must bring individual guest charges to the front desk so that they can be added to an account. This process, called **manual posting**, ensures that all outlet/ancillary charges are accounted for.

It is useful for all hotel employees to be familiar with their hotel's food and beverage operation so that they will be able to notify guests of what is available at the hotel. Many hotels regularly invite staff to dine at the various outlets in order to ensure that they remain familiar with offerings, specialties, hours of operation, and the like. In essence, by recommending the hotel's outlets to guests, the staff become part of the hotel's marketing effort.

Accounting

Because hotels operate just like any other business, someone must monitor and mange the money. The financial responsibilities of the accounting department can also vary with the size and scope of the hotel. Numerous food and beverage outlets and other ancillary revenue sources can affect the size of this department. Accounting also shares a duty, called night audit, with the rooms division. Accounting handles the following duties:

- Credit
- Accounts receivable
- Accounts payable
- Night audit

Credit is extended to individuals and groups based on certain preset criteria. Accounts receivable tracks the revenues due the hotel. Accounts payable manages the hotel's expenditures. Again, detailed discussion of the night audit function will come later, but basically it serves to reconcile the hotel's books on a nightly basis.

Accounting works very closely with most hotel divisions on a variety of issues. Credit may be extended to certain guests and groups, so the front desk and sales/catering must understand the role of accounts receivable. In fact, reservations must also understand the role of credit as initial reservations may be made with certain credit provisions. Accounts payable would play an important role in ensuring that the supplies for housekeeping are ordered and paid for on a timely basis. Of course, as has been stated, there is a large overlap between night audit and the front desk.

Accounting also manages the currency control process at the hotel. Front desk cashiers may handle many cash transactions in a given day. Although this specific process is addressed in a later chapter, it is important to realize the impact accounting has on the entire hotel.

Human Resources

In addition to the accounting function, hotels share other needs with most industries. Hospitality is an industry that relies on people. Hotels succeed only with the right personnel in the right places. It is the responsibility of the human resources department to find and retain these people. Within human resources, the staff performs the following duties:

- Payroll
- Benefits
- Recruitment
- Career development/ Training
- Conflict resolution
- New hire orientation

With staffing levels at some mega-size hotels reaching 1,000 employees, managing the payroll can be a daunting task. Nothing reduces employee satisfaction faster than an incorrect paycheck. Continuously monitoring trends in employee benefits ensures that the hotel remains competitive. Recruitment of new employees is perhaps the most important role of human resources. Creating and implementing various training and career enhancement programs has been proven to improve employee retention and reduce turnover. Human resources can also play a vital role as an impartial mediator in employee conflicts with each other and conflicts involving superiors.

Staffing and recruitment are perhaps the most important ways human resources can impact the entire hotel. Although final hiring decisions are usually left for the department heads, human resources acts as a "filter" by providing a pool of qualified candidates for the decision-makers to choose from.

Housekeeping, food/beverage, and night audit have traditionally high turn-over rates, so keeping this pool of candidates available is very important to those areas. Training programs on guest service and satisfaction impact the front office because they have arguably the most guest contact. The new hire orientation process ensures that new employees understand the basic hotel philosophies and processes before they begin their first day of training on the job. The orientation typically is conducted on a regular basis, say weekly or monthly (depending on the size of the hotel and its turnover rate).

Engineering

The physical structure of a hotel must be maintained and nurtured just like the people inside. The myriad systems within a hotel, including electrical, ventilation, heating/cooling, water, phone, computer, and others, must be continually checked and repaired. The building(s) themselves must also be maintained. Within engineering, the responsibilities are:

- Maintenance (repair and upkeep of the internal and external hotel structure and equipment)
- Groundskeeping (maintenance and upkeep of the facility grounds and landscape)
- Capital improvements

Capital improvement is the process by which a hotel undergoes renovation. The dispensation of these capital improvement funds, sometimes called **FF&E** funds (furniture, fixtures, and equipment) may reside with the hotel owner. FF&E funds are usually allocated in one of two ways: (1) **soft goods**, or those goods that are easily replaced (e.g., bedspreads, drapery, wallpaper, etc.) must be changed or updated often; (2) **hard goods** (sometimes referred to as case goods), or those goods that are associated with the infrastructure of the hotel. Items like the bed frame, lighting fixtures, and guest room furniture must also be replaced regularly to keep the facility up to date. Certain lodging associations, namely management contract and franchise, require that owners set aside a certain amount of each yearly budget for FF&E. Because of the disruptions that can occur with a hotel renovation, extensive planning by the director of engineering can help to minimize the impact on the hotel guests.

Hotel engineers maintain many parts of the facility by implementing a preventive maintenance program. A preventive maintenance program is structured so that engineers constantly inspect and monitor various aspects of a hotel to ensure that all items are in working order. The thought is that these programs help find small problems before they become bigger (and possibly more costly) problems. The "PM" programs, as they are referred to, rely heavily on observations from all staff.

Engineering works very closely with housekeeping in maintaining the quality of the physical guest room. Housekeepers are encouraged to report problems with a guest room's plumbing or electrical systems immediately to engineering for repair. The front office staff is usually the first to notice problems with the hotel common areas, as they are generally located in the lobby. Computer system malfunctions and PBX-related issues are also the responsibility of engineering. The catering staff reports problem areas in the banquet rooms to engineering as well.

Sales/Marketing and Catering

A full-service hotel that has meeting space requires a department to maximize that space. As the hotel success triangle showed, maximizing the revenue impact of this space, as well as the other two sides of the triangle, helps ensure that the hotel makes the most out of every available revenue source. Sales and catering encompasses three departments that directly impact the hotel success triangle:

- Catering sales
- Group sales
- Transient sales

The catering sales team works to sell the function space side of the success triangle. The group sales team sells sleeping rooms, the second side of the triangle. Combining transient sales (reservations) and group room sales endeavors to fully occupy the hotel's rooms each night, which in turn impacts the outlet/ancillary side of the triangle. This effort attempts to minimize the

GROUP RÉSUMÉS

Communication inside a hotel is vital. Many reports, memos, and other documents are created daily to ensure that each department is fully aware of the issues that may affect them. The sales and catering department creates many documents to make the hotel aware of groups that are due to arrive. One of these documents is called the **group résumé.** The group résumé summarizes all the sleeping room and catering requirements of a particular group. The résumé (also referred to as a group profile or group cover sheet) communicates with each department within the hotel. It summarizes the size of the group, the number of overnight rooms, the number and scope of on-property functions, and so on. Information pertinent to the kitchens, reservations, outlets, front desk, housekeeping, and other departments are included so that the requisite staffing and purchasing tasks are completed in advance.

opportunity cost of unsold rooms. The marketing responsibilities of the hotel (such as advertising) also reside with this group.

The transient sales team (reservations) with its "dotted line" reporting structure to the rooms division interacts with the front office often. The group sales effort, as was reviewed in earlier chapters, books groups into the hotel. These groups can impact the entire hotel in various ways. In addition to front desk and housekeeping, these groups affect the outlets, meeting space, and ancillary offerings. The group sales team must communicate relevant group facts and characteristics to the hotel. These relevant facts might include an early check-in, which would impact housekeeping, or a late checkout, which would impact the front desk. If the group is on their own for lunch on a given day, the food/beverage outlets would like to know in advance in order to prepare for possibly higher volume.

PRACTICAL AREAS

Six functional departments can be divided into two broad practical areas. Within the hotel industry, the level of guest contact defines the practical areas. Those with the most guest contact are considered front line, or **front of the house**. Those who serve more of a supportive role, with minimal guest contact, are considered **back of the house**. The relationship of the two practical areas is symbiotic. They need each other in order for the hotel to perform optimally. The rooms division, food/beverage, and sales/catering departments are considered front of the house. The human resources, engineering, and accounting departments are considered back of the house (see Figure 5-2).

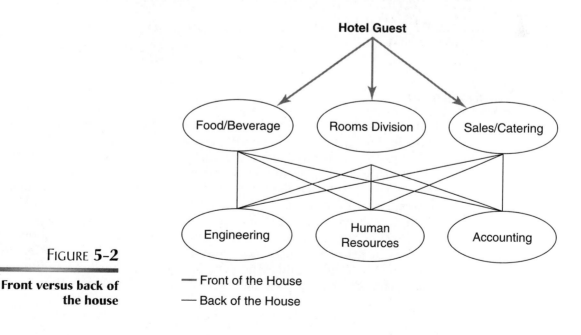

FIGURE **5-2**

Front versus back of the house

— Front of the House
— Back of the House

ORGANIZATIONAL DEPLOYMENT EXAMPLE

Functional departments and practical areas are generally accepted as integral to the organizational structure of all full-service hotels. An in-depth look at the specific titles and responsibilities of a hotel's organizational structure requires selecting a specific hotel profile. The most useful profile incorporates many levels of management within each functional area, while remaining realistic.

The organizational criteria for this example are as follows:

Organizational Criteria	Example Profile
Size classification	Large (401 to 1,500 sleeping rooms)
Location type	Resort
Product type	
● Service level	● Upscale service level
● Target market	● Standard target market

There are two distinct methods of hotel organization that differ in structure: traditional deployment and revenue-based deployment. The first method reviewed here is the traditional organizational method of hotel deployment. Later in this chapter, an analysis of revenue-based deployment is conducted.

> *"An executive is a person who always decides;*
> *sometimes he decides correctly, but he always decides."*
>
> —John H. Patterson

Top Level Management

From top level managers, to those working on the front line, the organization of the leadership structure serves to ensure that it functions properly. The first logical place to begin looking at the organizational structure of any organization is at the peak. The top level manager at any hotel is most commonly called the **general manager**, who is ultimately responsible for the hotel. The general manager may report to a regional manager if the lodging association of the hotel is with a chain or management company. Other associations may require that the general manager report directly to the hotel owner. In Europe, the general manager is often called the managing director or general director. Whatever the title, the general manager directly or indirectly (via other managers) coordinates the hotel's operational and sales efforts.

ABOUT MY JOB

General Manager
Kristin Wunrow

Very shortly after graduating from college, I stopped by a hotel and applied for a front desk agent position. I figured I could work some hours in a stress-free environment while I looked for a "real job." Who would've guessed that a front desk position could be the start of a life-long passion? I quickly learned that the front desk is the heart of the operation in a limited-service hotel. And I loved every minute of it.

What started as a part-time job suddenly turned into a full-time career. With my college years behind me, I decided that I was enjoying the hotel business. Because I was working at the "the heart of the hotel," I soon became a master of fielding complaints ("opportunities" is how the corporate people referred to them). I found myself actually enjoying the art of turning the situation around in favor of my organization. To go from the beginning of the conversation, where you might be apologizing to the guest for whatever might have happened, to the end, where the guest is actually thanking you for your help in resolving it, I had found my dream job. I knew I wanted to grow and get promoted to higher levels of responsibility, so I planted a couple of seeds in the mind of my manager. Low and behold, three months later I was promoted to front office manager at the same location.

I was now responsible for finding the perfect front desk candidates. Interviewing, hiring, training, supervising; I never thought I could make a whole week's work of this. During my time as front office manager, I interviewed what seemed like a thousand people claiming to be my perfect candidate. I had to figure out what I wanted at the front desk; who I wanted representing our hotel. I learned much from observing other managers. I realized that I could train anyone how to use a computer, or how to operate the switchboard. I could not, however, turn someone into a "people person." So the quest was on for the best personalities I could find. I was determined to have the best front desk staff in the city. This delighted my general manager immensely.

A year later, I moved 2½ hours away to become the assistant general manager of a hotel within the same company. In this limited-service hotel, there is no sales department. There is no accounting

(continued)

ABOUT MY JOB
(continued)

department. There is key staff—comprised of the general manager, assistant general manager, front office manager, executive housekeeper, and engineering supervisor. So my position was supposed to be approximately 70 percent outside sales and 30 percent in-house management. I found that this only works in a perfect world (or in a completely staffed hotel).

I became the world's greatest bedmaker. Or perhaps I was a world-class sheetfolder. Maybe I was the best accounts receivable clerk known in the history of hotels. In any case, I became a juggler of all imaginable hats. I had to learn how to go from cleaning rooms, to checking guests in at the front desk, to switching out a television set that wasn't working quite right, to going out and making a service call to a client, all without skipping a beat. I realized that I truly enjoyed all the hats I put on. I had the best of both worlds: I could have a great conversation with a guest while checking him in; or I could get to know an employee while working in his/her department.

The year quickly passed, and I received yet another career opportunity, which of course meant another geographical move. My experience had finally paid off—I was becoming a general manager.

I am now ultimately responsible for all goings-on in my hotel. Immediately after beginning my new position, I had to go through the tedious yearly budget process. I am responsible for controlling expenses while driving revenues to increase our gross operating profit and average daily rate (ADR). Working with numbers and spreadsheets, and toggling between computer programs completing reports for our corporate office have all become a part of my daily routine. I have to make a conscious effort to take a few moments out of each day to stroll around the hotel and talk to the guests and employees. After getting acclimated into my new position, I came to a conclusion. In order to eliminate the "juggling of hats" that many of us are still doing, I must, with the help of my key staff, reduce the turnover of employees at our hotel.

So, my time as a general manager for the most part has been consumed with creating and implementing the best incentive plan any of my employees has ever experienced, an incentive plan that rewards and motivates, one that makes our employees want to come to work each day. Our corporate executives believe that the guest should be number one. But I think differently. At our hotel, the guest is number two. In my opinion, the employee is number one.

ABOUT MY JOB
(concluded)

I truly believe that we need to take good care of our employees. Train them to deliver great service, motivate them to feel that this is more than just a job, recognize them for their great deeds, compensate them for a job well done, and retain them to create a consistent staff. If we take care of our employees, they will in turn take good care of our guests. The guests will tell their colleagues, families, and friends of the great service they received while at our hotel. They will stay with us again, and we will constantly build new clientele thanks to word of mouth. Our employees are happy, our guests are happy, our revenues are increasing—so the executives at our corporate office are happy—and all this makes me extremely happy. This is something they don't talk about in college. This is something you can learn about only through experiences. This is what is known as job security.

The Executive/Leadership Team

The senior-level managers who report directly to the general manager make up the hotel's leadership team. Sometimes called the executive committee, this group of managers directs one or more facets of the hotel's operation. The general manager usually sets the long-term management strategy of the hotel. The executive committee assumes the role of implementing that leadership vision. This group sets specific revenue goals and operational targets. In hotels operating in a franchise or management contract association, regional managers may be directly responsible for the strategic vision of each team member. Again, depending on the hotel's organizational criteria, the specific leadership team members may vary. The makeup of the leadership team invariably mirrors the structure of a hotel's functional departments. Each functional department has an executive committee member responsible for its operation. Our example resort may include the following managers on its executive committee (see Figure 5-3).

Rooms Division Manager/Resident Manager

The title "resident manager" can be traced back many years. It started as the name for the manager who actually lived at the hotel (hence the name *resident*) and was available at all hours. Long ago, it became evident that someone had

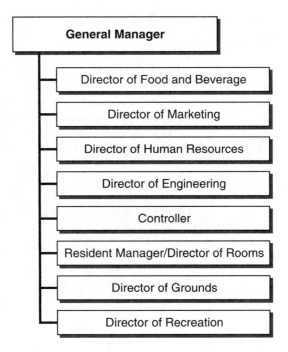

FIGURE 5-3

Executive leadership team

to be in charge of the hotel when the general manager was absent. It became apparent that the after-hours responsibilities of this **resident manager** would center on sleeping rooms because of the twenty-four-hour nature of hotels. Today, at most hotels, it is rare to find the resident manager residing at the hotel, but because of the age-old responsibilities of coordinating the operations of room-related hotel functions, the title remains. Some hotels have begun using the title rooms division manager or director of rooms for this position instead.

Director of Food and Beverage

The **director of food and beverage** runs each department that sells, buys, or prepares food and beverage products for hotel guests. The catering, restaurant/outlet, and kitchen staff report to him or her.

Director of Marketing

The **director of marketing** oversees the hotel's sales and marketing operation, directing the group and transient sales efforts to maximize room revenue. He or she also implements long-range goals, directs all advertising, and helps determine the hotel's yearly budget and marketing plan.

INDUSTRY PERSPECTIVE

Engineering

Jeff Beck
Director of Engineering
Indianapolis Marriott North

Beginning with the realization that the hotel is our guests' "home away from home" quickly focuses the engineering department. Start with the physical structure—its beauty—you can stand in front of her and feel an overwhelming sense of pride to know that you are responsible for her and that you will do whatever it takes to keep her beautiful.

Maintaining a hotel has several elements crucial to a smooth operation. Communication with other departments is number one. The front desk is the direct link between engineering and the guest. Constant communication is key in ensuring that all rooms are ready and in working order. The goal is to have a guest check in, enjoy the stay, and check out with no problems. However, if a guest does experience a problem, he or she usually notifies the front desk staff, who in turn sends an engineer to correct the problem. After the problem is corrected, the engineer follows up with the desk staff to relay that the problem is fixed. It does not end there. The information is then put into the guest history so that when the guest returns, the desk gives engineering a report of guest history problems so that we (Engineering) can take proactive measures to ensure that the room is 100 percent in working order prior to the guest's arrival. This helps to ensure that the guest will not have a repeat experience. Engineering may involve the front desk in a "second effort" program as well. Second effort simply means that follow-up communication is made with the guest who reported the initial program. The front desk should contact the guest and make sure that the situation was satisfactorily resolved. That goes a long way to ensuring guest loyalty!

Housekeeping is the backbone to the support system for Engineering. Housekeepers are in every room almost every day. They see the things that are wrong in the room and report to a supervisor, who immediately notifies engineering. This process helps ensure that everything is in working order for the guests—100 percent.

The next and a most important element is preventive maintenance. The Director of Engineering needs to establish a base—a core

(continued)

**INDUSTRY
PERSPECTIVE**
(concluded)

level of importance of every piece of equipment in the hotel. An inventory of mechanical equipment is compiled and then scheduled for maintenance accordingly. For example, on a washing machine, the motor is oiled once a month, the belts are checked every week, and the machine is cleaned daily. For the rooms, a continual process is necessary to keep them functional—a general rule is four times per year for every room.

Ownership is our pride, the building and everything in it is our work of art. We protect it, and much like an artist, when we complete something, we are proud to put our signature on it!

Director of Human Resources

The **director of human resources** is in charge of all hotel personnel. His or her responsibilities include recruiting employment candidates and complying with all governmental regulations when hiring and terminating employees. Payroll and benefits are often coordinated through this office.

Director of Engineering

The **director of engineering** is unique among executive/leadership roles in that he or she is involved in the physical aspects of the hotel's operation. The conditions of the interior and exterior structure of the hotel fall under his or her purview. Controlling the costs of heat/light/power as well as general maintenance are part of the engineering director's responsibilities. Long-term capital improvement planning and renovations begin with this manager.

Controller

The hotel **controller** is in charge of the hotel's financial reporting and cash flow management. The controller must monitor costs as well as help make cash expenditure decisions. The controller typically has input in the operational decisions of most hotel departments.

Director of Grounds

Unique to the resort hotel, the **director of grounds** is in charge of landscape and the surrounding area. If a resort happens to have a major attraction on property, such as a golf course, the director of grounds would maintain it. The director of grounds works closely with the director of engineering to ensure that the exterior of the hotel is in the best shape possible.

FIGURE 5-4

Hotel pool *(Courtesy Indianapolis Marriott North Hotel)*

Director of Recreation

Again, this position would only be found at a resort location type. Because a hotel must have a signature attraction to be labeled a resort, the **director of recreation** most often is in charge of that attraction. The operation of a world class tennis center or golf course on site would be under this manager's purview. The director of recreation works with the directors of grounds and engineering in maintaining pools (see Figure 5-4), play areas, beaches, fitness centers, and other recreational areas.

Department Heads

The next level of management in the organizational structure of this example hotel includes the departmental managers, or **department heads**. Reporting to the leadership team are these mid-level managers with responsibility for specific aspects of a department. These managers translate the strategic goals set by the leadership team to the staff. In turn, the department heads provide vital communication avenues to the leadership team from the front line managers and employees. The communication and integration of the various hotel departments generally occurs between department heads. It is at this level where much of the "work" is done. Department heads are the managers who are most directly involved in an area's day-to-day operations. Each executive committee manager may have one or more department heads reporting to him or her.

Rooms Division Department Heads

Front Office Manager. The **front office manager** is the department head responsible for a large portion of the most visible aspects of a hotel's day-to-day operation. He or she directs the day-to-day activities of the front desk and uniform services. Each of these areas has significant guest contact. The efficiency and service levels of each area under the purview of the front office manager are crucial to ensuring guest satisfaction. Most hotels include the PBX staff in the front office manager's line of authority. Working closely with the director of services, the front office manager reports to the resident/rooms manager. Reporting to the front office manager:

Job Title	Basic Responsibility
Front desk manager	Manage day-to-day operation of the front desk and coordinate communication with housekeeping. Typically assigned direct supervision of a shift.
Front desk supervisor	Work directly with the front desk staff ensuring quality and efficiency.
Front desk agent/ Guest service attendant	The actual titles vary, but the basic responsibility is universal: checking guests in and out of the hotel.
Bell captain	Supervises the bellstaff.
Bellstaff	Basic responsibility is to help guests into and out of their rooms.
Doorperson	Greet arriving guests and help them from their vehicles into the lobby.
Valet/Garage supervisor	Manage the valet parking and parking garage staff.
Valet parking attendant	Park and retrieve cars.
Parking garage attendant	Manage the entry and exits of the hotel's parking garage.
PBX supervisor	Manage the operation of the hotel switchboard and the staff.
PBX operator	Responsible for the smooth execution of internal and external communications.
Concierge manager	Basic responsibility is to manage concierge staff in assisting guests with any/all requests.

Director of Services. The **director of services** can be viewed as the "behind-the-scenes" version of the front office manager. The director of services is responsible for the hotel's housekeeping and laundry operations. Although not part of the front office directly, the director of services must ensure that the quality and cleanliness of the hotel's guest rooms and common areas are up to standard. This role is vital to the success of the front office. Together with the front office manager, the director of services must strive to quickly clean rooms and prepare them for sale once a guest has departed. Reporting to the director of services:

Job Title	Basic Responsibility
Housekeeping manager/ Executive housekeeper	Manage day-to-day operation of the housekeeping department and coordinate communication with the front desk.
Assistant executive housekeeper	Work directly with the housekeeping staff to ensure that all guest rooms are cleaned and that the hotel common areas are maintained.
Rooms inspector/ Senior housekeepers	Work hand in hand with housekeepers to ensure that standards of cleanliness are maintained by inspecting each room.
Housekeepers/ Room attendants	The actual titles may vary, but the basic responsibility is the same—clean guest rooms.
Housepersons	Basic responsibility is to help housekeepers by keeping them supplied with linens, towels, and amenities.
Laundry manager	Manage the hotel's internal laundry operation.
Linen room attendant	Ensures that an adequate supply of linen and towels is always on hand.
Tailor/Seamstress	Repair linens when applicable; also help coordinate employee uniforms.

These two department heads are in charge of most of the operations within the rooms division. For an illustration of the entire rooms division see the sample rooms division organizational chart illustrated in Figure 5-5.

Food and Beverage Department Heads

In a resort hotel like this one in the example, the food and beverage director would probably oversee a very large operation (see Figure 5-6). It would be

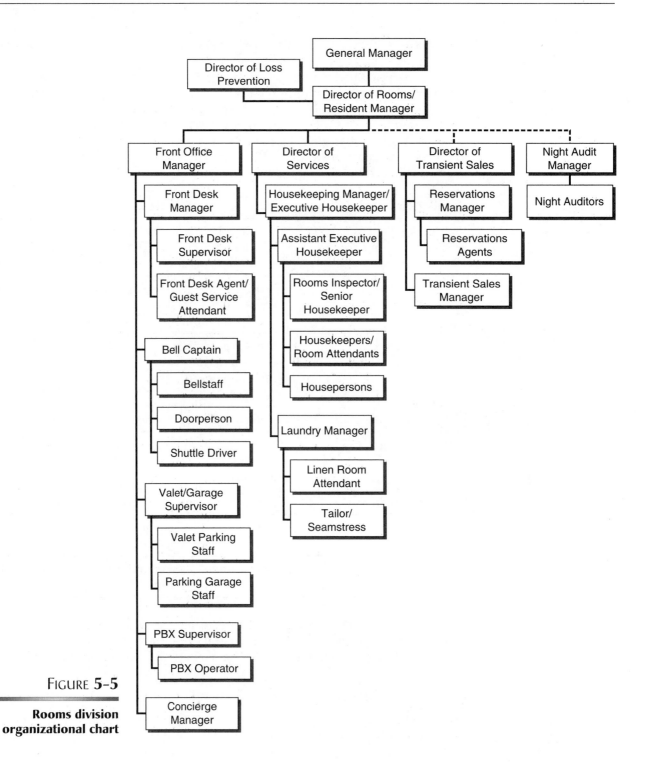

Figure 5-5

Rooms division organizational chart

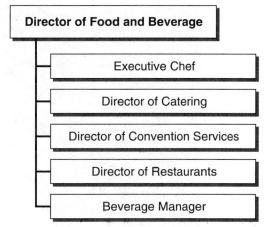

FIGURE 5-6

Food and Beverage department heads

vital to his or her success to have strong department heads managing the day-to-day operations of the outlets, restaurants, and catering services.

Executive Chef. The **executive chef** is responsible for the hotel's overall food production. He or she must control food costs while ensuring that the hotel's level of food quality is maintained. More of a manager than a hands-on chef, the executive chef monitors the food production of the hotel's restaurants, lounges, catering/banquet functions, and the in-house employee cafeteria. The executive chef typically reports directly to the director of food and beverage. In some smaller full-service hotels, there may not be a need for a director of food and beverage. In those cases, the executive chef assumes the same responsibilities and is part of the executive/leadership team.

Director of Catering. The **director of catering** is responsible for the catering side of the hotel sales effort. He or she must be able to direct all catering efforts on property. Often, the director of catering manages the catering sales staff as well as the operational catering staff directly. In this resort example, assuming ample amounts of meeting/banquet space (see Figure 5-7), the director of catering may only be responsible for non-group, or **local catering**. Local catering functions are events that are not tied to any group guest rooms. Weddings, proms, banquets, and other events within the social market segment are considered local catering. The director of catering works with the executive chef in developing catering menus to be used for all banquet functions. In this resort example, the director of catering will work in tandem with a director of convention services.

Director of Convention Services. The director of convention services (often abbreviated CS) is responsible for servicing all **group catering**. Group catering functions are those meetings, events, and meal functions tied to a block of

Figure **5-7**

Grand Wailea meeting space *(Courtesy KSL Resorts)*

group guest rooms. The group sales team would book a group, and the CS department would handle all functions held on site. The CS director must work closely with the director of catering in ensuring all catered functions operate smoothly.

Director of Restaurants. The director of restaurants oversees the food and beverage outlets and room service. Whereas the executive chef is responsible for the actual outlet product (food), the director of restaurants concentrates on staffing, décor, beverage, and other aspects of operations. The director of restaurants works with the executive chef and director of food and beverage in developing new outlet concepts and revising menus.

Beverage Manager. The beverage manager is responsible for ensuring that all outlets have a sufficient supply of beverage for continued operation. He or she must also work closely with the catering department to ensure that the beverages that have been ordered by groups are on hand when the function date arrives.

Sales Department Heads

Director of Group Sales. The director of group sales is responsible specifically for the group rooms sales effort (see Figure 5-8). On a day-to-day basis, the

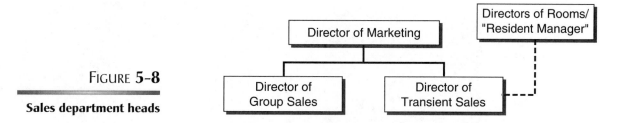

FIGURE **5-8**

Sales department heads

manager supervises and assists in the decision making of the senior and junior salespeople. Often, the director of group sales is personally responsible for key/focus accounts that have important and/or long-term impact on the hotel. Reporting to the director of marketing, the director of group sales is accountable for achieving group room revenue targets. He or she often works closely with the director of transient sales to maximize overall room sales. He or she must also work with the directors of catering and/or convention services to ensure that the group catering contribution is best utilized.

The director of catering was reviewed in the analysis of the food and beverage department. Again, the director of transient sales is pictured with a dual reporting structure because reservations has a significant impact on the rooms division.

Engineering and Human Resources Department Heads

The functional departments of engineering and human resources are never as large as some of the other departments. Because they are considered back of the house, they may go unnoticed by the casual observer. Each of these two departments typically has only one department head (see Figure 5-9).

Chief Engineer. The **chief engineer** coordinates the day-to-day maintenance of the hotel's physical structure. Because sleeping rooms are the main product of any hotel, the chief engineer may spend most of his or her time checking and assigning sleeping room repair duties. Often, in a proactive approach, the chief engineer will assign preventive maintenance (or PM) duties to staff before repairs are needed. The chief engineer also performs daily checks on the hotel's meeting space, outlets, and common areas (see Figure 5-10).

FIGURE **5-9**

Human Resources and Engineering department heads

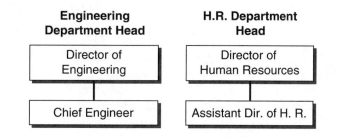

FIGURE **5-10**

Common area *(Courtesy Omni Severin Hotel)*

Assistant Director of Human Resources. The assistant director of human resources works closely with all other department heads to maintain employee satisfaction and to ensure that proper employment procedures are followed. He or she is often called upon to screen potential applicants in initial employment interviews. In this resort example, the assistant director of human resources may find that his or her workload may change significantly throughout the year based on the seasonality. As was reviewed earlier, resorts may experience differences in demand based on when their attractions are open or at peak level. The resort in this example (assuming it is located in say, Arizona) may experience a big drop in demand during hot summer months and a big increase during favorable winter months. Because of this large swing in demand, the assistant director of human resources may have to adjust the work force accordingly. It is not unheard of for large resorts to vary their staffing levels by 75 percent or more due to seasonality.

Accounting Department Heads

Assistant Controller(s). In a large hotel, such as this example, two or more department heads may support the controller (see Figure 5-11). The assistant controllers are typically responsible for specific accounting duties. The assistant in charge of operations may oversee the reporting and accuracy of documentation regarding the outlets, ancillary revenue sources, and attractions

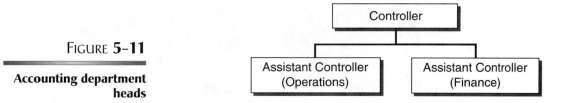

FIGURE 5-11

Accounting department heads

within the resort. The assistant in charge of finance may oversee the credit policies, night audit, and the payables/receivables function. Smaller hotels may have only one assistant or none at all. However, with the myriad transactions that occur in larger hotels, a lone controller couldn't possibly keep tabs on everything.

RESORT DEPLOYMENT EXAMPLE

Within the example of a large resort, other department heads would be in place. Certainly unique to resorts, these department heads would vary based on the size and scope of the hotel's attractions. As seen in Figure 5-12, these positions are focused on the management of certain recreational and physical landscape aspects of the hotel.

Some mega-size resorts may have even more department head level managers than listed here. Resorts that lease out space for vendors to open shops on premise (e.g., gift shops, beauty salons, massage, jewelry, clothing, etc.) may designate a department head to monitor the operation of those shops. Because signature attractions can be so varied, it is not feasible to list all the different possibilities. It should be noted that the career opportunities at large and mega-resorts would be greater than at smaller hotels because of

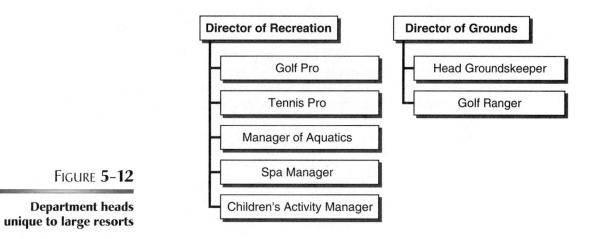

FIGURE 5-12

Department heads unique to large resorts

FIGURE **5-13**

Claremont activities
(Courtesy KSL Resorts)

these varied areas and responsibilities. The sheer number of outdoor activities available at the Claremont Resort shown in Figure 5-13 illustrates just how much a director of recreation would be responsible for.

TRADITIONAL VERSUS REVENUE-BASED DEPLOYMENT

The traditional organization scenario divides the sales effort into two camps, employing the concept that room sales are unique and that food and beverage sales are separate. As a result, those involved in group and transient sales report to one executive/leadership team member, and the catering sales people report to another. All food and beverage departments, including catering sales and the outlets, report to the person in charge of the hotel's food and beverage arm. The person who directs the sleeping room sales effort manages both the transient and group salespeople. The traditional organizational chart includes roles for executive committee members who focus on the rooms division (resident manager) and food and beverage (director of food and beverage) operations independently of each other.

The revenue-based organizational chart (see Figure 5-14) eliminates the resident manager position and adds a different leadership position, director of operations.

As the title implies, the **director of operations** is in charge of the fundamental operational functions of the hotel. All operational departments that are not involved in the selling of a hotel product report to this manager. In this revenue-based deployment, managers who work in a sales (proactive revenue) capacity report to one leadership team member, and those who work in an operational capacity (reactive revenue) report to another.

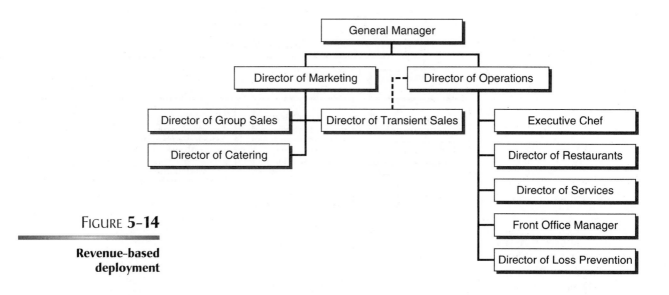

FIGURE **5-14**

Revenue-based deployment

The director of operations, in essence, combines the responsibilities of the food and beverage director and the resident manager. The synergy of having the operational departments report to one leader can positively impact the hotel. The synergy is evident in that overall guest satisfaction is directed by one individual. The message can remain constant throughout the disparate areas of guest contact. Sometimes referred to as an assistant general manager or a senior assistant manager, the director of operations position is often viewed as a stepping stone to the position of general manager.

FUNCTIONAL DEPARTMENT MANAGEMENT TEAMS

Each of the executive committee members, and their respective department heads, would manage groups of entry-level and middle managers. These management teams can be large or small, depending on the functional area. Traditionally, the largest management teams are a part of the following departments:

- Food and Beverage
- Sales and Catering
- Rooms Division

An in-depth look at the management team structure of the rooms division occurred earlier in this chapter. It should be noted that close study of the other departments can be better accomplished using other texts. Nonetheless, the organizational charts in Figure 5-15 and Figure 5-16 highlight the

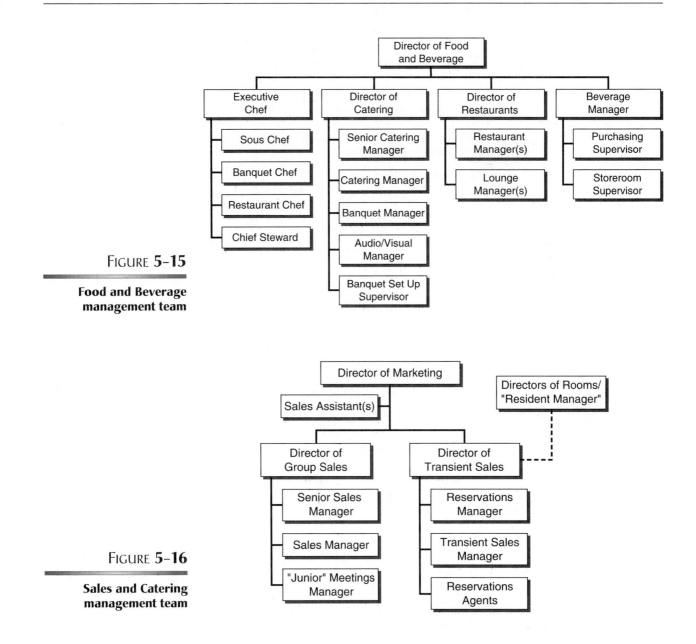

Figure **5-15**

Food and Beverage management team

Figure **5-16**

Sales and Catering management team

basic management team structure of both the food and beverage and sales and catering departments.

The collection of preceding organizational charts highlighted specific areas and management levels within a large resort hotel. Figure 5-17 illustrates how they all come together for a large-size downtown hotel (omitting members unique to resorts), in traditional deployment.

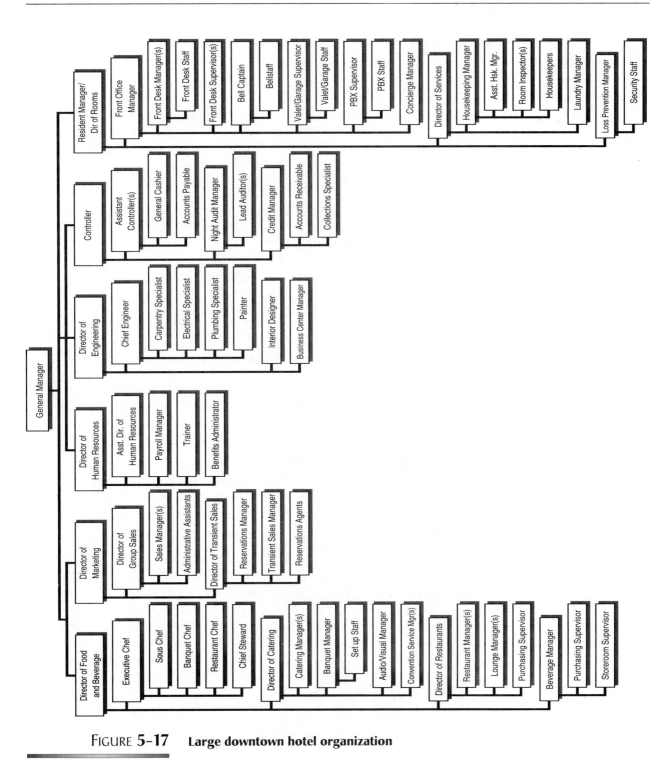

FIGURE 5-17   Large downtown hotel organization

This chapter touched briefly on many different careers in the hotel industry. In addition to the rewarding careers in the rooms division, a larger hotel can offer a great variety of challenging jobs. A common question asked by students is "How do I begin a hotel career?" Without the ever-important qualifier of "previous experience" on a résumé, how can one best enter the hotel industry?

Education is the critical first step to entry into the hotel industry. The inevitable answer must be "What are your career goals?" If your goal is to eventually become a general manager, your career path would be different from one who wants to lead the rooms division as a director of rooms.

BEGINNING A CAREER

Facilities of every size, location, product type, and service level are always looking for new employees. Some of the larger chains employ a staff of several individuals whose sole purpose is to travel the country's higher-learning campuses seeking talent. Small chains and independents must use other means. The sheer size of the industry makes the possibility of working at a facility a very real one. There are several ways of entering this field, each requiring perseverance and initiative.

Management Training Programs

Most of the larger hotel chains offer extensive management training programs for recent graduates. Hyatt, Marriott, Sheraton, Hilton, and Westin (among others) each have prearranged training programs that last anywhere from six months to a year or more. Each new candidate will work in most or all of the hotel departments during this time to gain experience in all facets of operations. Upon completion of these programs, these new recruits are often assigned a junior management or supervisory role at a hotel. Some management training programs will conclude the last portion of training in the department of choice of the individual. There may not be a permanent position available in the preferred department of the hotel providing the training, but the trainee will eventually be placed at a hotel that does if that is his or her goal. The most prevalent entry-level management position in the rooms division is front desk manager.

Internships

If a management-training program is unavailable, interested candidates may be able to seek paid internships. Though not as formal as a management-training program, these internships are often focused on providing broad-based exposure to a variety of departments. Repeated internships during the course of education (summers, for example) may allow for focusing on a particular discipline.

Sales offices have many marketing and promotional projects that require no more than three months' work, which are perfect for summer interns. Catering operations that face an increase in demand during the holiday season may also employ interns. The rooms division may also see increased activity when the hotel is in season.

Volunteering

If formal training opportunities at a facility are not available, gaining experience in meeting planning may be the road into a hotel. Nonprofit organizations and charities of all kinds are always looking for assistance in planning fund-raisers and other events. Experience gained in working with a facility from the other side (meeting planner) may catch the eye of a director of catering or sales. The volunteer who is able to manage a large group check-in in conjunction with a hotel's front desk may generate interest from the front office manager.

Cross-Departmental Experience

Recent school graduates may find themselves frustrated with a lack of a specific department's opportunities at their hotel of choice. If other departments are offering training or internship programs, job seekers would not hurt themselves by looking into them. The hotel industry is renowned for promoting from within. Quality employees are rewarded with new opportunities. A housekeeping supervisor or assistant front desk manager will find the chances of gaining entrance into sales and catering much greater than what they would be outside of the hotel.

Perhaps most relevant to the rooms division is the experience gained dealing with guests and the operation of the front office. The

(continued)

front desk manager will bring customer rapport skills gained from guest interaction to the sales office, not to mention an in-depth knowledge of the rooms division as well. A sales manager can bring a wealth of knowledge on the intricacies of groups to the front desk.

FOSTERING A CAREER

Whether a hotel employee works for a major chain, or an independent, that worker must always be thinking about how best to enhance his/her career. Assuming that these workers enjoy what they do, what are the keys to their long-term success? The best approach to fostering a career is to predetermine the career path as much as possible.

A good starting point is to sit down and map out long-term career goals. A list or a chart should be made detailing where they hope to see their careers one, five, and ten years down the road. Do they envision themselves as a general manager eventually? Do they want to rise through the ranks and lead a team as a director of rooms or food and beverage? Perhaps they are quite content with where they are currently and feel good about doing just that. No matter what the specific goals are, the yearly plans should reflect where they want to be and how to get there.

One-Year Plan

The one-year plan should really be a reflection of an employee's most recent job evaluation or review. A yearly plan should focus on those areas where the supervisor feels improvement is needed. It is most useful when set up as an "action plan" to act on right away. These action plans should list specifically what areas need to be worked on and the best ways of doing so. A supervisor's input is vital in that the supervisor controls the employee's short-term career destiny. Such input on the action plan will help the manager get a grip on the specific expectations of management and their ideas on how best to achieve them.

Five-Year Plan

The five-year plan should really be a blueprint of what the individual wants his or her next position to be. If content in their careers, workers still need to prove to themselves and management how they will stay productive there for many years. Do they want to become a front office manager or move into food and beverage soon? It should all be written down. To move up the ladder, the individual must map out how to get there. Start immediately by asking superiors how they themselves got to where they are and the time it took them. Positioning oneself as a leader and a team player in day-to-day activities is a very good step. Exceeding expectations consistently is a must. If possible, employees should take on extra projects and responsibilities whenever possible.

Being the first one to jump into a difficult situation establishes a good reputation. Always being supportive of management and teammates positions one as someone whose only interests are those of the team. The employee will find that consistency over five years will put him or her in a position to dictate what the next position will be.

A good ongoing career management tool for hotel employees (and students interested in the hospitality field for that matter) is to consistently keep abreast of trade journals. Publications such as *Hotel & Motel Management, Meetings and Conventions,* and *Events and Hotels* offer a wide range of topics that are timely and relevant. Association newsletters from groups like the American Society of Association Executives and the Religious Conference Management Association can give people the meeting planner's point of view on the industry. Individuals interested in the food and beverage side of hotels should seek out *Restaurant Business, Cuisine,* and *Hotel Restaurant* magazines for similar insight. Other magazines and newsletters can provide resources for research, career opportunities, and networking.

Ten-Year Plan

A ten-year plan is more of a rough outline than anything else. Hotel employees may have more or fewer options depending on the type and size company they work for. If they work for a chain, and they want to be promoted quickly, a good idea is to be open to relocation. Human resources managers at larger chains will have some type of career profile on all staff that other facilities may look at when they have openings. Often, these other facilities will look at employee profiles before the employees themselves ever know of another opportunity.

(continued)

HOTEL CAREER
MANAGEMENT
(concluded)

This profile will outline salary, performance history, experience within the company, education, management suggestions or career path, and relocatability. It is a good idea for all professionals to review their profiles from time to time to ensure accuracy and make changes to reflect where they want to be. Marriage, new families, and other changes in personal status may necessitate changes in employee profiles.

If an employee lives in an area where the hotel company has more than one operation, he or she may still have career opportunities without having to relocate. Called cluster cities, these areas allow for career movement from operation to operation in the surrounding region within easy commute. Large cities like New York, Chicago, and Los Angeles are often considered cluster cities because hotel chains regularly build more than one hotel there.

CHAPTER FIVE **REVIEW**

KEY TERMS

common areas
night audit
director of loss prevention
manual posting
FF&E
soft goods
hard goods
group résumé
front of the house
back of the house
general manager
resident manager
director of food and beverage
director of marketing

director of human resources
director of engineering
controller
director of grounds
director of recreation
department heads
front office manager
director of services
executive chef
director of catering
local catering
group catering
chief engineer
director of operations

REVIEW QUESTIONS

1. Name the six functional departments within a hotel.

2. Of those six, which are considered front of the house and which are back of the house? Why?

3. What is the difference between traditional and revenue-based deployment?

4. What are uniform services and what departments within the front office do they encompass?

5. What executive/leadership team members are unique to resorts? Briefly describe their job roles.

6. Explain the history and background behind the title Resident Manager.

7. List the organizational criteria that dictate a hotel's organizational structure.

8. "Everything begins with the _____ division."

9. Explain the unique organizational reporting structure reservations has.

10. What is the importance of the loss prevention/security department?

DISCUSSION QUESTIONS/EXERCISES

1. Request a copy of the organizational chart of a full service hotel located in a downtown area and of a full service hotel located in a resort area. Compare and contrast the organizations. Answer the following questions.

   a. Who is the top manager? What is the title?

   b. How many "management layers" does the downtown property have?

   c. How many "management layers" does the resort property have?

   d. How similar are the charts?

   e. What differences do you see in the charts?

   f. What basic functions are covered in both?

   g. Do you see different titles assigned to the same function?

   h. If you were a steward in the downtown property, what department do you fall into?

   i. If you were a landscaper in the resort property, what department do you fall into?

   j. Do you find either organization chart more appealing than the other? Why or why not?

2. Arrange to interview the general manager of a large downtown hotel. Answer the following questions and share with the class.

   a. What is the name of the hotel you have selected?

   b. What is the location of this property?

   c. What is the size of this property?

   d. What is the name of the general manager?

   e. How long has he/she worked at this property?

   f. How long has he/she worked for this chain?

   g. What position did he/she have prior to becoming the general manager?

   h. How many properties has he/she worked for during his/her career?

   i. What is his/her background in the hotel industry?

   j. How was his/her very first job in the hotel industry?

   k. What management style does he/she prefer?

   l. Did he/she have a mentor in the industry?

   m. Who are the members of the leadership team at this property?

   n. What is the best advice he/she can give you as a novice to the industry?

   o. What was the most interesting thing you learned from this general manager?

3. Arrange the following elements of an organizational chart in the manner dictated by the revenue-based deployment model.

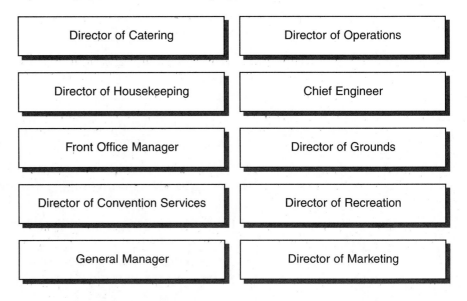

Director of Catering	Director of Operations
Director of Housekeeping	Chief Engineer
Front Office Manager	Director of Grounds
Director of Convention Services	Director of Recreation
General Manager	Director of Marketing

INTERNET RESOURCES
Hotel Career Web Sites

These sites are great Web tools for the job seeker. Most sites offer listings sorted by location and position. The job listings change often, so those interested in employment should make visiting them a habit.

<http://www.1whcareers.com>

<http://www.hoteljobresource.com>

<http://www.hospitalityjobs.com>

<http://www.hospitalitycareers.net>

<http://www.hotel-jobs.com>

<http://www.hcareers.com>

<http://www.resortjobs.com>

<http://www.hotelmanagers.net/Homepage.htm>

<http://www.hotelandcaterer.com>

<http://www.monster.com>

<http://www.hotjobs.com>

For additional hospitality and travel marketing resources, visit our Web site at <http://www.Hospitality-Tourism.delmar.com>.

Front Office Overview

OBJECTIVES

After reading this chapter, you should understand:

- The arrival chronology
- Processes involved in group and transient arrivals
- Guest billing arrangements
- Check-in and checkout processes
- Front office communications and staffing

INTRODUCTION

The registration process is arguably the most important part of the hotel hotel experience for a guest. It is during this time that lasting impressions are made. It has been said that 75 percent of a guest's total satisfaction with a hotel is determined during this process. A successful hotel must do whatever it can to ensure that the guest is satisfied with every aspect of registration.

THE ARRIVAL CHRONOLOGY

Analysis of the registration process begins with a look at the arrival chronology. **Arrival chronology** is the term used to categorize the stages a transient or group guest go through upon arrival to a hotel. This arrival chronology allows for analysis of the front office departments that come into contact with the hotel guest. It should be noted that the arrival chronology begins upon arrival to the hotel. It does not describe the initial contact with a guest. Often, that first contact is with the reservations department. That process is addressed later in the reservations chapter.

Stage One—Greeting

The first hotel employees who come into contact with most guests when they arrive are members of the uniformed services division of the front office. Depending on the size and makeup of the hotel, the first person to greet a hotel guest will be either a doorperson or valet/garage attendant. This first impression is very important. Always with an eye towards total guest satisfaction, the initial greeting begins the process of establishing a favorable impression of the hotel.

In larger hotels the parking valet is the first to greet people arriving to a hotel. In many cases, they are the last employees people see as well. Thus, this job role requires that the employee have a gracious and hospitable demeanor. A pleasant smile and warm welcome set the stage for guest satisfaction.

This position can be physically demanding as well. It requires strength enough to load and unload luggage from vehicles. It also requires running to and from where the cars are parked. Most hotels are designed with a main drive-up entrance that is covered with a porte cochere. This enables guests to arrive and depart with a partial shield from the elements. This shield protects the valet attendants only when they are loading/unloading cars; they need to be appropriately dressed for the weather.

In many downtown location types, the hotel may not have access to adequate parking facilities for their guests. The hotel may need to rely on other vendors to supply parking spaces. Utilizing an outside vendor for products or services is called **outsourcing**. In many cases, hotels choose to outsource. In addition to parking, hotels may outsource grounds maintenance, recreational activities, guest transportation, and other services.

In terms of guest parking, there are generally two options available to guests. The first option is valet parking. Valet parking allows guests to leave their vehicles by the front door and have them parked by an attendant (this is where the name valet attendant is derived). The other option, if available, is for the guest to park his or her own car, referred to as self-park. Because of the labor involved, the valet parking option is more expensive for guests than the

FIGURE **6-1**

Guest greeting *(Courtesy Omni Severin Hotel)*

self-park option. A hotel may have its own parking garage or adjacent parking lot where guests may self-park.

The next person to come into contact with guests and others arriving to a hotel is the doorperson. The doorperson, though not as prevalent today as it once was, is another opportunity for the hotel to promote guest satisfaction. This "greeter" should be pleasant and outgoing. Many legendary doorpersons have created a large base of loyal guests who return for that one individual alone. The doorperson helps in the transition from the arriving vehicle to the lobby area (see Figure 6-1). They impact departing guests as well in that they summon taxicabs and limousines as needed. In smaller hotels, the role of the doorperson may be incorporated into the duties of the bellstaff.

Stage Two—Transition

Perhaps the most widely recognized job role within the industry is the bellperson (bellman, bellhop, and bellboy are no longer acceptable terms), who is responsible for the assistance of guests to their rooms and to explain the hotel and room features to each guest. Escorting a guest to the room is called **rooming a guest**.

Beyond rooming guests, members of the bellstaff are called upon to assist other departments when needed. Valet parking, housekeeping, restaurants, and others often have cyclical demands that the bellstand can help fill.

ABOUT MY JOB

Doorman
Jeff March

The best thing about my job as the doorman at a major hotel is the interaction that I have with the guest. I am the first person they meet as they arrive and the last one they see as they pull away. Many people call me an ambassador. I do a little bit of everything for the guest.

If the concierge is not available, I have the chance to recommend the restaurants, bars, and sites to see here in the city. I help people find their way by giving directions. I make a lot of contacts with local ticket brokers and reservationists to help the guests have the best possible time while visiting the hotel and the city. I don't want them to forget what a great experience they had while staying at our hotel.

It gives me great satisfaction to see the guests enjoying themselves and having fun. I only have three or four minutes with guests on their way in or out of the hotel, and during that time it is my job to make them smile! Impressions are everything, and if I make a good impression on the guests, then in turn the hotel makes a good impression on them and they want to come back to see us!

Delivery of messages, faxes, and room gifts (flowers, fruit baskets, etc.) are also bellstaff duties.

The primary bellstaff duties are to assist guests from the door to the front desk, and then from the front desk to their guest room. Depending on the size of a hotel, the bellstaff may actually serve multiple roles. Some may act as door-persons, and others may assist people with their cars. In large hotels, the bell-staff may not even greet a guest until after check-in. This is because the front desk area may be so large that arriving guests do not need assistance in finding it. After the check-in process, the bellstaff will either greet the guest for the first time, or revisit to determine whether assistance is needed. When assistance is needed after check-in, the front desk may ask for a **front**, which is the term used to alert the bellstaff that a guest is ready to be escorted to their room.

The **bellcaptain** is the leader of the bellstaff. He or she directs the bellpersons and ensures that staffing levels are adequate. Staffing is very important. The bellcaptain must review the daily arrival and departure reports and future occupancy forecasts to determine how many people to schedule. An **arrivals report** lists the guests due to arrive that day, and the **departures report** lists those due to check out. A general rule is to staff 1 bellperson for every 75 arriving or departing guests. Luxury hotels or those hotels wishing to increase their levels of service may staff 1 bellperson for every 40 to 50 guests that arrive or depart.

Because the majority of income the bellstaff employees earn is from gratuities, the bellcaptain must ensure that each team member receives an equal number of fronts. An ironic term used by the bellstaff applies to duties that do not always generate a gratuity. A last is a bellstaff duty that does not typically generate a gratuity (flower delivery, message delivery, etc.). The bellcaptain may use a **front log sheet** such as this sample to ensure equity in assigning fronts and lasts:

XYZ Hotel Front Log

Bellstaff Name	Time of Front*	Room Number	Rooming?	Check Out?	Other
John	8:12	235		X	
Sally	9:45	124		X	
Pedro	10:05	223		X	
John	14:25	456		X	
Sally	15:00	555			Flowers
Pedro	15:15	633	X		
John	15:17				Overnight Package
Pedro	16:23				Fruit Basket

* Because the front office regularly deals with guests of many nations and cultures, it is a very good idea to coordinate as many processes and procedures using the 24-hour clock as possible. Most of the rest of the world does not use A.M./P.M. designations. Front office employees who can readily express times in the 24-hour mode reduce misunderstandings and improve guest satisfaction.

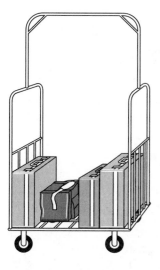

FIGURE **6-2**

Bellcart

Assisting guests with great amounts of luggage requires a bellcart. A **bellcart** is a large brass cart on rollers that bellstaff use to carry luggage to and from a room (see Figure 6-2).

Once in the guest room, members of the bellstaff should explain the features of the room and the hotel itself. In addition, they should turn on lights and open curtains if applicable. The bellstaff should memorize a guest familiarization checklist which would include:

- How to use the room key

- How to use the television, VCR, DVD, and in-room movie service

- Showing the room service menu and other hotel in-room collateral

- Briefly showing them the telephone and explaining how to reach the PBX operator and how to reach the bellstand if needed

- A brief review of fire and other emergency procedures as deemed necessary by hotel management

THE HOTEL SHUTTLE

The bellcaptain also oversees the usage of the hotel shuttle. Some hotels, primarily airport location types, offer complimentary shuttle transportation to and from the local airport. The shuttle itself is typically a 12- to 15-seat vehicle that has the hotel name and logo clearly marked on its exterior. The number of shuttles and the frequency of their trips to the airport are dependent on the hotel's size and traditional demand from the airport. A typical hotel will schedule "airport runs" every 15 minutes. The shuttle driver should announce his/her departure from the hotel in the lobby to notify waiting guests. The hotels that use a shuttle must train their drivers that they play a role in the arrival chronology and that their guest service skills are important. The shuttle driver may come into contact with the guest first.

Smaller hotels or those with infrequent requests for transport to the airport may keep a shuttle on hand for special requests. In those cases, members of the bellstaff may operate the shuttle as needed.

Stage Three–Registration

Once a guest has arrived and has made it to the front desk, the registration process begins. It is at this point where most guests have begun to create an impression of the hotel in their minds. The front desk personnel must continue to focus on guest satisfaction. Hotels that create a warm and inviting atmosphere around the front office area ensure that the registration process goes smoothly (see Figure 6-3).

FIGURE **6-3**

Lobby/Marriott *(Courtesy Indianapolis Marriott North Hotel)*

Check-in

Getting people into guest rooms quickly, efficiently, and accurately is the primary responsibility of the front desk. The mechanics of checking guests in is fairly self-explanatory. In summary, checking guests in entails processing individual reservations, assigning the proper guest rooms by ensuring that room preferences are maintained, and obtaining a method of payment.

Each day, based on the arrivals report that is generated, the front desk knows how many guests are due to check in. Each individual reservation is known in advance, so the front desk should be able to manage what rooms are available. Coordinating the available rooms with each guest's room preferences is an important task. Room preferences, as reviewed earlier, are defined as the individual guest's choice in room type, configuration, and designation.

The process of matching room preferences to available rooms is called blocking. **Blocking** is a process where a specific room is reserved for a specific guest. Blocking a room to match an arriving guest's room preferences contributes greatly to guest satisfaction levels. The process of blocking these rooms each day may fall to a front office employee called a **rooms controller**. The rooms controller uses the arrivals report and compares it to the hotel's room inventory. The rooms controller must factor in room preferences as well as projected arrival times. Special requests such as cribs and rollaway beds are also blocked in advance as needed. The blocking of rooms applies to transient and group guests.

Most hotels assign a priority level to which rooms are blocked first. Guests who are members of a hotel's guest loyalty program, VIPs as designated by management, and those who are paying premium rates are usually given top priority. The rooms controller must watch any rooms blocked that are not in V/R status very carefully. Communication with the housekeeping department ensures that all arriving guests are blocked into rooms that achieve a V/R status prior to their arrival.

Unexpected early arrivals or incorrect documentation of room preferences may require the rooms controller to change the existing blocks. This process, called "blowing the block" can create problems. The rooms controller must ensure that one block isn't created at the detriment of another arriving guest. It is for this reason that the rooms controller works closely with the front desk, housekeeping, and reservations department.

As the guest approaches the front desk, he/she should be greeted warmly, further emphasizing guest satisfaction. This is accomplished by implementing the **10x10 rule**, which has two parts. The first part states that a guest's perception of an entire stay is, in large measure, instilled in the first 10 minutes upon arrival. The other part states that the front desk must greet a guest 10 feet before he/she approaches the desk. An employee who begins a conversation with a guest at least 10 feet away creates a favorable impression. This makes the guest feel welcome by encouraging his/her approach.

Once the guest has approached the desk, the employee should greet the guest with a smile. In the course of their conversation, the guest's name should be used at least twice, again, continuously reinforcing the commitment to guest satisfaction.

The mechanics of an actual check-in are illustrated later in this text, but the following steps summarize the process:

1. Guest's name is verified, to include correct spelling.

2. Once reservation is found, a reservation summary is given vocally to the guest. This summary includes verification of room preferences, arrival/ departure dates, and confirmed rate.

3. If the room is not preblocked, the employee must find a room in V/R status that fits the parameters of the reservation summary. If the proper room is not available at this point, the guest should be given the choice of either (a) waiting for their preferred room to reach V/R status, or (b) taking another available room. Placing guests in "wait" status, as it is referred to, should be kept to a minimum. A guest should be placed in wait status only for rooms that are vacant but not yet clean. Keeping one guest waiting for another guest to check out and for the room to be cleaned places undue hardship on the waiting guest. A wait status should never exceed one hour in duration or guest satisfaction could plummet.

4. The next step is to determine whether the guest is a member of the hotel's guest loyalty program and/or whether the guest is participating in other promotional tie-ins (e.g., airline frequent flier miles, car rental points, and credit card promotions).

5. Before a key is released to a guest, the method of payment is determined (see next section). Assuming that the method of payment is determined, the employee should give the room key to the guest. Some hotels have preprinted keys with the room number. The room number should never be spoken aloud for security reasons.

6. If required, this is the point in the check-in process where a front is requested from the bellstand.

Determining Method of Payment

A recurring theme throughout this text is that hotels are in the business of hospitality. Hotel owners, as with any other business owner, are in business to make money. Because a hotel's primary item for sale is the guest room, the collection of room rates is crucial to the success of the business. This responsibility of collecting room rates falls on the front desk. The collection of this revenue begins at check-in, in the process of determining method of payment.

There are three ways a guest room can be paid for. The first, and most common, is by credit card. The credit card is obtained at the time of booking and is used as a guarantee for some forms of reservations. Most hotel computer systems can check to ensure that each card is valid and that a sufficient amount of credit is available on the card. This is called obtaining a **card approval**. Based on the number of nights needed on the reservation and the rate that it was booked at, the computer can calculate the approval based simply on the anticipated revenue.

The second method of payment is cash. Guests choosing not to use a credit card may provide a cash deposit prior to or at the time of check-in. Cash payments should be collected prior to assigning the guest room. For security and fraud concerns, the hotel will require the full room rate, taxes, and what is referred to as **anticipated usage amount**. This usage amount is the cash deposit required to cover estimated use of hotel facilities and services (e.g., in-room phones, in-room movies, room service, etc.). Guests wishing to "sign" these and other services to their room must provide additional cash. Guests choosing not to do this may face their phones and movies being turned off, room service will require a payment at the time of delivery, and so on.

Checks, which are simply a form of cash payment, can be verified in a manner similar to credit cards. Funds to cover personal checks can be verified through the issuing banks. Traveler's checks and certified checks do not need approvals because they are issued in exchange for payment at the time of issuance.

The third method of payment is less reliant on the front desk, but is a valid method of payment. **Direct billing** allows an individual or group to pay for goods/services incurred during a stay or function at a later date. Within a hotel, guests and groups are routinely extended credit. Each time a guest checks in with a credit card as a method of payment, the hotel provides goods/services under the assumption that the credit card company will reimburse it at a later date.

Groups with direct billing privileges may have their attendees' room charges included on their bill. This may be in addition to planned banquet or outlet/ancillary charges. The individual with direct billing may only be billed their outstanding guest account. Extending direct billing privileges requires that the hotel impose proper credit guidelines. The credit approval process must be strictly adhered to in order to ensure that no credit is extended to an individual or organization unable to pay, called a **credit risk**.

Credit is issued solely within the hotel's judgment. The terms "billing or signing privileges" are used because credit is not a right, but a privilege. Individuals who travel often to the same hotel may work with the hotel's accounting department to set up direct billing. Typically, if traveling on a company's expense, a letter of authorization from the organization is required to set up billing. In addition, most hotels require that an individual or group complete a direct billing application prior to extending them credit. The **direct billing application** is a form requesting some level of credit from a hotel. This application will contain four basic parts:

1. **Organization information**—comprised of organization size, purpose, history, address, years in existence, company officers, and any other such identifying information.

2. **Financial information**—bank account history, number(s), and balance(s), IRS status, and the like.

3. **References**—hotels and other vendors who have extended credit to this organization will be contacted in order to verify an ability to pay.

4. **Independent references**—companies such as Dun & Bradstreet can, for a fee, provide financial background and credit ratings for organizations.

Figure 6-4 illustrates what a sample direct billing application might look like.

Certain hotel chains extend direct billing privileges to their most loyal guests. Those that earn the highest levels of a guest loyalty program may, because of their frequent traveling, appreciate direct billing. **Walkouts** (also referred to as "skippers") or those that leave a hotel before properly settling their accounts may have to be billed (extended credit) because there is no other way of collecting the funds due.

FIGURE **6–4**

Direct billing application

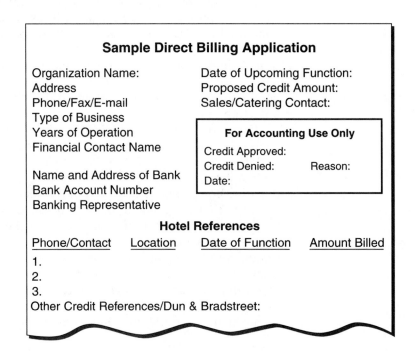

Sample Direct Billing Application

Organization Name: Date of Upcoming Function:
Address   Proposed Credit Amount:
Phone/Fax/E-mail   Sales/Catering Contact:
Type of Business
Years of Operation
Financial Contact Name

Name and Address of Bank
Bank Account Number
Banking Representative

For Accounting Use Only

Credit Approved:
Credit Denied: Reason:
Date:

Hotel References

Phone/Contact	Location	Date of Function	Amount Billed
1.			
2.			
3.			

Other Credit References/Dun & Bradstreet:

ABOUT MY JOB

Front Desk Clerk
Stephany Brush

As a front office agent, I have the opportunity to make an impression on the guests' stay. Sometimes I have more of an impact than any other employee with whom they come into contact while at my hotel. This is what I love about my job! I am one of the first people they meet as they arrive and one of the last people they say goodbye to as they depart. During their stay, I am the key contact person to whom they direct their every question or point out any concerns. I love to find out about my guests—where they are from, why they are in town, and what their interests are. You can learn a lot about the guests in the short amount of time that you have with them at check-in and throughout their stay.

I know that if I greet my guests with a big smile and a happy hello at check-in, it may help them to forget about the delayed flight they had, or the rush hour traffic that they were stuck in while traveling. I am here to offer assistance to make their stay enjoyable, memorable, and to make them want to return. As my guests depart, I like to ask them how everything was, ask how they enjoyed the city, and tell them to come back and see us next time. I love to see guests return time and again. It is great to recognize faces and call them by name! It makes them feel special and that someone does care about them and their experience.

In many hotels, the group sales and catering department will have a listing of organizations that have been approved for direct billing furnished by the accounting department. This list is continually updated to reflect the credit standing of each organization. Large chains have been known to preapprove major accounts for direct billing at all affiliated hotels. These **national accounts** will not have to go through the billing approval process at each individual hotel they wish to do business with.

Stage Four—Completion

Once the registration process at the front desk is complete, the guest usually commences on to their guest room. There are instances, primarily in the transient guest arrival, where a stop is made to the concierge desk before continuing on to the guest room.

Concierge

Concierge departments are not as all encompassing as they once were. It once was considered a senior management position. European hotels still rely on the concierge to handle many management duties. Today in North America, they have evolved into general assistance personnel.

Some hotel chains have tied a specific room configuration to the concierge. The "concierge floor" offers an enhanced room configuration to guests as well as access to an exclusive lounge area (as reviewed in an earlier chapter). The concierge lounge may require a guest room key for access. The concierge employee may be stationed in this lounge during its hours of operation, or he or she may be located in the lobby itself. Some hotels require concierge presence in both areas.

The hotel concierge should be able to provide a wide range of services to any guest. They are viewed as a valuable tool in enhancing guest satisfaction. Some of their services include:

- Reservations for airlines, other hotels, car rentals, restaurants.

- Securing tickets for theater and sporting events as well as nearby attractions. They arrange for tours, interpreters, babysitters, and other services.

- They should be knowledgeable of the hotel and local area. Maps, driving directions, and brochures should all be available.

PBX (Private Branch Exchange)

Once guests have begun their stay, they may come into contact with another front office department but probably will never see anyone from that department. The PBX department comes into play for guests when they choose to communicate (within the hotel, or outside). The PBX, or "switchboard" as it is referred to, manages all incoming and outgoing communications. Phone calls, faxes, and mail are routed through PBX. PBX operators are trained in guest relations and hotel emergency procedures. Security and PBX work hand in hand in situations that involve guest safety because they are best positioned to communicate to all hotel guests and employees. Often, PBX operators use handheld radios ("walkie-talkies") to communicate with other hotel personnel.

PBX operators are viewed as the "gatekeepers" of a guest's privacy. Room numbers should never be revealed. If a call comes in asking for a specific room number, the operator should ask the caller to verify the name associated with the guest room. Under no circumstances should the identities of hotel guests be revealed by PBX staff.

Many hotels have automated wake-up call systems that are monitored by PBX. The PBX staff may have the option of changing the message daily to include date and local weather information. When delivering a personalized

ABOUT MY JOB

Head Concierge
Jackie Schult

My name is Jackie Schult. My title is head concierge, but I view my role as more of an ambassador. I love being the link between hotel visitors and the community. I take great pride in making each and every guest feel welcome and comfortable. My desk is located in the middle of the lobby. I am easily accessible to anyone who strolls by. My job is to make sure that the guests will see and do what they want, when they want. When a guest arrives to the room, I phone that guest to check on the room and see whether any assistance is needed at that time. Daily I arrange tours of the city, baseball tickets, set up reservations in a variety of restaurants, theater tickets, transportation, translators—you name it and I will get it done. I make sure that every guest from around the world feels right at home.

I would love to share this example with you. A gentleman called me, saying it was his anniversary. He had the guest room reservation but just did not have the time to arrange anything else. His anniversary was that night, 12 years. I said, "Let me help you create a special evening!" I called him back at work within 30 minutes and had the following set for him:

- The gentleman and his wife checked into the hotel at 4:00 P.M.
- I upgraded him to a suite.
- In the suite, we arranged candles, champagne, and had a dozen red roses (to mark the 12-year anniversary).
- Transportation picked them up at 6:00 P.M.
- I had dinner reservations made for 6:30 P.M.
- After dinner, transportation took them on a tour of the city and stopped in on a famous local coffee shop for dessert.
- Back to the hotel after an unforgettable evening.

After the gentleman and his wife returned home they phoned me to say thank you for making that evening a night to remember. That phone call is why I do what I do. I like to feel that I have contributed to an experience in our city and at this hotel. Memories are the only thing you can hold on to. That is what I try to do for the guests—create memories!

wake-up call, the PBX operator should use the guest's name (see Figure 6-5). When a wake-up call fails to reach the room occupant after three attempts, hotel management/security should be notified to check that room personally.

PBX is responsible, in addition to members of the front desk who handle incoming calls, to deliver messages to guests. The modern hotel has two ways of passing along message information to guests. The most common is via voicemail. Incoming calls and pertinent messages from hotel staff may by placed directly on the voicemail room extension of a guest. Another method, if the message is in text form, or if the guest is hearing impaired, is to provide the message information via video display. Guests can access a message center from their television sets. Guests are made aware of all messages by a blinking "message waiting" light on the room phone.

In order for all the elements of the arrival chronology to function efficiently, the hotel itself must be designed well. As illustrated in Figure 6-6, the lobby level of a hotel should position its front office area as close to the main entrance as possible.

In this diagram, the hotel guests can easily move from each stage of the arrival chronology. In addition, elevators and outlets are positioned in such a way that guests will find them easily from the front office area.

FIGURE 6-5

PBX operator *(Courtesy Omni Severin Hotel)*

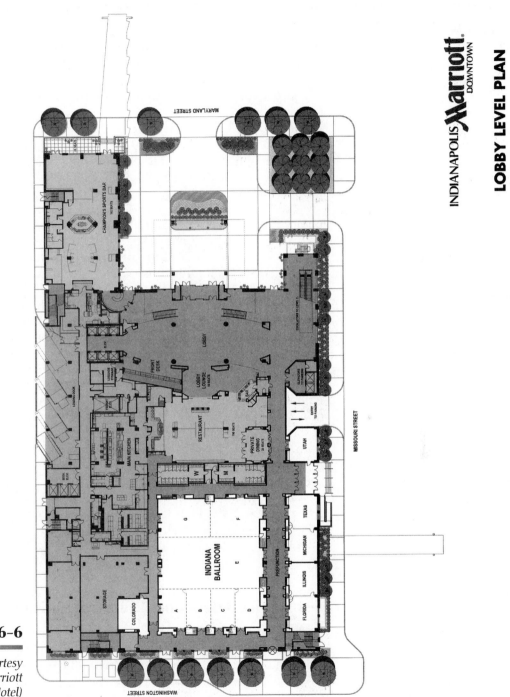

FIGURE **6-6**

Lobby diagram (Courtesy Indianapolis Marriott Downtown Hotel)

ABOUT MY JOB

PBX Operator
Penny Woodruff

My job is very important to me, and the responsibilities are quite extensive. When a guest calls in either from outside the hotel or while staying at the hotel, I am the first voice he/she hears. My voice and attitude make the first and lasting impression on our guests. They make an initial judgment about what type of hotel we have based on me. I strive to make that impression a good one. I am proud of my job in that respect.

I often think of myself as the nerve center and heart of this hotel. I also have other duties I am responsible for, beyond the switchboard. I am in charge of all the phone lines (called trunks) and the maintenance of those lines in the hotel. If a meeting room needs a direct outside phone line, I arrange for this line to be hooked up and working properly. I also work with the phone company when in-depth requests are made for phone lines in meeting rooms or sleeping rooms (e.g., ISDN lines, videoconferencing, etc.). Another responsibility I have is when an emergency occurs (hopefully not very often), I coordinate with security to ensure the safety of the guests. This entails not only answering the incoming calls with a pleasant voice but also ensuring that every guest in the hotel is given correct information if they call me. We coordinate evacuation plans if needed and work with the various state and local law enforcement agencies to make sure the guests are accounted for. Also, in the case of that rare complaint by a guest in the hotel, I am the person who takes responsibility of making that guest happy. If for some reason I cannot make that happen, I get the correct hotel person in touch with that guest. Our goal is to make each guest completely satisfied with his or her experience at our hotel. So, when staying at my hotel, be prepared to have a pleasant enjoyable stay, starting with my voice as the first contact!

Guest Service Attendant—The Front Office Hybrid

Some hotel chains, Marriott for example, have begun to experiment with a new arrival process. The guest service attendant, or GSA, is a unique job description in that it combines many front office positions into one. Instead of having separate roles in valet/parking, bellstaff, and front desk, the GSA assumes all those roles. The GSA is, in essence, "assigned" an arriving guest.

That GSA assists the guest into the hotel and gets him/her to the room. This process requires a preregistered guest who does not need to proceed to the front desk for any reason. Room preferences have been met ahead of time, and the credit card used in the initial reservation is assumed to be the preferred method of payment.

This new process has met with some success. The average arrival/check-in time for guests can be reduced. The GSAs themselves are able to perform more duties in a given day than their counterparts in other hotels. One drawback ironically stems from this faster check-in process. Some guests perceive walking up to the front desk as an integral part of the hotel "experience." For some, diminishing the overall hotel experience can lead to less satisfaction.

Group Arrivals

The front desk chronology for transient guests may differ slightly from that of group guests. The group guest may proceed directly to the front desk; thus avoiding Steps 1 and 2 of the chronology. The arrival chronology of a group guest differs from the transient guest primarily when there is a group arrival. A **group arrival** occurs when a large number of guests from the same group arrive at once. Usually this occurs with group tours (motorcoaches). Sometimes charter flights for groups result in everyone checking in at once because they too arrive in charter motorcoaches. Group arrivals may require special staffing because a large number of people arriving at once may adversely impact a front desk. To reduce the impact on the front desk, a hotel may implement special group arrival procedures. The two most common group arrival procedures are a remote check-in and pre-key/key pack measures.

A **remote check-in** can be thought of as an extension of the front desk. Using signage identifying the group, a separate table is set up to accommodate the arrivals. Also referred to as "satellite" check-in, the remote desk can be equipped with computers and credit card machines to offer a complete check-in process. The hotel will also dedicate front desk personnel to manage the group's check-in process at this desk. Taking this demand off the front desk lessens the adverse affects of waiting in line for other guests. It also speeds up the check-in process for the group itself. Other registration information pertaining to the group (e.g., meeting agendas, meeting locations, activity options, etc.) may be available at the remote check-in desk as well. This personalized check-in service is often negotiated into group contracts. Of course, smaller groups may not need this service because their numbers may not adversely affect the operation of the front desk.

The **pre-key/key pack** system begins the check-in process before guests arrive. To pre-key is to pre-assign guests a room and issue a key. The actual "key pack" is simply a document to hold the key. Guests are checked in using the credit/payment information received earlier from the group sales department. This system is only appropriate within certain billing parameters. Typically, during final stages of negotiation, the group salesperson determines the method of payment a group desires. Three are three common methods of payment for groups:

1. **Sign All Charges (SAC).** This billing arrangement allows for each member of the group to "sign" all their charges to the group. The group will pay for everything. "Signing privileges" are extended to guests who have established a method of payment. To "sign" charges to a room or group is to be extended credit. If this payment method were agreed upon, the attendees would not have to supply the hotel any method of payment. Groups using the SAC billing method can be issued key packs directly, never having to visit the front desk or remote check-in location.

2. **Sign Room and Tax (SRT).** This arrangement allows for the group to pay the room and tax charges for the attendees. This is a common billing arrangement for groups wishing to reward their attendees (incentive trips). The guest is still responsible for all nonroom and tax charges, called **incidentals**. Although a method of payment from each individual is still needed, they may proceed up to their rooms with their key packs and return to the front desk at a later time.

3. **Each Pays Own (EPO).** This payment method stipulates that the group attendees must pay all their own charges. Hotels avoid allowing the pre-key/key pack option here because all guests must present some form of payment before being allowed into a room.

The pre-key/key pack system can be available to certain transient guests as well as groups. If guests make a reservation using a credit card, and the front desk (prior to arrival) meets their predetermined room preferences, they can be checked into a room. This process lessons the load on the front desk because guests can simply pick up their key and proceed to their rooms. The preregistration process is needed for hotels employing the guest service attendant.

It is not uncommon for the hotel salesperson who booked the group to be on hand during a group arrival. It portrays a feeling to the group that their business is valued and that all facets of the hotel are working together to ensure a successful check-in. Executive-level managers are also known to greet groups on occasion.

Other operational issues arise with the arrival of groups. Luggage associated with a large group may overwhelm the bellstand. This would impact the bellstand specifically during the arrival and departure of the group in question. A solution used by many hotels is to implement what is referred to as bag deliveries and bag pulls. A **bag delivery** is the term used when a group's luggage is delivered to individual rooms at some point after the group has checked into the hotel. The bellstaff, using the same practice popular with cruise lines, deliver luggage with proper guest identification tags to assigned guest rooms. The **bag pull** is basically the opposite procedure. At a predetermined time in the day (usually when all group attendees are in session), the bellstaff go into each room and "pull" each attendee's luggage. This luggage is then stored until the group is ready to depart.

When the bellstaff are called upon in this manner, a gratuity is expected from the group, not the individual guest. This gratuity can vary in price due to location type and service level. The designation "in and out" is used when affixing a gratuity for delivering and retrieving luggage for guests. The understanding is that the bellstaff would have received a separate gratuity for the delivery (the "in" phase) and the retrieval (the "out" phase). This in and out gratuity for the bellstaff can apply to transient guests as well. Upscale and luxury resorts, for example, often apply this bellstand gratuity directly to the guest's room as a mandatory fee. Though a point of contention for some, this direct gratuity charge does relieve guests from one out-of-pocket expense.

The arrival chronology is summarized in Figure 6-7. There are stages in which a transient or group guest can differ, but the interrelationship of the front office departments remains important. Only when all departments work together can an arrival be conducted flawlessly.

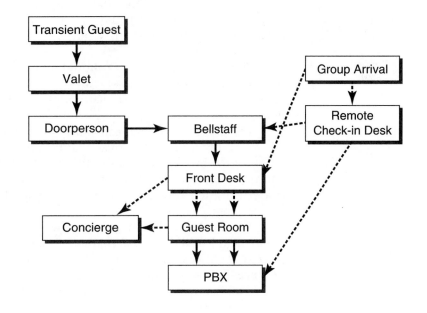

FIGURE **6-7**

Arrival chronology

DEPARTURES

The checkout process is generally less involved than the check-in process. Assuming that all the pertinent information was gathered during the check-in phase, the checkout should be smooth and fast. The checkout phase is the last opportunity to affect guest satisfaction on property. Concluding a guest's stay with a lasting positive memory contributes greatly to the possibility of a return visit. This memory helps lay the foundation for the brand loyalty reviewed earlier.

There are three primary ways a guest can check out of a hotel: at the front desk itself; via a guest-directed computer checkout system; or via an automated system. Each achieves the same result, but there are specific characteristics involved with each.

Front Desk Checkout

When a guest comes to the front desk to check out, many of the same principles involved in check-in apply. Once the guest has approached the desk, the employee should greet him/her with a smile. In the course of their conversation, the guest's name should be used at least twice, again continuously reinforcing the commitment to guest satisfaction. The guest's name is verified, to include correct spelling. This is a time some employees make the mistake of associating a guest's name with a room number. "Checking out of room 124, Mr. Smith?" The room number should never be spoken aloud by the employee, because the guest may still return to the room to retrieve luggage, family, and so on. For security purposes, it is always best to never reveal a guest's room number.

The front desk employee should inquire about the stay. Any outstanding service issues should be resolved at this point (see Chapter 14). Allowing a guest to depart with unresolved issues invariably leads to a guest who will not return.

The guest's hotel bill, called a folio, should be reviewed by the guest to ensure accuracy. The employee should not review the bill unless the guest points out a discrepancy. This is because the charges incurred may be private, and the guest may not feel comfortable with a stranger looking at what they charged to their room. (The actual makeup of a guest folio is reviewed in a later chapter.)

The employee should then ask the guest if the previously chosen method of payment is still the actual method of payment. Some guests, who choose to place a credit card down upon check-in, do so to enable them to sign hotel products and services to their room. It is within their discretion to pay a portion or all of any balance incurred with cash or check. Check verification procedures would apply, of course.

Once the bill reconciliation is complete, the employee would ask if the guest needs luggage assistance. If so, a front would be called to the bellstand. The front desk employee would then conclude the process by thanking the guest for choosing their hotel and asking him/her to return again in the future. The front desk employee should offer to make a reservation for any guest who indicates a possible return to the area. That proactive gesture also builds guest loyalty.

Guest-Directed Computer Checkout

The guest-directed computer checkout (also referred to as video checkout) is available at most hotels. The in-room television acts as a video display terminal for hotel guests. Guests can review their accounts at any point during their stay using this system. This system also allows for visual display of text messages as reviewed earlier.

Once the guest has reviewed the folio and decided to check out, he/she would input the appropriate commands on the computer keyboard connected to the television. The folio would then automatically print out at the front desk. The desk would place a sealed copy of the folio in a clearly marked area where the guest can pick it up before departing.

This checkout option is only available to guests with a valid credit card established as method of payment, or guests with the sign all charges (SAC) billing arrangement. Guests with declined credit cards, or those on a cash basis, must still go to the desk to settle their accounts.

Automated Checkout

The automated checkout system (also called "express checkout") is implemented by the hotel, on behalf of the guest. Because the departure date was verified upon check-in, the hotel knows what a guest's scheduled checkout date is. Using the automated system, the hotel would print out a folio for all guests that are to depart. This is usually done by the night audit staff. The actual folios are then delivered to each room and slid under the door. Night shift bellstaff or security personnel typically deliver the folios.

The departing guest simply reviews the folio for accuracy and can depart without ever having to stop at the desk. The express checkout is not useful for those guests who incur charges after the folio was printed (e.g., breakfast, phones calls, etc.). In those cases, guests would still need to return to the desk to retrieve a more accurate folio. As with the guest-directed computer checkout, the automated system would not apply to those guests using cash as a method of payment.

FRONT OFFICE OPERATIONS

Hotels operate 24 hours a day, 365 days a year. Excluding some seasonal resorts, most hotels operate continuously. Sleeping rooms, outlets/ancillary venues, banquet services—everything must be available for guests. That means the hotel personnel responsible for operating and maintaining those services must be staffed continuously as well. Being that the guest room is the primary justification for the hotel's existence at all, nowhere is the need for continuous staffing more evident than the front desk. The front desk must operate, in some manner, 24 hours a day.

Because the front desk is such a vital department within the rooms division, it requires strong oversight by managers. The front office manager or front desk manager(s) in large and mega-size hotels must be able to manage a staff of front desk agents and lead by example. The scope of responsibilities of these managers depends in large part on the size of the hotel, its location type, and its product type. The specific duties vary widely based on these factors, but the most universal functions are communication, staffing, and operations administration.

Communications

Communication with front office staff is very important. Making staff aware of occupancy levels and projected arrivals/departures are the most fundamental communication needs. Front desk agents and the bellstaff need to know what to expect and when to expect it. Group arrivals (time, numbers, remote check-in, etc.) will be communicated to the front office in advance via a group résumé. As has been reviewed, the group résumé is a hotel document that communicates to all vital departments any aspect of a group that may affect them. Managers should review these résumés daily and inform their staff as appropriate.

Because hotel front desks operate on a 24-hour basis, a need exists to communicate with other managers and staff who may work other shifts. Guest information that requires in-depth explanation or other hotel issues that may impact the front office are often communicated via the **pass on log**. The pass on log takes the form of a large book in which managers write notes to other managers. Similar to the logbooks used in the military, the pass on log serves to document daily activities and other issues so that a permanent record exists. If a PBX operator called in sick, for example, the pass on log would notify the next front office manager to expect that department to be short staffed. A very late arriving guest should be noted in the log as well so that the night audit staff would know to expect them.

Communication with other departments is important as well. The relationship between the front office and housekeeping is vital to successfully maximizing room revenue. The arrival and departure reports generated by the front desk manager are often reviewed by the housekeeping manager to ensure that room status reconciliation is error-free. Because the front desk is centrally located and should be the easiest area for any guest to locate, they often receive complaints from groups first. The front desk must communicate these issues to the group sales and catering department immediately to ensure follow-up. Communication with other uniform services departments is ongoing for front office management. Monitoring the workload of the bellstand, PBX, and valet areas is vital in maintaining guest and employee satisfaction.

Most hotels have areas behind the front desk that serve as a central gathering place for employees and managers. These areas serve as facilities for desk agents to discuss issues of the day, and take breaks. In these areas, the managers typically list the number of arrivals and departures for the day as well as other pertinent information. If a hotel is aware of other issues (such as impending bad weather, competitors who are sold out, or if the hotel itself is in a sellout situation), a notice to all employees will be posted in this area. This area serves as another means of communication for management. Often, these break areas are equipped with some type of indicator light or audible buzzer. If the front desk suddenly becomes busy, the staff at the desk push a button to notify those in the break room that the desk needs assistance.

Staffing

The 24-hour nature of front office operations requires constant staffing. The day in the front office is usually divided into three shifts. The first shift typically begins between 5:00 A.M. and 7:00 A.M. The first shift staff (often referred to as the A.M. shift) and management arrive to relieve the night audit staff (night audit is reviewed in depth in another chapter). The second shift (P.M. shift) typically arrives prior to the hotel's scheduled check-in time, between 1:00 P.M. and 3:00 P.M. This shift remains on duty until relieved by the night audit team (between 9:00 P.M. and 11:00 P.M.). A "swing" shift may be needed depending on the hotel size and projected arrivals/departures. Swing shifts may be needed at any point in the day. A swing shift may be needed to facilitate a group arrival, or serve as back-up staffing when other front office employees are given breaks.

The scheduling of each shift and the number of employees needed per shift largely depends on rooms forecasts. Forecasting is addressed in-depth in the chapter covering reservations, but in brief, a rooms forecast informs the hotel of upcoming occupancy levels. Short-term forecasts (looking to 3 to 14 days out) indicate fairly accurately the volume a front office might see. This volume, therefore, dictates the number of employees needed on a shift.

Front office managers do their own labor forecast using longer-term rooms forecasts (60 to 90 days out). Realizing that future demands may not be handled well by current staffing levels gives the managers time to hire more staff. Hotels that experience major swings in demand due to seasonality are good examples of why labor forecasts are important. Senior hotel management also reviews labor forecasts to ensure that labor cost is managed well.

Value-Added Services

The front office provides services to hotel guests beyond the primary duties of getting them into and out of their rooms. The front desk, because it is the traditional guest focal point, provides some value-added guest services beyond check-in and checkout. Again, the scope of these services varies from hotel to hotel, but two important value-added guest services are safe-deposit boxes and mail/document delivery.

Safe-Deposit Boxes

The **safe-deposit box** is a secured storage vehicle that allows guests to store their valuables during a hotel stay. Often, guests may wish to store items of importance, such as money, jewelry, passports, and the like. These safe-deposit boxes meet a guest need, while at the same time reducing a hotel's potential liability. In accordance with each state's laws, the limitations of the value of items placed in a safe-deposit box must be posted clearly in guest rooms (typically on the in-room tariff sheet). Hotels that do not post these value limitations may not be able to claim any statutory limitation of liability.

Guests wishing to use a safe-deposit box are given a special registration card to fill out. This card lists the:

- Guest's name
- Guest's address
- Guest's room number
- Date

The safe-deposit registration card is then placed in an "in use" file at the front desk. This confidential file is kept secured by management; no guest or employee should have access. The front desk then assigns a safe-deposit number from the available boxes. Guests themselves must always place the valuables in the boxes. These boxes are then locked in a secure area that can only be accessed with a combination of two keys. The front office manager has access to a master key, but the individual boxes can only be opened with the master key and the guest-issued box key. Items too large to be placed in a safe-deposit box may be placed in the hotel's safe at the front office manager's discretion.

Once the safe-deposit box is surrendered, the guest completes a "surrender of safe-deposit box" form that typically is printed on the reverse of the box registration card. Upon surrender of the box, the front office manager must verify that the box is indeed empty. The forms are retained by the front desk for up to six months. Random audits may be conducted by the hotel to ensure that all safe-deposit boxes are in working order.

It should be noted that hotels do assume a level of liability by offering the service of safe-deposit box storage. These levels of liability differ from state to state. Some hotels will post signage claiming "no liability for lost or stolen articles." The safe-deposit registration cards may include similar verbiage. However, even with these disclaimers, hotels generally must assume some level of liability, based on state law.

Mail and Document Handling

Guests who stay at a hotel for one or more nights may receive mail and overnight packages. Guests staying for as few as one night, or nonguests attending a meeting, may receive faxes. Hotels can ensure a high level of guest satisfaction by properly handling these documents. Between the hours of 8:00 A.M. and 9:00 P.M., if mail, faxes, or packages are received, the guest should be contacted in his/her room. If the guest is not in the room, or if these items are received outside of these hours, a message should be delivered. All incoming faxes should be placed in a sealed envelope. When possible, the hotel should attempt to deliver these items to the guest. The actual delivery of these documents/packages is usually done by the bellstaff.

A mail log is maintained in the front office to track small overnight packages and regular mail received. All items received for guests should be kept for at least 10 days. Each day the front office should check to see if the intended guest has arrived. Mail should be returned after the 10-day waiting period.

Operations Administration

Front office managers need to be good communicators first and foremost. Proper staffing levels are required to operate efficiently. The operations conducted in the front office can be quite varied. An overview of the front office manager's responsibilities in terms of operations is best revealed by analysis of a sample job description. The following job description lists the processes and procedures a typical front office manager would need to know in order to perform the job efficiently.

ABC Hotel
Front Office Manager Responsibilities

Emergency Procedures
- Senior management notification
- Emergency phone numbers, pagers, cell phones
- Reserve power and water supplies
- Police, fire, ambulance

Guest and Employee Relations
- Guest losses
- Guest accidents and illness
- Employee accidents and illness
- Employee absences, sick leave, leave of absence, bereavement
- Guest complaint management
- Lost and found procedures
- Guest loss/Theft reporting
- Liability and insurance management

Credit Policies
- Check-cashing procedures
- Paid outs, petty cash, credit card cash advance
- Delinquent guest-account management

Security
- Fraud
- Theft
- Trespassing
- Employee conduct

Scheduling and Staffing
- Hotel document management
- Scheduling
- Hiring and termination procedures
- Employees attendance requirements
- Dress code

Training
- Employee training
- Ongoing management training

Disciplinary Guidelines
- Employee disciplinary procedures
- Mentoring and coaching processes

Communication Management
- Pass on log
- Forecasts
- Group résumés
- Arrivals
- Departures
- Out of order
- Guest preferences

ABOUT MY JOB

Assistant Front Office Manager
Michelle Quick

My interest in hotels started just after graduating college with a degree in Retail Management, when I was trying to figure out what I wanted to do with my life. It was suggested that my personality, very outgoing and friendly, would be a great fit for hotels. I felt the best start for me would be at the front desk. My career started in as a front desk agent where I was trained on the day shift, then moved to the evening shift. I enjoyed being one of the first impressions the guest had of my hotel. I was eager to learn as much as I could, taking on all evening tasks, and other duties.

My supervisor noticed my enthusiasm, and early on in that same year, he rewarded me with the position of Guest History Coordinator. I was moved back to the day shift. My main focuses as Guest History Coordinator were setting up the house each morning for the repeat guests to our hotel and guests of the corporate frequent guest program and training all new Front Office Agents. What a kudos to me because I had only been at the hotel for three months.

During my tenure, I added some other responsibilities to the position. Our hotel was the host of many NBA and NFL teams. These are very detailed and time-consuming groups. It was in my

(continued)

ABOUT MY JOB
(concluded)

opinion that these types of groups needed someone dedicated at the front desk to take care of all their specific needs. That someone was me! I enjoyed molding these new responsibilities into my day-to-day job, and I held this position for 1½ years, at which time I was promoted to Transient Sales Manager. My room night goals were attained on a monthly basis, and I was able to increase the hotels' business due to my penetration of the local market.

I held this job for a short nine months, when a position of Front Office Assistant Manager became available. I always felt as though my true calling was in operations, so I jumped at the new opportunity. I love the fact that no day is ever the same. When a guest is upset, they come to the front desk, and I have the ability to turn their negative situation around into a positive one by my interaction with that guest. This job also has allowed me to be the one person in charge of the entire hotel after the department managers left for the evening and weekends. My day-to-day involvement does not stop at the front desk. Part of my responsibilities include membership on the Heat Team, the in-house emergency response team trained to be the first persons at the site of an alarm or an emergency. However a shift ends, I am continually amazed at how many opportunities in the day I have to impact very important decisions that could affect the outcome of a guest's or group's stay at my hotel. It was over these 2½ years that I gained the perspective I needed to lead at the front desk. I now see new employees as eager and as fresh faced as I was. I feel it is my responsibility to motivate, train, and promote all qualified staff members. After all, I want to give each the same opportunities that were afforded to me!

Shift Checklists

Operations administration differs from shift to shift. Each shift has different duties to perform. Documents are usually developed to aid each shift manager in completing every assigned task. These checklists vary with each hotel. These checklists outline what needs to be done and when a task should be completed. A sample A.M. checklist is illustrated in Figure 6-8.

ABC Hotel and Towers-AM Front Office Checklist

Date:
Front Office Manager On Duty:
Arrivals: Departures: Projected Occupancy:

7:00 A.M.

_____ Meet with night audit to review pass on log and outstanding issues
_____ Determine current occupancy. Verify and cross-reference with forecast
_____ Print and file Contingency Report*
_____ Run room preference report
_____ Run credit card authorization report and cash balance report
_____ Verify V/R room status

8:00 A.M.

_____ Review occupancy strategy
_____ Verify all incoming reservations
_____ Verify with reservations any same day changes, cancels
_____ Review room status
_____ Review groups to arrive with staff
_____ Determine walk-in rate

9:00 A.M.

_____ Run and re-file contingency report
_____ Review all arriving VIP's, reserve rooms accordingly
_____ Meet with front desk manager, bellcaptain, PBX supervisor, concierge manager
        to discuss day ahead

10:00 A.M.

_____ Review occupancy
_____ Run duplicate reservation report. Verify absence of double-bookings, spelling
        similarities

11:00 A.M.

_____ Review room status
_____ Print arrivals report

1:00 P.M.

_____ Review Occupancy
_____ Run and re-file contingency report
_____ Restock desk supplies

2:00 P.M.

_____ Begin employee shift changes

3:00 P.M.

_____ Review pass on log with PM shift manager
_____ Review overtime agent status
_____ Complete remaining paperwork and end shift
        Re-evaluate walk-in rate as needed

*Note, the contingency report is run several times throughout the day by front desk managers. A contingency report lists every guest in-house, guests due to arrive/depart, room statuses and rate information. Because most hotels are reliant on the computer for information, a contingency report provides backup in case of system failures. Because factors inside the hotel change constantly, the report should be run often.

FIGURE **6–8**

AM checklist

CHAPTER SIX **REVIEW**

Key Terms

arrival chronology
outsourcing
rooming a guest
front
bellcaptain
arrivals report
departures report
front log sheet
bellcart
blocking
rooms controller
10x10 rule
card approval
anticipated usage amount

direct billing
credit risk
direct billing application
walkouts
national accounts
group arrival
remote check-in
pre-key/key pack
sign all charges (SAC)
sign room and tax (SRT)
incidentals
bag delivery
bag pull
pass on log

Review Questions

1. Why is the registration process so important?
2. Explain the different guest billing options and the requirements of each.
3. What areas of the front office are impacted by the arrival chronology?
4. How does the physical layout of the hotel affect the arrival chronology?
5. Why is communication so important in the front office?
6. Define PBX.
7. Explain the premise behind the Guest Service Attendant.
8. Define the term "bag pull."
9. What are the three ways a guest can check out of a hotel?
10. What are the two primary value-added services available at the front desk?

Discussion Questions/Exercises

1. What other ways could hotels speed up the registration process? What steps in the arrival chronology could be shortened? eliminated? Some hotels have begun experimenting with a check-in kiosk. Similar in design to an automated teller machine (ATM), it allows guests with advance reservations to simply swipe a credit card and a room key is issued. What are the advantages and/or disadvantages of such a system?

2. Using the general rule for staffing bellpersons, how many staff members would be required each day based on the following?

Day	Arrivals	Departures	# Staff Needed
1	213	95	
2	189	231	
3	305	291	
4	257	326	
5	222	367	

3. The following is an excerpt from a group résumé.

XYZ Hotel Résumé–Regional Home Builders Association

Group Room Information:

Date	Arrivals	Departures
May 1	11	0
May 2	22	0
May 3	116	1
May 4	12	27
May 5	0	79
May 6	0	54

Arrival:

Remote check-in with bag delivery. Group Hospitality Suite available upon arrival to all guests. Lemonade and cookies to be served continuously 2:00 P.M.–5:30 P.M. Housekeeping to refresh room per hour.

Guest/Contact Information:

Meeting Planner:	Sue Bockman
VIP/Title:	David Wheeler (President), Bob Adelman (Executive Director), Julia Morgan (Vice President), Sue Bockman (Planner)

Activities:

Golf Tournament, May 4. Ocean Course, first tee time is 8:30 A.M. Expecting 25 foursomes. Box lunches to be on the carts. Beverage cart to be provided comp.

Departure:

Bag pull @ 7:15 A.M. Individuals to pay miscellaneous incidentals only. Room, tax, food, beverage, and recreation to be billed to the master account.

Answer the following questions as if you were the front office manager.

1. What is the group name?
2. Who is the main contact?
3. How long is the group in house?
4. What items are going to impact your bellstaff?
5. What items are going to impact your front office staff?
6. What other items will impact your staff?
7. What questions do you have that are unanswered?

CASE STUDY

Pass On Log

Following is an excerpt from a pass on log.

Time of Entry	Comment
15:00	Reviewed a.m. activities with GM. Expecting full house tonight.
15:55	PM Housekeeping attendant has gone home ill. Requested an AM attendant to stay over to cover shift. Emma can stay until 18:00.
16:20	7 Stayovers with 86 still due in. Not accepting walk-ins.
17:15	Still have 4 rooms Vacant Dirty.
18:00	2 rooms left Vacant Dirty — Emma cannot stay any longer.
18:15	Guest called to find out where her room service dinner was. I followed up with the kitchen. They had burned the steak; they will give her a new one comp. Guest was happy. Have Chef send apology note.
18:45	15 Arrivals left — 12 Vacant Ready rooms.

| CASE STUDY | **Pass On Log** *(concluded)* |

Time of Entry	Comment
19:00	Mr. Smith came down to change credit cards. He received the message that his card had declined. He was very apologetic.
19:30	5 Arrivals — 2 Vacant Ready Rooms.
19:35	I had to clean the 2 rooms Emma didn't get to.
21:00	Filled last two rooms — glad I cleaned them earlier! 1 Arrival left.
22:00	Noise complaint in room 305. Security and I contacted the guest; he had a bit too much to drink. Need to watch.
22:05	Guest pick up at airport. Need to send shuttle. This could be bad, as we have no rooms left.
22:15	Had to walk last guest to the Maple Leaf Inn. He was understanding. Called Rachel there and made the arrangements. Guest will return in the morning. Note, upgrade upon return to hotel.
23:00	Reviewed p.m. activities with night audit manager.

1. Write a narrative about what happened at the hotel on this evening.

2. What would have happened if the hotel did not clean the two remaining rooms?

3. If you were this manager, what would you do differently?

4. The log noted instances of guest service and contact. Why is this important to make note of?

INTERNET RESOURCES
Trade Journals/Online Resources

Learn more about other ways to operate the front office as well as other hotel departments. It is always prudent to read the industry journals. Many of these journals have their own Web sites.

Cornell Hotel & Restaurant Administration Quarterly	<http://www.hotelschool.cornell.edu/publications/hraq/>
Hospitality Net	<http://www.hospitalitynet.org/>
Hospitality News	<http://www.hotel-online.com/Neo/News/>
Hotels	<http://www.hotelsmag.com/>
Hotel and Motel Management	<http://www.innvest.com/hmm/>
Hotel News Resource	<http://www.hotelnewsresource.com/headlines.htm>
Hotel Online	<http://www.hotel-online.com/Neo/>
International Hotel & Restaurant Association	<http://www.ih-ra.com/>
Lodging Hospitality	<http://www.lhonline.com/>
Lodging News	<http://www.lodgingnews.com/>

For additional hospitality and travel marketing resources, visit our Web site at **<http://www.Hospitality-Tourism.delmar.com>.**

Room Rate Structure

OBJECTIVES

After reading this chapter, you should understand:

- The Hubbart Formula
- Different methods of calculating room rates
- Room rate designations
- Rate measurements

INTRODUCTION

Hotel room rates are similar in many ways to airline fares. They are both quantifiable and qualifiable. Given that on any given flight, there may be 20 or more different prices being paid for the same service, hotel rooms will vary in cost for the same basic product. They are quantifiable in that they can be measured and structured to meet certain criteria. They are qualifiable in that large amounts of discretion are allowed in which rates are implemented and when. Later chapters deal with how and why these room rates are implemented; this chapter gives a background on their origins and a summary of the most prevalent room rates in today's marketplace.

RATE STRUCTURE

Throughout this chapter the term average daily rate is used. The **average daily rate (ADR)** is an average of all the rates sold at a hotel on a given night. It obviously isn't the highest, nor is it the lowest booked rate. It is an accepted term that is primarily used to determine a starting point in understanding a hotel's rate structure. The combination of all the rates offered at a hotel is called the **rate structure**.

The Hubbart Formula

Where would a hotel manager start in determining the fair price for a guest room? What is a fair value? This question has daunted innkeepers from the beginning. Charge rates too high, and no one will stay with you. Setting rates too low, and the owner makes less money. For many years in the beginning of the modern hotel era, hotel managers simply guessed. As unscientific as this approach sounds, it did work to an extent. After a hotel has been in business for a while, managers would know by instinct and past experiences what rates to set. In some ways, this instinctual approach had merit. It allowed for flexibility and swift market response.

That approach stopped being effective when new lodging management associations emerged. As owner-operated and owner-managed hotels looked to expand and evolve into chains and franchise operations, they needed to borrow capital. It is the banking industry that forced a change in the way hotels set their rates. The guessing approach didn't translate well into the language of income statements. In order for financing to become available, a standardized rate formula was developed.

In the 1940s the American Hotel Association (the precursor to today's American Hotel and Lodging Association) asked a gentleman by the name of Roy Hubbart to develop a way to compute room rates.[1] Mr. Hubbart came up with a method to calculate a hotel room rate based on the costs incurred in operating the hotel and a reasonable return on investment for the investors. Going beyond simple room cost, the Hubbart formula allowed the hotel to scientifically illustrate to a banker what the return on investment would be.

This quantifiable approach was well received. Financing for any business enterprise has always been contingent on return on investment and forecasts. Though this rate formula has its detractors today, it was a valuable milestone in the evolution of the industry. Here is how the Hubbart formula works.

The Hubbart formula incorporates three different sections, or schedules, into its calculations: Schedule I looks at specific financial calculations; Schedule II looks at the rates per occupied room; Schedule III incorporates square footage into the analysis.

Schedule I attempts to determine the costs incurred with the hotel operation and incorporate a reasonable return on investment (or **ROI**). Operating expenses, taxes/insurance, and depreciation are understood to include all the same criteria used to determine room cost (Figure 7-1). What the Hubbart formula does differently from strict room cost analysis is to incorporate a fair market ROI for the investor. This ROI level can vary widely, but it is understood to be a fair market value based on equity and interest expense on debt. The numbers used in the Hubbart formula examples presented here (Figure 7-1, Figure 7-2, and Figure 7-3) are for illustrative purposes only.

Schedule II of the Hubbart formula (Figure 7-2) uses the figure reached at the end of Schedule I to determine the average daily rate the hotel would need to charge to meet its obligations—those obligations being operating costs and owner ROI. Schedule II is similar to the opportunity cost calculation in that it considers the total number of room nights available for sale in a year (365 days times the number of rooms available per night). It goes further in that it takes into consideration an estimated occupancy percentage. Determining this occupancy percentage is where the Hubbart formula gains detractors. What would be a fair occupancy percentage? Some hotel markets consistently run very high occupancy levels. Other areas are susceptible to market fluctuations. Hotel room supply in an area can vary, as does the demand. Occupancy expectations must be based on detailed analysis of competition, market supply, local economic factors, and population, among others. A very general rule of thumb is to insert an expected occupancy figure of 70 percent. The 70 percent figure is used by many as a benchmark of performance, prior to reviewing market factors.

Schedule II yields a required average rate of $46.07, based on an occupancy of 70 percent. Again, the variables in determining occupancy can sway this number. When comparing the Hubbart formula to room cost calculation, the results are close but not the same. With the same data, the Hubbart calculations would yield a higher room rate than the room cost analysis. There are two main reasons for this:

1. Room cost analysis does not include the ROI provision that Hubbart does. In strictly looking at the costs incurred in room sales, profit would not come into play.

2. Room cost includes opportunity cost. The cost of maintaining each room for every night is included in determining room cost. The Hubbart formula assumes an average occupancy.

While useful in determining an average rate for a generic hotel, Schedules I and II of the Hubbart formula do not take into account the variables in the modern hotel structure. Few hotels today build all their rooms to the exact same specifications. Variances in room type, size, and configuration could command higher rates than a standard room. With Schedule III (Figure 7-3), the Hubbart formula attempts to address the issue of these varying rooms by making an assumption that larger rooms are more expensive to maintain. With that assumption, the Hubbart formula incorporates a square footage

Hubbart Formula Example - Schedule I

Operating Expenses:	*Example*	
Rooms Department	$450,000	
Telephone Department	$75,000	
Administrative and General	$200,000	
Payroll Taxes and Employee Benefits	$225,000	
Advertising and Promotion	$75,000	
H/L/P (Heat, Light, Power)	$150,000	
Repairs and Maintenance	$125,000	
Total Operating Expense		$1,300,000

Taxes and Insurance		
Real Estate and Personal Property Taxes	$75,000	
Franchise Taxes and Fees	$25,000	
Insurance on Building and Contents	$30,000	
Lease Costs (Equipment and/or Vehicles)	$45,000	
Total Taxes and Insurance		$175,000

Depreciation at Book Value		
Building	$175,000	
FF&E (Furniture, Fixtures and Equipment)	$125,000	
Total Depreciation		$300,000

Fair Market Return on Investment (ROI) Property		
Land		
Building		
FF&E		
Total Fair Market ROI		$500,000
TOTAL:		$2,275,000

Deduct (Income from sources other than rooms)		
Income from store rentals/leases	$25,000	
Profit [Loss] from food and beverage operations	$175,000	
Income from other sources (ancillary revenue)	$15,000	$215,000
Total Income from Other Sources		

Amount Needed from Room Revenue to Cover Costs and Realize a Fair Market ROI		$2,060,000

FIGURE **7-1**

Hubbart Schedule 1

Hubbart Formula Example - Schedule II

		Example
1. Amount Needed from Guest Room Sales (Schedule I)		$2,060,000
2. Number of Guest Rooms Available		175
3. Number of Rooms Available on an Annual Basis Item 2 multiplied by 365 (175 x 365)	100%	63,875
4. Less Allowance for Average Vacancy	– 30%	–19,163
5. Number of Rooms to be Occupied Based on Average Occupancy	70%	44,712
6. Average Daily Rate Required to Cover Costs and Provide Reasonable ROI (Item 1 divided by Item 5)		$ 46.07

FIGURE **7-2**

Hubbart Schedule 2

Hubbart Formula Example - Schedule III

	Example
1. Amount Needed from Guest Room Sales (Schedule I)	$2,060,000
2. Square foot Area of Guest Rooms	70,000
3. Less Allowance for Average Vacancy (70,000 x 30%)	–21,000
4. Net Square Footage of Occupied Rooms (70,000 x 70%)	49,000
5. Average Annual Rental per Square Foot (Item 1 divided by Item 4)	$ 42.04
6. Average Daily Rental per Square Foot (365 divided by Item 5)	$0.12

FIGURE **7-3**

Hubbart Schedule 3

provision. This provision requires a measurement of the total square guest room area. This measurement is simply a sum of the square footage available in each guest room. Using the same hotel from the example, assume that it has a total square guest room area of 70,000 square feet.

In Schedule III, an average square foot calculation of $0.12 was determined to be needed to meet the costs and reasonable ROI determination. The flexibility of this calculation allows the hotel manager to apply different rates to differing room types and configurations. Again, assuming that the better rooms are the larger rooms, a higher average rate could be applied to the better room types. For example:

A standard guest room may have an area of 375 square feet. A junior suite may have an area of 450 square feet. The average daily rate of the standard room would be $45 ($0.12 × 375). The suite would command a higher rate because of its bigger area $54 ($0.12 × 450).

Cost Rate Formula

There are many other ways to set the required rates in a hotel. There is no "perfect" way to determine the rate. One unique method is called the **cost rate formula**.[2] The cost rate formula is based on the construction cost of the hotel. The average room rate should equal $1.00 per $1,000 of total construction cost (total cost would include the land and the physical structure). If a 175-room hotel cost $10 million to build, the average rate would be $57.14 ($10 million divided by 175 divided by $1,000).

Market Tolerance

One of the more time-consuming methods in establishing a hotel's average daily rate is called the **market tolerance** method. Before a hotel is constructed, an owner may simply call around to hotels of similar product type, location type, and size. Called the **competitive set**, these hotels would serve as direct competitors to the newly built hotel. An ongoing record of what transient rates are offered on any given night would give the new hotel an idea of what the market tolerance is in the area. Although this isn't the most scientific approach, it does do better than simply guessing what the rate should be.

It is common in the industry for hotels in a competitive set to call each other to see what rate each is offering each night. Called "shopping," or "call-around," these hotels must never share who they are when they make the call. It is illegal for hotels to get together and set their rates as one unit. Called price fixing, it is a violation of antitrust laws. The market tolerance rate method isn't a violation in that there is no attempt to price fix. Many industries "shop" their competition. The prevalent "low price guarantee" is an example of vendors who know when they have the lowest price. It is when the competitors band together to raise prices that a crime is committed. One must be cognizant of antitrust laws in that the potential for abuse is high.

ROOM RATE DESIGNATIONS

The difficult part of determining room rates is finding a starting point. The Hubbart formula and the other methods of establishing an average daily rate help hotel managers with that first step. That initial rate calculation enables hotels to build an overall rate structure. The rate structure, or combination of all the rates offered at a hotel, will vary from property to property. Actual dollar values will of course vary as well based on hotel product type, location type, size, and market conditions.

The individual room rates within the rate structure are allocated a value based on certain characteristics. The **room rate designation** is the term used to specify the rate threshold within the overall structure. In other words, the rate designation defines what position a specific rate will take within the overall rate hierarchy. As with a chessboard, one knows immediately that the queen is a more powerful piece than the knight is. The rate designation allows any hotelier to get a good idea as to a rate's value in relation to the other rates. The room rate designation does not specify an actual dollar value; it simply "ranks" all the rates within the rate structure.

Understanding each of the different rate designations within the structure is crucial to maximizing overall room revenue. Hotel managers must continually review the rate designations they incorporate within a hotel's rate structure. The most common designations include:

- **Rack rate**—The **rack rate** is understood to be the highest published rate a hotel can charge for a specific room. Rack rates can differ between room types, configuration, and designation. On the back of most hotel room doors, a **tariff sheet** will be posted. This tariff sheet will list the rack rate for that particular room. In most cases, hotels must adhere to the rate structure posted on the tariff sheet. Certain states allow for exceptions during unusually high demand events, such as yearly sporting competitions. The hotels that change their rack rates for these events must post that information on the in-room tariff sheets well in advance.

- **Corporate rate**—This designation is designed to promote the corporate market segment. It is offered generally to any guest who knows to ask for it. Typically, the corporate rate reflects a 10 to 20 percent discount off of the rack rate. The corporate rate is widely accepted as the transient **target rate** for most hotels. The target rate is simply an average rate goal a hotel sets to achieve for a certain day or market segment. Both the group and transient room sales teams have their own target rates, which they strive to reach. Understanding that some rates will be lower and some higher, the target rate serves as the predetermined average goal.

● **Volume account rates**—Also called preferred rates, the volume account rate trades a further discount off of the corporate rate in exchange for a guaranteed number of room nights within a specific time frame. Organizations who know that they have a certain level of transient volume that they can bring to a certain hotel can negotiate for this volume discount. The level of this discount is contingent upon the volume. Hotels will base their volume requirements on many factors. Primary among the requirements is a set time frame. Whether on a monthly, quarterly, or yearly basis, the volume account must be measured to ensure that room night production levels are maintained. Whatever criteria are used, these volume accounts are usually assigned a grade based on production. Hotels will predetermine the number of room nights required to achieve each grade, and assign a rate discount accordingly. For example:

— "A" Accounts are entitled to a 20 percent discount off corporate rate.

— "B" Accounts are entitled to a 15 percent discount off corporate rate.

— "C" Accounts are entitled to a 10 percent discount off corporate rate.

● **Government rate**—Within most major cities, federal and/or state governmental agencies set predetermined rates that they will reimburse their traveling employees for. This reimbursable rate is called a **per diem**. A per diem for governmental employees usually covers hotel, meals, and other out-of-pocket expenses. These per diems are set a year in advance and published so that all interested hotels can offer it. The Federal government, as well as other state and local agencies may set their per diems at the same dollar amount. However, in many instances, the federal and state per diems are not the same. Setting a per diem too low may preclude governmental employees from staying at a nicer facility. It is not uncommon for hotels to lobby the government to raise the per diem if it is deemed too low. Those traveling on government business are usually asked for identification upon check-in before being granted the government rate. Large corporations (such as IBM) often set per diems as well in areas where no volume accounts have been set.

● **Seasonal rates**—Resorts and other location types that see a fluctuation in demand due to weather or the operation of a nearby attraction will vary their rates accordingly. Offering a different rate for in-season and out-of-season (also called off-season) allows the hotel to alter their rate structure to compensate for this cyclical demand. A seasonal rate designation can apply to other rates as well. In-season corporate rates, for example, will definitely be higher than out-of-season corporate rates.

● **Weekday/Weekend rates**—Hotels of all location types see fluctuation in demand during certain days of the week. The hotel industry looks at the days of the week slightly differently than the public might. The determination of what days are considered weekday and which are considered weekend is based on the next morning of occupancy. Guests who stay at a hotel on a Friday or Saturday night are staying on a weekend night because the next morning is a non-workday. Those staying Sunday through Thursday are considered weekday occupants because the next morning is a traditional workday. Traditionally, hotel location types see their weekday and weekend demand levels as illustrated in Figure 7-4.

These figures will vary based on market factors, but traditionally the hotel location types will see their demand fluctuate with the days of the week. Resort hotels (in season) will see demand grow on weekends and drop during the week. Airport hotels traditionally have higher demand when business travel increases during midweek, and lower on weekends when most travelers are home. Downtown hotels have a strong weekday demand cycle that corresponds to meetings and conventions. Suburban hotels will see

FIGURE **7-4**

Weekday/weekend demand

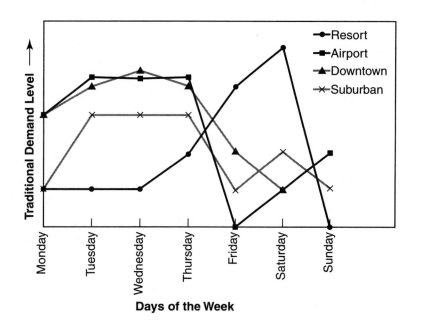

steady mid-week demand and a drop off on weekends. A spike can occur on Saturdays if suburban hotels have strong demand from the social market.

- **Membership rates**—Organizations such as the American Automobile Association (**AAA**) and the American Association of Retired Persons (**AARP**) have a large constituency of members who enjoy travel. Recognizing this, these organizations have developed travel guidebooks and other aids to help their members choose a hotel. These hotels must meet two main criteria in order for them to be recommended: (1) a certain level of quality, service, and cleanliness; (2) a special rate. These membership rates are typically 50 percent off rack rate. Hotels benefit from offering these rates because of the loyalty that members of these organizations exhibit. If it is recommended by their organization, the members can be sure that the hotel has met the two main recommendation criteria. By offering these membership rates, the hotels are allowed to display the logos of the AAA and AARP. The members will then find it easier to seek out hotels that offer these membership rates. Another benefit of offering membership rates is the free advertising given to participating hotels by being listed in the organizations' guidebooks.

- **Industry rates**—Those who work in the travel industry (travel agents, employees from other hotels, meeting planners, etc.) are often extended the professional courtesy of discounted rates. Industry rates can vary from 30 to 50 percent off rack rate, depending on the location and seasonality factors. The one restriction most hotels impose is a valid form of industry identification. The International Association of Travel Agents (**IATA**) is a recognized industry group that issues a number for all legitimate travel agencies and their employees. A business card or paycheck stub may suffice as well. This industry rate should not be confused with what is referred to as an "employee rate." Many chains offer their employees a discounted rate at affiliated hotels when they travel. They see this as an effective way to promote awareness of sister hotels and to instill a form of guest loyalty on the employee. These rates vary greatly, but can be as much as 75 percent off rack rate.

- **Walk-in rate**—This type of rate designation may vary from night to night. It is set each night by the front office or rooms manager based on the remaining unoccupied rooms in the hotel. A walk-in is a hotel guest who arrives without a reservation. Literally "walking in off the street" these guests can help fill any remaining hotel rooms. With few remaining rooms, the walk-in rate may be set fairly high to maximize room revenue. An empty hotel may reduce the walk-in rate significantly.

- **Premium rates**—Schedule III of the Hubbart formula looked at establishing an average room rate based on the size of the hotel room in question—The assumption being that larger rooms were nicer rooms. But, because that formula only created a starting point for the rate structure, a specific rate designation for these nicer rooms is needed. Room configurations above standard, those with views or other amenities, can command a room rate premium. Premium rates are applied to any room that offers something "extra." There are two methods of implementing the premium designation: (1) Fixed premium rates are set, standard rates quoted for each configuration regardless of demand. They do not vary. (2) Variable premium rates are determined based on the other available rates. A specific premium is determined for each configuration. Variable premium rates simply add the specific premium to the initial rate quoted for a standard room. Rooms with a special view might command a $20 premium over the same room type with no view (for example, corporate rate + $20). A guest wanting a junior suite may pay a $100 premium over the initial rate quote ($100 + government rate).

- **Advance purchase rates**—A relatively new trend in hotel rate structures, an advance purchase rate offers a greater discount based on the number of days in advance it is booked. A 7-, 10-, or 21-day advance purchase rate will have a corresponding lower price. How far in advance a hotel sets its advance purchase rates depends largely on its booking cycle. As was reviewed previously, the individual booking cycle is the time between when an individual reservation is made and when that reservation is due to arrive. The booking cycle can be anywhere from a few days to a few months. The transient demand is low outside the traditional booking cycle and increases drastically within it. A hotel wishing to lengthen that booking cycle (and hence getting more reservations booked farther in advance) will offer advance-booking rates with greater discounts further out. The advance purchase rate concept was copied from the airline industry. Similarly, they are often nonrefundable and can carry a penalty for any change.

- **Half-day rates**—Some hotels offer certain guest rooms as an alternative meeting room. Most often these are suites, but some hotels have built specially designed sleeping rooms complete with small conference tables and limited audiovisual equipment. These rooms are often utilized for just a few hours to conduct interviews and small conferences. Because the room is not used for the entire night, a half-day rate may be assigned based on half the value of the rack rate. Half-day rates are also commonly offered at airport hotels in major gateway cities. Travelers arriving in from a long flight may come at all hours of the day. They may require a room for a few hours' sleep and a quick shower to freshen up. A half-day rate may be imposed in these cases as well.

● **Package rates**—A hotel package combines one or more hotel products or services to make the new entity more attractive. Called **bundling**, a hotel will package the room (and its rate) with another service or amenity. Often this entails pricing the package below the cost of purchasing the items separately. Most traditional hotel packages combine a room with a meal (e.g., breakfast). The perceived benefit to the guest can be monetary savings, convenience, or both. Package rates can incorporate nonhotel items as well. Variations on the hotel package can consist of:

— *Meal packages.* The most common are the American Plan (AP), which includes three meals a day with the room. (Not to be confused with all-inclusive rates, which resorts often incorporate into their rate structure. An all-inclusive rate will bundle all meals, drinks, activities, and gratuities into the room rate.) The Modified American Plan (MAP) includes two meals (typically breakfast and dinner) and the room. The Continental Plan (CP) includes continental breakfast and a room. (**Note:** The European Plan is commonly mistaken for a package, but no meals are included. It is simply another way of asking for the room rate only.) The All-Suite Plan (SP), a relatively new package rate, combines the room with breakfast and cocktails in the evening. This rate is the standard plan for all-suite properties.

— *Vacation packages.* These bundle room rates and one or more of the following: airline tickets, transportation, tickets to local attractions or shows, and "themed" amenities. A themed amenity could include sunglasses and suntan lotion for a "Fun in the Sun" package. A honeymoon package could include champagne and strawberries with the room. A "Night on the Town" package might include a limousine ride and dinner. Shopping packages may include discount coupons to local shops and a foot massage for tired feet. A concert package might include a ticket to a show and the musical artist's latest compact disk in addition to the room. Savvy hotels have even bundled their sleeping rooms with sought-after items. Tickets to a sold-out show that are bundled with a hotel room virtually guarantee a sale (whether the guest stays there or not).

— *Meeting packages.* These can be valuable for the busy meeting planner. A Complete Meeting Package (or CMP) rate typically includes coffee breaks, lunches, dinners, and/or audiovisual equipment, the cost of the meeting room and a sleeping room all bundled together. Sometimes referred to as a Comprehensive Meeting Package, the CMP rate is often offered at conference centers with sleeping rooms. Variations of the meeting package may not always include the sleeping room. The DMP, or Day Meeting Package, includes everything the CMP rate did except for the sleeping room.

● **Per person rates**—All the aforementioned rate designations are usually based on single occupancy. As was introduced in the chapter on the guest room, a single occupancy room has only one occupant. A single occupancy rate assumes the same. To review, rooms that are occupied by more than one guest are called double occupancy (two guests), triple occupancy (three guests), and quad occupancy (four guests). It is rare for a standard room to house more than four people. Based on the number of people, hotels may charge a preset amount for each additional occupant. Similar in design to the premium rates, per person rates can be variable or fixed. Sometimes called the **rate spread**, the difference between the single and double occupancy rates can range anywhere from 10 to 25 percent. This additional cost is due to the fact that hotel rooms suffer a greater "wear and tear" with more occupants. Hotel rooms that house many people will, over time, require more maintenance and a greater frequency of renovations. There are a few hotels that do not charge per person rates because they value the outlet and ancillary revenue that additional occupants will surely generate.

● **Group rates**—Although analysis of group rates merits an entire text, they do make up a portion of a hotel's rate structure. It is difficult to categorize these rates as a specific designation because they can differ greatly. A group rate is determined by many factors. Group rates, as was reviewed earlier, are typically lower than transient rates because they are booked in advance and are contractually obligated. They also provide revenue to the other two parts of the hotel success triangle (namely catering and outlet/ancillary revenue). For the purposes of this text, it is important to note that the number of groups and their differing rates may affect the other rate designations within a hotel's rate structure.

RATE MEASUREMENT AVERAGES

Each of the various room designations will equate to a specific dollar amount based on the many factors discussed earlier. Measuring each of these rates is important in determining hotel performance. How many corporate rates were sold last night? How high were the group rates? What are the average rates of each sleeping room? These questions and many others like them are best answered by reviewing rate averages. The most common rate average measurement was reviewed earlier—average daily rate. Its intended use, in conjunction with the Hubbart formula, was to select a starting point for a hotel's rate structure.

The term "average daily rate" is broad and has another meaning. Average daily rate can also be used to determine the total (cumulative) average rate paid at a hotel on a given night. Its abbreviation (ADR) is universally understood to stand for the revenue generated by all occupied sleeping rooms divided by the number of rooms. The ADR measurement is used by most in the industry to compare a hotel's performance in relation to past years and to other hotels in a competitive set. Other rate measurements averages include:

- **Gross average rate**—determined by the combination of room revenue generated by all the sleeping rooms divided by the total number of rooms. ADR was determined by using the revenue from strictly occupied rooms. The gross average rate includes all rooms (occupied or not).

- **Net average rate**—determined by calculating the room revenue generated strictly by occupied and paying rooms. Whereas ADR looks at all occupied rooms, net average rate excludes comps and out-of-order rooms. A comp (industry term for complimentary) is a room given away on a gratis basis for a special guest. Hotels give comps away for many different reasons. Groups with many rooms at a hotel are often given 1 comp for every 50 occupied rooms. Casino hotels may give comps away to their high rollers. An unhappy guest may be asked to come back again on a complimentary basis. An out-of-order room (OOO) is "not occupiable" for one reason or another. Repairs due to damage or renovations may render a room inappropriate for occupancy. An OOO room is said to be taken out of inventory, which literally reduces the number of rooms available at a hotel. Both comps and OOOs are excluded from net average rate because they were either not occupied or did not generate revenue. Comps literally translate into a rate of $0. This does not mean that there is no cost incurred. As was reviewed in the analysis of room cost, all rooms incur a cost regardless of the value of the rate (H/L/P, taxes, etc.). Opportunity cost is incurred every night. Each comp and OOO room reflects a lost opportunity to sell the room. It is for that reason hotels generally attempt to limit the number of comps and OOO rooms on any given night.

- **Group average rate**—calculated from occupied rooms of groups of 10 or more rooms per night. The group average rate is often lower than the average daily rate or net average rate due to the fact that group rooms include comps and most group rates are lower to begin with.

- **Transient average rate**—the companion measurement to group average rate. The transient average rate looks at the revenue generated from all non–group-occupied and revenue-generating rooms.

- **Market segment averages**—both transient and group rooms are comprised of their own specific market segments. Each of these can be analyzed on its own to determine the average rate for that particular market segment. For example, within the transient market, an average rate can be viewed for business and pleasure segments. The group market can analyze the rates averaged for the corporation, association, and other market segments. More in-depth analysis can be conducted on market subsegments by averaging their rates as well.

- **Room specific averages**—Another type of average rate is based on the room itself. Average rates can be based on room types (e.g., double average rate), configuration (e.g., suite average rate), and designation (e.g., non-smoking average rate).

NOTES

1. Hubbart, R. (1952). *The Hubbart Formula for Evaluating Rate Structures of Hotel Rooms.* New York: American Hotel and Motel Association.
2. Vallen, G., and Vallen, J. (1996). *Check-in Check-out.* Chicago: Richard D. Irwin.

CHAPTER SEVEN **REVIEW**

KEY TERMS

average daily rate (ADR)	tariff sheet
rate structure	target rate
ROI	per diem
cost rate formula	AAA
market tolerance	AARP
competitive set	IATA
room rate designations	bundling
rack rate	rate spread

Review Questions

1. What are the benefits of offering AAA/AARP rates?

2. How is the Hubbart Formula useful in determining room rates? What are its drawbacks, if any?

3. What is a room rate designation?

4. What are the benefits of bundling?

5. What was the American Hotel and Lodging Association called in the 1940s?

6. Why does Schedule II of the Hubbart Formula yield a higher room rate than strict room cost analysis?

7. Using the cost rate formula, what reasonable rate should a hotel charge that cost $20 million to build and has 400 guest rooms?

8. What is a target rate?

9. What does IATA stand for?

10. What is a walk-in, and how are walk-in rates determined?

Discussion Questions/Exercises

1. Why is price fixing such a concern within the hotel industry? What would happen in an area of few hotels if they got together to set rates? How could this apply to other industries, say the airline industry? What control would an airline possibly have over fares in a city that was served only by them?

2. Call a large city hotel early in the morning on a weekday. Request a rate quote for a day that is at least 21 days from today. What is the lowest rate available?

   ● Call the same hotel later that afternoon. Request the lowest rate available for the same date. What is the rate now?

   ● Call the same hotel the next morning. Request the lowest rate available for the same date. What is the rate now?

   ● Do the same exercise for a date that is only three days from today. What assumptions can you make based on the rates you were quoted?

3. As a consumer, what types of package rates would be attractive to you? What items would need to be bundled together to make that package? Why do package rates thrive at resorts and less so at other hotel types? Develop packages targeted to three specific market subsegments and share them with the class.

| CASE STUDY | **Room Rate Structure #1** |

Background

A 500-room property has recorded the following data from the previous day:

- Total rooms occupied: 423
- Total room revenue: $64,452.51
- Total group revenue: $42,206.53
- Total group rooms: 271
- Three groups in-house:
    1. The Smithers Data Corp group held 56 percent of all the group rooms and 48 percent of all the group revenue.
    2. The rate for the Power and Light Group was $120 (single occupancy).
- Transient rooms were booked in the following segments:
    30% rack rate
    50% corporate and volume rates
    10% membership rates
     8% package rates
     2% government rates
- $15,800,000 is the guest room sales goal for the year.
- 70 percent occupancy is the occupied room goal for the year.
- A competitive call-around to competitors finds that two of four hotels in this hotel's competitive set are sold out on this night.

Using these data, answer the following questions:

1. What is the overall occupancy percentage?
2. What is the ADR (average daily rate)?
3. What is the transient average rate?
4. How many rooms did each transient segment receive?
5. What was the room block and average group rate for Smithers Data Corp?
6. What would the average daily rate be required to be to cover costs and provide reasonable ROI? (Hubbart Formula)
7. What conclusions can be drawn from this night's actual hotel data?

(continued)

Room Rate Structure #1 *(concluded)*

8. What are the multiple-occupant rates for the Power and Light Group?

   Double:

   Triple:

   Quad:

9. If the rack rate is $175, most likely, what would these rates be?

   Corporate:

   Volume Account A:

   Volume Account B:

   Membership Discount:

Room Rate Structure #2

Call two local hotels and fill out the following chart:

Hotel Name:		Hotel Name:	
Number of guest rooms		Number of guest rooms	
Rack rate		Rack rate	
Corporate rate		Corporate rate	
Volume rate (request a rate for a large local company)		Volume rate (request a rate for a large local company)	
Weekend rate		Weekend rate	
Package rate		Package rate	

Compare the two hotels. What are the discount percentages between rates? What do the packages include? Does the weekend rate go up or go down? What does this mean in terms of the demand pattern? Which is the better deal? What are the hotel ratings? Which is the recommended property?

The Property Management System

OBJECTIVES

After reading this chapter, you should understand:

- The Property Management System
- How PMS is integrated within other hotel systems
- Why a hotel would implement a PMS hierarchy
- How to check-in a guest

INTRODUCTION

Hotels use a variety of computer systems to manage the operations of their front office. Called a property management system (**PMS**), these computer systems manage a variety of tasks. A hotel PMS manages a guest's check-in and checkout, cash transactions at the front desk, outlet/ancillary transactions, reservations, housekeeping, night audit, and other tasks. The PMS impacts the rooms division before, during, and after the arrival chronology.

SELECTING THE PMS

PMS's, by nature, differ greatly. Due to the wide variety of hotels currently in the marketplace, PMS's have evolved to meet the differing array of needs. Each hotel must consider several factors that influence the type of PMS they use before finding one that best fits their needs.

The first step in deciding on the right PMS is to conduct a **needs analysis**. A needs analysis is a process where hotel owners and senior managers determine the required scope of their PMS needs. The needs analysis documents exactly what processes a particular hotel will require from its PMS. Factors such as the hotel size, product type, location, and target market affect this analysis. A large resort, for example, with numerous outlets and ancillary services, will need a much more comprehensive system than a small suburban hotel would. The sheer number of transactions and users involved in day-to-day operations of this resort would require a much more robust system. It should be noted that not all lodging ownership associations allow for independent PMS procurement. In most cases, franchise and management contract hotels must use the PMS chosen for them by their chain. Often, chains maximize savings by implementing the same PMS at all affiliate hotels. This standardization reduces costs as a result of volume purchasing. An additional benefit for the chain is that they have to provide computer help desk support for only one system. Supporting several systems is costly. The independent, owner-operated, and owner-managed hotels are free to choose the system that best suits their individual needs.

Once the needs are determined, the appropriate software should be secured. PMS software is a computer program designed on a particular programming platform. There are several PMS's on the market currently that operate on different software platforms. Older PC systems are MS-DOS based; newer PC systems use a Microsoft Windows™ platform. Other software platforms available are written in Linux, still others are written specifically for Apple computers. The functionality of the software platform is important when selecting the PMS. Questions the decision makers should ask themselves are: "How easy is the system to learn?" and "Does it do everything I need it to?" The needs analysis conducted ensures that the PMS software is appropriate for a particular hotel. Nearly all PMS suppliers allow potential purchasers to view a software's capabilities through demonstration trials. Hotels that are given a mandated PMS by their chain typically receive a system with many more capabilities than needed. The chain will determine the appropriate system for their largest, most complex hotel operations. Therefore, smaller hotels in that chain receive a system with a greater capacity than they require. This scenario is much more attractive to a hotel than receiving a mandated system that does not meet the needs outlined in the needs analysis.

Once the software is decided upon, the hotel must consider the requisite hardware needs. Hardware is understood to be the actual machine the software runs on. The software itself often dictates the hardware needs. The chosen software will require specific processing speeds and memory capability of its hardware.

"640k ought to be enough for anybody."

—Bill Gates in 1981

The end users of the chosen configuration are the hotel employees and managers. The areas where an employee or manager can access the PMS are called **PMS workstations**. Each PMS workstation will include the software, hardware, and computer monitor. In the modern hotel, many of these workstations are also loaded with additional software. Depending on the needs of the end user, other applications (such as e-mail, word processing, spreadsheets, and Internet access) might be available at a particular workstation. These additional applications must also be considered when determining the hardware needs.

Hotels must consider the aesthetic impact of the hardware as well. PMS workstations will need to be placed in many areas of the hotel. The workstations are most often located in the front office (at the front desk; behind the front desk; in reservations, PBX, and accounting). However, additional workstations are generally needed at the bellstand, concierge desk, in housekeeping, and at the various outlets throughout the hotel. Often, these workstations are in plain sight of guests, so the size and "look" of the machines must be appropriate.

Hotel PMS stations, whatever the hardware and software configuration, are generally linked to each other in some type of network. A PMS network also referred to as a LAN (local area network) allows each station to communicate with the other. This communication is vital, as hotels must know the status of their facility in real time. That is, every PMS station will know the status of every room and every guest. The PMS station will show a room as checked out as soon as the front desk employee completes the transaction. The housekeeping department will instantly realize that they have another room to clean. Once that room is cleaned, the front desk will immediately determine that they have another room to sell. The efficiencies created by PMS networks are very valuable in maximizing revenue.

PMS's are more than communication tools. They can also be thought of as extensive databases. They store guest information and preferences. This information is valuable because it enables a hotel to target its marketing effort. PMS's capture demographic and other information on each guest. Direct mail, newspaper, and other forms of advertising media are much more effective when targeted to a specific demographic or region. Trends in guest preferences,

FIGURE **8-1**

PMS at the front desk
(Courtesy Omni Severin Hotel)

such as an increase in requests for nonsmoking rooms, can help hotel managers reconfigure rooms during a renovation. If cribs are being requested more frequently, managers can purchase more and increase the safety inspections of the current inventory.

Whatever platform and configuration is used, the fundamental PMS structure is the same. The most important aspect of any PMS is its ability to manage a hotel's room inventory (see Figure 8-1).

GUEST ACCOUNT

Most PMS's are organized based on a series of menus. Within the PMS, the **guest account** tracks all the data that pertains to an individual guest. The guest account contains two separate menus. The **guest registration menu** contains all the pertinent information garnered from the initial reservation and during the stay (i.e., name, arrival/departure, room preferences, method of payment, and other miscellaneous information). The **guest accounting menu** will be used to track all credit/debit transactions related to the guest's stay. Figure 8-2 illustrates how these two menus come together to create the guest account.

FIGURE **8-2**

Guest account

**The Guest Account -
Two Parts of the Same Whole**

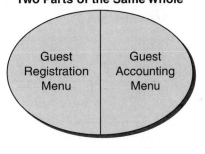

Guest Registration Menu

The data contained within the guest registration menu helps track all the information pertinent to the guest's stay. Each PMS will contain this information in some format. Though the order and verbiage may differ, the following lists the information contained within the registration menu:

Required Field	Meaning
Guest Name:	Name of individual's account
Arrival Date:	Date of check-in
Departure Date:	Date of checkout
Address:	Address of guest
Phone:	Phone of guest
Reservation Status:	This field is unique in that it lists different information on one line. A guest's reservation status will indicate two things: (1) Prior to check-in, it will indicate what type of reservations was made; (2) After check-in, it will list the status of the guest's stay. Prior to check-in the reservation status line will list a (G) for a guaranteed reservation or a number (4 or 6) which would indicate a non-guaranteed reservation (i.e., 4 or 6 P.M. hold). Once the guest has checked in, the reservations line may indicate (I), which means they are in-house. An (O) would indicate they checked out. (D) would indicate a deleted reservation, which might happen if the guest cancels the reservation, or there was an obvious error in the reservation itself (i.e.: duplicate reservation).

(continued)

Required Field	Meaning
Room Number:	Actual room assigned
Room:	Lists the room type, configuration, and designation
Room Rate:	Actual rate paid
Room Status:	Lists the current room status of the room reserved (i.e., V/R, O/D)
Method of Payment:	Cash, check, credit, or direct billing
Billing Method:	EPO (Each Pays Own), SRT (Sign Room and Tax), SAC (Sign All Charges). Note, some PMS's may combine billing method and method of payment on the same line like this: CA/EPO (Cash/Each Pays Own) or CC/SRT (Credit Card/Sign Room and Tax), etc.
Guest Loyalty #:	Frequent stay program number
Frequent Flier #:	Airline incentive partnership
Special Requests:	Early/late check-in or checkout requests for an upgrade, etc.
Comments:	This field is generally a "free form" field that lets front desk personnel communicate to one another regarding a specific guest. This field may be used to notify the front desk that the guest has a message waiting, or that a credit card has expired.
Market Code:	The market code is used to track the accuracy of the guest room rate.

Figure 8-3 illustrates what this might look like in an actual PMS menu screen.

Guest Accounting Menu

The guest accounting menu will contain a limited amount of information relating to the guest's reservation. Its primary purpose is to document every financial transaction relating to the guest. Each time a charge is posted, a credit issued, or a payment made, it will be reflected in this display. Though the order and verbiage may differ, the following lists the information contained within the accounting menu:

Guest Registration Menu

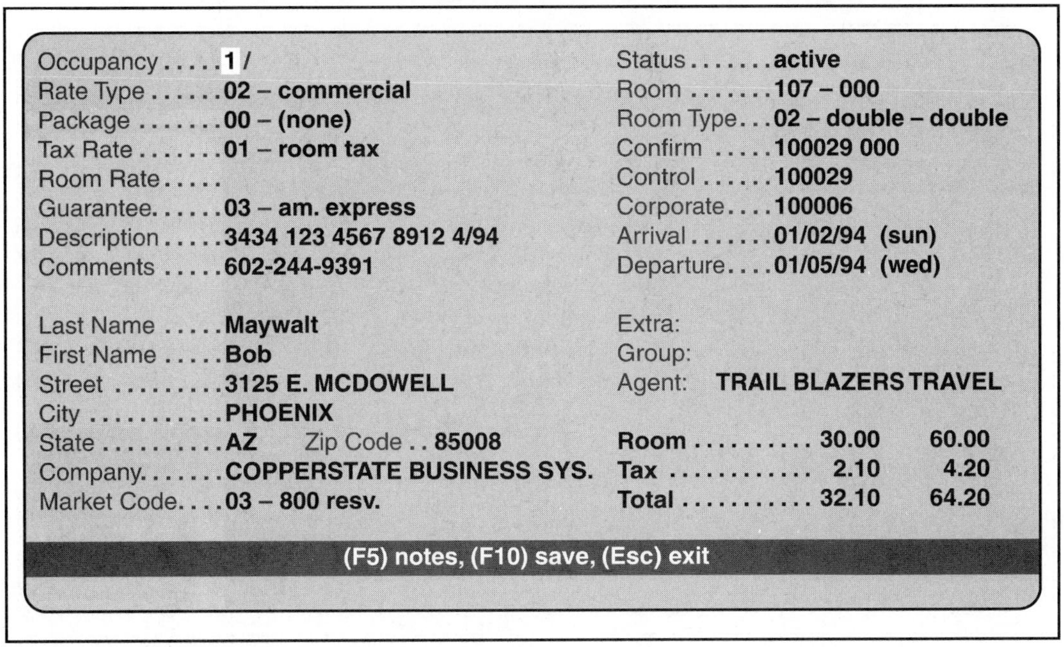

```
Occupancy.....1/                          Status.......active
Rate Type......02 – commercial            Room .......107 – 000
Package .......00 – (none)                Room Type...02 – double – double
Tax Rate.......01 – room tax              Confirm .....100029 000
Room Rate.....                            Control ......100029
Guarantee......03 – am. express           Corporate....100006
Description.....3434 123 4567 8912 4/94    Arrival.......01/02/94  (sun)
Comments .....602-244-9391                Departure....01/05/94  (wed)

Last Name .....Maywalt                    Extra:
First Name ....Bob                        Group:
Street .........3125 E. MCDOWELL          Agent:   TRAIL BLAZERS TRAVEL
City ..........PHOENIX
State .........AZ     Zip Code .. 85008   Room .......... 30.00      60.00
Company.......COPPERSTATE BUSINESS SYS.   Tax ............. 2.10      4.20
Market Code....03 – 800 resv.             Total ........... 32.10     64.20
```

(F5) notes, (F10) save, (Esc) exit

FIGURE **8-3**

Guest registration menu

Required Field	Meaning
Guest Name:	Name of individual's account
Arrival Date:	Date of check-in
Departure Date:	Date of checkout
Room Number:	Actual room assigned
Payment Method:	Cash, check, credit, or direct billing
Reservation Status:	Lists the current room status of the room reserved (i.e., V/R, O/D)

The remainder of the accounting menu summarizes the financial transactions of the guest. Each transaction is issued a line number so that the record is easy to follow. The date of the transaction is also recorded. A reference space

Guest Accounting Menu Display

Guest Name:	**M/M Jones**		Room Number:	**123**
Arrival Date:	**12/1**		Payment Billing Method:	**CA/SRT**
Departure Date:	**12/3**		Reservation Status:	**1**

Line #	Date	Room/Acct	Reference	Credit	Debit	Empl.
1	12/1	123	Room Rate		100.00	AI
2	12/1	123	Room Tax		6.00	AI
3	12/2	123	Room Serv.		38.50	JB
4	12/2	123	Movie		8.00	KM
5	12/2	123	Room Rate		100.00	AI
6	12/2	123	Room Tax		6.00	AI
7	12/3	**132**	Gift Shop		12.95	JB
8	12/3	**132**	Gift Shop (line 7)	12.95 (TR)		JB
9	12/3	123	Bar		10.00	SD
10	12/3	123	Bar	10.00(CO)		SD
11	12/3	123	Check Out	285.50		

Balance Due: 0

FIGURE **8-4**

Guest accounting menu

is usually provided as a free-form cell for any additional information needed to document the transaction. The final item of note is the record of the employee who made the transaction. The next chapter focuses on guest accounting principles and will review the guest accounting menu in detail. Figure 8-4 illustrates a sample guest accounting menu.

THE CHECK-IN

For the front desk, the PMS is used continuously to check guests in and out of the hotel. This process, as has been reviewed, is crucial in effectively managing room inventory. It is also a very good way to illustrate the operation of a PMS. This section illustrates the check-in of a walk-in guest, that is, a guest with no prior reservation.

If the hotel finds itself in need of occupancy on a certain night, the front office manager will notify all the front desk agents. He or she will determine a walk-in rate for the evening. This rate is determined by how many rooms are left to sell that night. If a day arrives, and not every room is sold, the hotel must do its best to fill the remaining rooms. Due to opportunity cost, any unsold room will be lost forever, so the walk-in rate must be set carefully. Too high, and guests go elsewhere. Too low, and money may be "left on the table."

The mechanics of checking in a walk-in guest are very similar to making an advance reservation. The information needed is nearly identical. Therefore, a front desk agent must be cognizant of all the details needed in any reservation. Most reservation agents can assist in checking guests in because of this similarity. The following series of PMS screens show step by step what information is needed to check in a walk-in guest.

Step 1(Figure 8-5) is to identify the arrival and departure information, and if need be, verify with management the availability of sleeping rooms.

Step 2 (see Figure 8-6) is to identify the room type the guest prefers. The agent should do their best to match the guest's room preferences with what is available.

Step 3 (see Figure 8-7) is to use the PMS to determine what available rooms in the hotel inventory match the guest's room preferences.

Step 4 (see Figure 8-8) is to assign a specific room number based on what PMS indicated was available.

Step 5 (see Figure 8-9) is to determine the tax status of the guest. If the guest works for agencies of the government, or certain not-for-profit organizations, he or she may be tax exempt.

Step 6 (see Figure 8-10) is needed to determine method of payment.

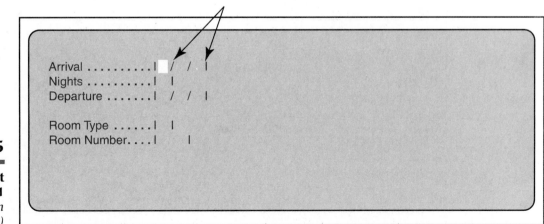

FIGURE 8-5

Walk-in guest
Step 1
(Adapted from
TPE Research)

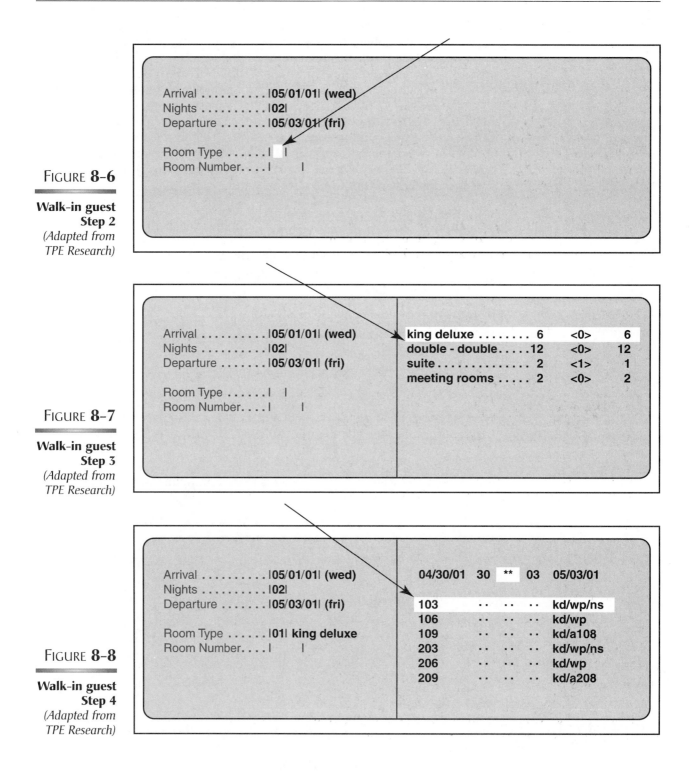

FIGURE **8-9**

**Walk-in guest
Step 5**
*(Adapted from
TPE Research)*

```
Occupancy . . . . . .      /
Rate Type . . . . . . .  00 – (none)
Package . . . . . . . .  00 – (none)
Tax Rate . . . . . . .  01 – room tax
Room Rate . . . . . .
Guarantee . . . . . . .  00 – (none)
Description . . . . . .
Comments . . . . . . .

Last Name . . . . . . .
First Name . . . . . . .
Street . . . . . . . . . . .
City . . . . . . . . . . . .
State . . . . . . . . . . .    zip code . . . . .
Company . . . . . . . .
Market Code . . . . .  00 – (none)
```

```
tax exempt . . . . . . . . . . . . . . . . . . . . . (00)
room tax . . . . . . . . . . . . . . . . . . . . . . (01)
sales tax . . . . . . . . . . . . . . . . . . . . . . (02)
. . . . . . . . . . . . . . . . . . . . . . . . . . . . . (03)
```

FIGURE **8-10**

**Walk-in guest
Step 6**
*(Adapted from
TPE Research)*

```
Occupancy . . . . . .      /
Rate Type . . . . . . .  00 – (none)
Package . . . . . . . .  00 – (none)
Tax Rate . . . . . . .  01 – room tax
Room Rate . . . . . .
Guarantee . . . . . . .  00 – (none)
Description . . . . .
Comments . . . . . . .

Last Name . . . . . . .
First Name . . . . . . .
Street . . . . . . . . . . .
City . . . . . . . . . . . .
State . . . . . . . . . . .    zip code . . . . .
Company . . . . . . . .
Market Code . . . . .  00 – (none)
```

```
(none) . . . . . . . . . . . . . . . . . . . . . . . . (00)
cash/checks . . . . . . . . . . . . . . . . . . . . (01)
mc/visa . . . . . . . . . . . . . . . . . . . . . . . (02)
am. express . . . . . . . . . . . . . . . . . . . . (03)
diners club . . . . . . . . . . . . . . . . . . . . . (04)
direct bill . . . . . . . . . . . . . . . . . . . . . . (05)
paid-out . . . . . . . . . . . . . . . . . . . . . . . (06)
. . . . . . . . . . . . . . . . . . . . . . . . . . . . . (07)
. . . . . . . . . . . . . . . . . . . . . . . . . . . . . (08)
. . . . . . . . . . . . . . . . . . . . . . . . . . . . . (09)
. . . . . . . . . . . . . . . . . . . . . . . . . . . . . (10)
. . . . . . . . . . . . . . . . . . . . . . . . . . . . . (11)
. . . . . . . . . . . . . . . . . . . . . . . . . . . . . (12)
. . . . . . . . . . . . . . . . . . . . . . . . . . . . . (13)
. . . . . . . . . . . . . . . . . . . . . . . . . . . . . (14)
. . . . . . . . . . . . . . . . . . . . . . . . . . . . . (15)
```

Step 7 (Figure 8-11). In this step, the front desk agent is able to make notes relevant to the guest for other employees. Because this guest is paying by check, a good practice is to note the check number in the registration menu. Also, this disabled guest may need assistance later, so another note was made.

Step 8 (Figure 8-12) is to gather personal identification information, such as name, address, phone, and company name, if applicable. A driver's license or some other proper from of identification should be shown.

Step 9 (Figure 8-13) is to verify the rate market code. Every rate in the rate structure is assigned a market code in PMS. This code is read by the system, and the computer determines the appropriate rate. The market code is needed to serve as a "check and balance" to the sleeping room rate assigned. The market code must match the rate. This is needed to uncover any possible fraud by front desk employees (e.g., reducing a rate for a friend).

Step 10 (see Figure 8-14) is the final step. The rate is typically assigned at the time a market code is issued. However, because this was a walk-in, and the walk-in rate changes, this rate was assigned last.

FIGURE 8-11

**Walk-in guest
Step 7**
*(Adapted from
TPE Research)*

Occupancy ...... /		Status .... **add**		
Rate Type .... **00 – (none)**		Room .... **103 – 000**		
Package .... **00 – (none)**		Room Type .... **01 – king deluxe**		
Tax Rate .... **01 – room tax**		Confirm........... **000000 000**		
Room Rate		Control **000000**		
Guarantee ...... **01 – cash/checks**		Corporate		
Description ...... **CHECK NUMBER 1234**		Arrival .... **05/01/01 (wed)**		
Comments		Departures .... **05/03/01 (fri)**		
GUEST HAS SEEING EYE DOG				
Last Name		Extra:		
First Name		Group:		
Street		Agent:		
City				
State .... zip code		**Room ....**	**0.00**	**0.00**
Company		**Tax ....**	**0.00**	**0.00**
Market Code ..... **00 – (none)**		**Total ....**	**0.00**	**0.00**

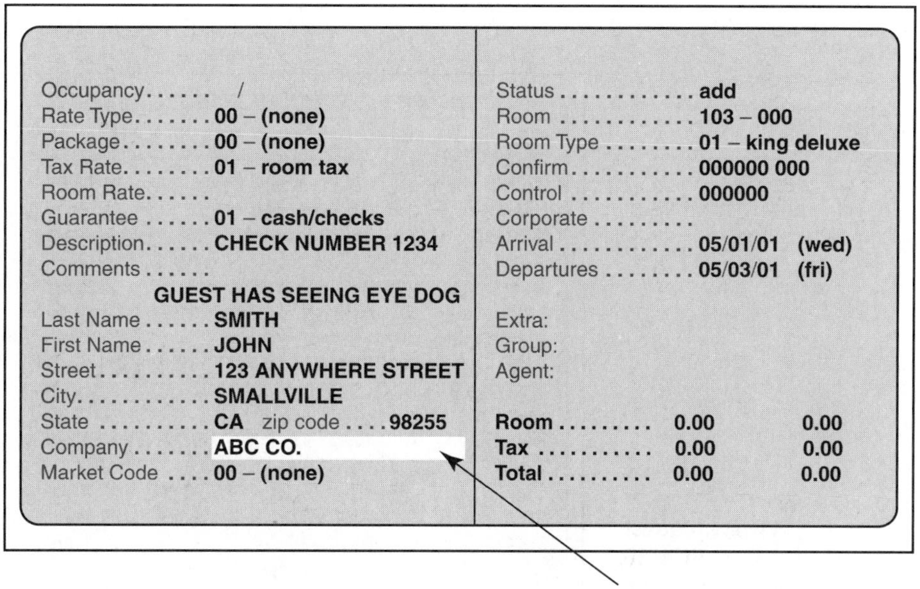

FIGURE 8-12

**Walk-in guest
Step 8**
*(Adapted from
TPE Research)*

Occupancy...... /	Status .... **add**
Rate Type....... **00 – (none)**	Room .... **103 – 000**
Package........ **00 – (none)**	Room Type .... **01 – king deluxe**
Tax Rate........ **01 – room tax**	Confirm.......... **000000 000**
Room Rate......	Control **000000**
Guarantee ..... **01 – cash/checks**	Corporate ....
Description..... **CHECK NUMBER 1234**	Arrival .... **05/01/01 (wed)**
Comments	Departures .... **05/03/01 (fri)**
GUEST HAS SEEING EYE DOG	
Last Name ..... **SMITH**	Extra:
First Name..... **JOHN**	Group:
Street........ **123 ANYWHERE STREET**	Agent:
City........... **SMALLVILLE**	
State .... **CA** zip code **98255**	**Room** 0.00 0.00
Company ...... **ABC CO.**	**Tax** 0.00 0.00
Market Code ... **00 – (none)**	**Total** 0.00 0.00

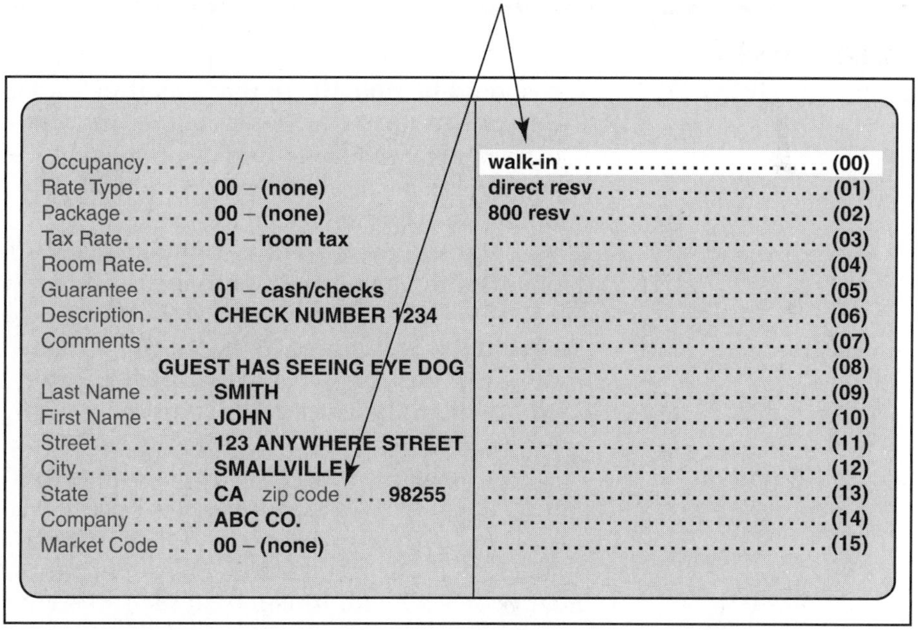

FIGURE 8-13

**Walk-in guest
Step 9**
*(Adapted from
TPE Research)*

Occupancy...... /	**walk-in** .... **(00)**
Rate Type....... **00 – (none)**	**direct resv** .... **(01)**
Package........ **00 – (none)**	**800 resv** .... **(02)**
Tax Rate........ **01 – room tax**	.... **(03)**
Room Rate......	.... **(04)**
Guarantee ..... **01 – cash/checks**	.... **(05)**
Description..... **CHECK NUMBER 1234**	.... **(06)**
Comments	.... **(07)**
GUEST HAS SEEING EYE DOG	.... **(08)**
Last Name ..... **SMITH**	.... **(09)**
First Name..... **JOHN**	.... **(10)**
Street........ **123 ANYWHERE STREET**	.... **(11)**
City........... **SMALLVILLE**	.... **(12)**
State .... **CA** zip code **98255**	.... **(13)**
Company ...... **ABC CO.**	.... **(14)**
Market Code ... **00 – (none)**	.... **(15)**

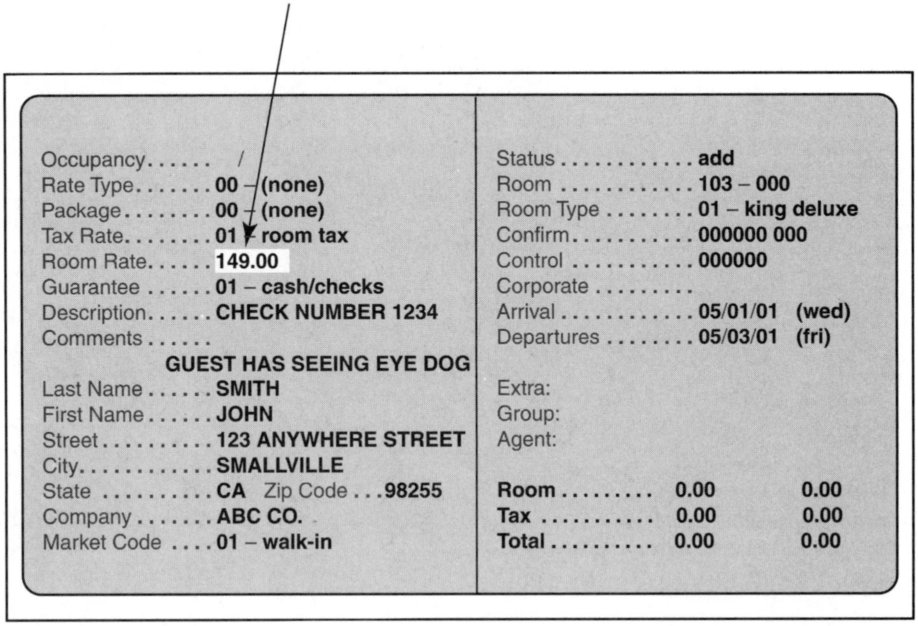

FIGURE **8-14**

**Walk-in guest
Step 10**
*(Adapted from
TPE Research)*

BEFORE PMS

It should be noted here that this text has focused solely on hotels that utilize PMS's in some manner in front office operations. It is extremely rare today to find any hotel that does not utilize a PMS in some form or another. PMS's are available for even the smallest limited-service budget hotel.

Prior to the advent of computers and PMS integration, hotels operated in a manual environment. A hotel was said to be a "manual hotel" if all room status reconciliation, guest registration, and accounting were done by hand. Hotel rooms were laid out behind the front desk in what was called a **room rack**. The room rack would identify each room type and configuration at a glance. Managers would mark each room on the rack (usually with some form of color-coding) to note the room's status (occupied, vacant, dirty, etc.). Messages, letters, and other guest correspondence were kept in the room rack until retrieved. Today, it is rare to find any hotel operating in a manual environment. Older texts can be referenced for more information on the subject.

Once the registration process is complete, the PMS may print a registration card. A **registration card** summarizes much of the information contained in the guest registration menu of PMS. The information on the card is used to verify the accuracy of that information in PMS. Arrival/departure information, spelling of the guest's name, and assigned rate should be reviewed by the guest to ensure that both parties understand and approve the transaction. The registration card is the successor to the hotel registration book, or log. Prior to the advent of computers, hotel guests would "sign in" to verify that they were actually staying at the hotel.

Arriving guests should sign the registration card as they would the hotel log. The signing of the registration card creates a binding agreement between the hotel and the guest. Guests with a prior reservation should have a pre-printed card waiting for them at the front desk. Some PMS's allow for rapid printing of registration cards; others require a special printer configuration. In those cases, the walk-in guest would have to fill it out by hand. Figure 8-15 illustrates a sample registration card.

Even though the registration card is useful for both the hotel and guest, many hotels neglect to ensure their use. Pre-key/key pack and other developments aimed at making the check-in process faster and easier for guests inhibit the signing of registration cards. The major drawback for the hotel is that the guest makes no agreement with the hotel in writing. Disputes on rate and other charges may arise later if no firm verification was made between the hotel and guest.

The Registration Card

FIGURE **8-15**

Registration card

Room Number _____   **Nice Hotel and Towers**   Card # 001
123 Nice Avenue, Anywhere, USA

Arrival Date _____ Departure Date_____ Payment _____
Room Preference_____ Rate_____

Signature _____

(By signing above, I hereby confirm all details contained herein are correct and agree to abide by hotel policies)

Check-in Time is 3PM (15:00)   Check Out Time is 12:00

Guest Name _____
Company_____
Address _____
Telephone_____

PMS HIERARCHY

Each PMS menu contains specialized information and reporting capabilities for a specific rooms-division area. Several of these menus lead the user to even more specialized menus and reporting options. The organization of these menus and their interrelationship is called a **PMS hierarchy**.

The primary menu within most PMS's, that is, the general starting point of the hierarchy, is the front office menu. The front office menu typically contains options to conduct every possible transaction that a rooms division employee might need to make. A front office menu can then lead the user to other menus, namely:

- Reservations menus
- Registration menu
- Night audit menu
- Housekeeping menu
- Uniform services menu

Each of these menus, based on their position within the hierarchy, requires a specific level of authorization for access. The ability to access the different menus is tied to the users job description and authority level. A front desk employee would have access to the registration menu, but would not need to have access to the housekeeping menu because that is not his/her primary responsibility. A rooms division manager would have access to every menu because he/she is responsible for all the departments. The restricting of access reduces the number of errors that might arise with unfamiliar menus.

A PMS hierarchy starts with the most broad menu (front office) and narrows its scope as each menu gets more specific. The more specific the menu, the smaller the range of options contained within it. This again is tied to the authority level and "need to know" concept of providing only enough PMS options to get a specific job accomplished. Figure 8-16 illustrates a sample PMS hierarchy.

As the illustration showed, each rooms division area was allowed access to only the options it needed to get the job done. The uniform services, for example, only need to know how to find a guest and if need be, leave a message. The PBX operator has no business attempting to manually block a room, for example.

PMS SYSTEMS INTERFACE

The PMS must be able to communicate with other hotel computer systems in order to maximize efficiency. The interface process begins with the reservations system. Depending on the hotel in question, the reservations system may be quite different from the PMS used. If the systems are indeed different, a process of "passing along" reservations occurs where the reservations system

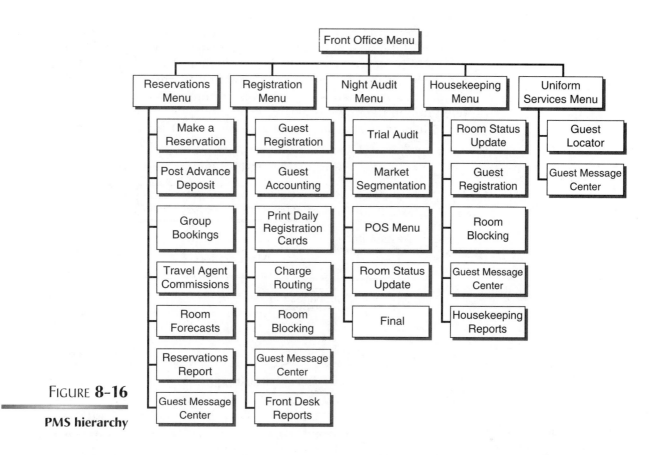

FIGURE **8-16**

PMS hierarchy

provides the PMS with upcoming arrivals. This information is then processed by the PMS, and a guest account is created. Typically, PMS's receive new reservation information for arrivals three days out. Even though the guests are not scheduled to arrive for 72 hours, changes do occur. Any early arriving guests would be without a room unless the PMS was made aware of the reservation.

The point of sale (**POS**) systems may also be running on different platforms. In an automatic posting environment, a similar process of "passing along" occurs. Outlet/ancillary charge data is given to the PMS. The difference between this process and the information shared from the reservations system is that this information is passed along and posted to the guest account immediately. This is to ensure that a guest does not check out prior to paying for all incurred charges.

The PMS can also interface with a sales and catering management system. Within sales and catering operations, various computer programs are available that allow the team to manage groups and the function space within a hotel. Some chains have developed their own systems, whereas others use prepackaged systems such as Delphi, Breeze, and Miracle. These systems allow the sales and catering team to view and block function space on a computer and manage the group guest room contribution. The interface of these systems to PMS ensures that two of the sides of the hotel success triangle are managed efficiently.

Finally, depending on the hotel's configuration, a PBX system interface may be in use. Most PMS's include a robust PBX call management feature, but the actual switchboard units must also communicate with PMS. These units often run on their own software.

The interrelationship of these systems is illustrated in Figure 8-17.

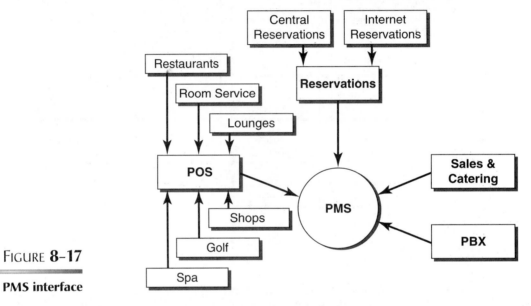

Front Office PMS Systems Interface

FIGURE **8-17**

PMS interface

THE EVOLUTION OF PMS

The next generation of PMS's are being designed to be Web browser enabled. This feature may have a tremendous impact on the current PMS interface structures. In the current environment, the PMS must be written with computer code that enables it to "talk" with the disparate systems it is integrated with. The reservations system is a perfect example of this. If two systems are not compatible, that interface becomes inefficient.

With a Web browser built into the PMS, the different systems can use the Web as the communication avenue. This, in a sense, uses the Web as the intermediary between disparate systems. Reservations, POS, and other systems would have a much easier time "communicating" with PMS. Web-enabled PMS's will also create easier data sharing between individual hotels in a chain. The individual PMS databases at the hotel level can be combined into a much larger data warehouse. This would create immense marketing efficiencies across the chain.

INDUSTRY PERSPECTIVE

Technology in Hospitality

Technology Manager
Jason L. Bean

Technology in the hotel industry seems disparate at best. Although it's not uncommon to hear about your preferred hotel chain having a Web site or being able to search for and find a hotel online at another travel supplier's Web site, it seems the use of technology in the everyday workflow of running a hotel is sparse. In my job, I've worked with many hotels that don't even have e-mail access for their employees. When I meet hotel staff that let me know that they do not have this most basic form of new communication tool, I sarcastically ask if their managers would like me to call them on their rotary phone and try to sell them my 8-track collection.

For hoteliers, the technology needs for their company can be broken down into two major components that encompass every person they will contact: their employees and their customers. Not only is access to up-to-date technology imperative, but adequate training on the use of these systems and resources as well. The front desk of a hotel should at the very least have access to all major computer user assets, including but not limited to mainstream office software titles, e-mail, and Internet access. This not only enables them to more effectively communicate with coworkers and upper management, but also with their customers and corporate clients. Many times I have requested information from a hotel, so that I can update their Web page or other marketing materials, only to discover that they cannot send me a file in a preferred format or open a file I may send to them. This type of resource and information allows the front desk staff to quickly alert me to changes in their service offerings, updates to their property, as well as the availability of last minute purchase deals and rebates for our respective clients.

In pushing the limits of how a property could use technology to equip its staff to more effectively handle the requests of customers, imagine a housekeeping staff equipped with remote contact devices that would locate the closest employee to the guest in need and communicate that need without any direct human communication or contact. This same system could also be used to send inventory requests back to a central location to be filled and delivered at the next room cleaning, or more urgently if requested.

(continued)

The most obvious use of technology that a hotel should make use of is those areas that directly impact a prospective customer's contact or communication with the hotel. As stated earlier, many hotels have great Web sites that allow from the most obvious of services, booking a reservation, to lesser-known services like finding an appropriate restaurant for a business dinner within walking distance to your hotel, or taking a virtual tour of the property. However, a Web site shouldn't just be another way to make a reservation. It must be a form of dialogue between supplier and customer that cannot be more efficiently shared in any other way. By this I mean that if every customer knew exactly what was wanted and where, we could just make a phone call to the hotel's 800 number and be done with our reservation.

Personally, when I visit a Web site, I want to get information from that Web site that cannot be received in any other single location. I want information on rates (standard and specials), weather, location, room amenities, maps, distance, directions, points of interest, hotel ratings, restaurants, nearby corporate facilities, and more. And not only would I like for you to tell me what other sister properties you may have in the area if my first choice is sold out, let me know about a competitor's property across the street. You want another chance at my business? Give me a discount to use at another property on my next stay.

As a guest, not only do I want information available to me on the Web before I make the reservation, I want high-speed access once I'm in my room. I believe hotels should make corporate agreements with nationwide Internet service providers (ISPs) that would allow me to use high-speed Internet connections at your hotel free if I'm already a member of that ISP, at the very least a competitive rate. If I'm a true road warrior, I more than likely have a preferred hotel company I choose to give my regular patronage to. I should be able to sign up to a hotel's frequent guest program and use my "points" for free access at any of your properties. I should be able to order room service online, access messages online, check out, make dinner reservations at local restaurants, and confirm ground transportation needs during my stay and upon my departure. With the exponential growth of wireless devices, allow me to make download directions to local points of interest from your property as well.

Somewhat in conjunction with online services, a hotel needs to make sure they are using one of the global distribution systems

(Amadeus, Apollo, Galileo, or Sabre to name a few) to most effectively market property agencies. There is a great need of understanding in a hotel's sales office, how their agency clients use these systems to book their properties. There are many limitations to finding or selling hotels through these systems. Many will shirk the responsibility on the GDS's, but I believe hoteliers need to be proactive in their involvement with insisting change in some of these systems. Many of these systems are now integrated with corporate preferred and managed online booking systems. Limitations in the GDS's directly inhibit the ability and ease of business travelers to find the properties desired.

Closely related to this problem of finding the preferred property is also now booking the preferred rate. It's regularly becoming a problem of making sure contracted, negotiated rates are available to be booked directly through the system, without the need for a phone call to verify a rate. Most travel agents agree, unless a client specifically asked for a property and for them to contact the hotel directly to verify a rate or availability, they would be more likely to try and sell a hotel they knew they could book through the system without any problems. If your hotel is sold out, do **NOT** display your property in my system as having availability, only to let me know to search for one of your other properties in the area.

Also, hotels need to be aware of how their listing a **GDS** can affect the ability for someone to find the property desired. If you're closer to one airport in a multiairport city, do not list your property as being closer to the larger, busier airport. Join your property search function to all airports in the city. Use standard naming conventions in all your property's listings. As stated before, because of the way a hotel's name is listed in one GDS, our customer can't search for a hotel by the actual brand name of the property.

These are just some of the ways technology can directly affect the bottom line of making the all-important dollar. Use technology to make it easier for agencies to find and sell your hotel, for your employees to service guests as quickly and most efficiently as possible, as well as provide services to guests that will keep them loyal customers for years to come. Something I've learned recently in my experience in the industry: It's not necessarily the free tickets travelers are interested in for their frequent flyer points, it's the way they are treated for being recognized as an important customer to the company.

CHAPTER EIGHT **REVIEW**

KEY TERMS

PMS	guest accounting menu
needs analysis	room rack
PMS workstations	registration card
guest account	PMS hierarchy
guest registration menu	POS

REVIEW QUESTIONS

1. Name and describe the different hotel computer systems that interface with the PMS.

2. What menus make up the guest account?

3. What is the importance of setting an appropriate walk-in rate?

4. Why would a hotel set up its PMS hierarchy to prohibit access to certain menus for employees?

5. What is the importance of the rate market code?

6. Explain the goals of a PMS needs analysis.

7. Name examples of sales/catering software currently on the market.

8. Define a LAN.

9. What are the usual prerequisites to being tax exempt for hotel guests?

10. Explain the importance of documentation in the hotel industry.

DISCUSSION QUESTIONS/EXERCISES

1. In what other ways could the evolution of the Internet be applied to the hotel industry? Could other hotel duties, such as purchasing, recruiting, and communication, be improved? In what ways? Could there ever be a limit to automation in this industry? When would the guest experience suffer, if at all?

2. Contact a small hotel that has no chain affiliation and a large chain affiliated hotel. Inquire as to the type of PMS each uses. Answer the following questions.

   a. What is the name of the hotel you selected?

   b. Does this hotel have a PMS?

   c. Is this hotel a manual hotel?

   d. What type of reservation system does this hotel utilize?

   e. What type of system is utilized to check a guest into the hotel?

f. Do the reservation system and the check-in system communicate with each other?

g. Do the POS system and the front office system communicate with each other?

h. How does the room status become reconciled?

i. Does this hotel have much turnover in staff?

j. Compare and contrast the two different hotels.

k. Would you like to work at this hotel? Why or why not?

PMS EXERCISE

This exercise is intended to expose the student to a different PMS. The industry has many varieties available on the market, so becoming familiar with the differences will better prepare students for the workplace. This is a Web site available to download anytime courtesy of Execu/Tech Systems, Inc.

Step 1: Go to the Web site <http://www.execu-tech.com> (see Figure 8-18).

Step 2: Fill out the basic information. (**Note:** You will not be solicited in any way. Simply indicate student, or instructor as appropriate.)

Step 3: Complete Execu/Touch Point of Sale 30-Day Evaluation.

Step 4: Complete download.

Step 5: Begin exploring the program. (**Note:** This is a 30-day free evaluation demo.)

Step 6: Navigate the main menu.

Step 7: Using the skills learned in the text, how does this information correlate to the everyday business of front office operations and management?

FIGURE 8-18

Execu/Tech Web site
(Courtesy Execu/Tech Systems, Inc.)

INTERNET RESOURCES
Property Management Systems

The PMS screenshots shown in this text are only a few examples of the vast array of systems available in the marketplace today. PMS developers are constantly innovating and improving. The ever-changing scope and capabilities of property management systems, as well as other technologies have created a new discipline. The Hospitality Information Technology Manager is rapidly becoming an important individual in a hotel. Some schools are offering degrees in this specialty. The following Web sites are glimpses of just some of the systems currently on the market. Many offer on-line demos that students can view.

Hospitality Technology Solutions	<http://www.innhanse.com/>
TPE Research	<http://www.tperesearch.com/>
Multi-Systems Inc.	<http://www.msisolutions.com/>
InnSystems	<http://www.innsystems.net/index.html>
Resort Systems Inc.	<http://www.resortsystemsinc.com/index.html>
TCS Systems	<http://www.guesttracker.com/>
Hotel Data Systems	<http://www.hoteldata.com/>
Micros	<http://www.micros.com/>
Aremissoft	<http://www.aremissoft.com/>
Metropolis Technologies	<http://www.metropolis-tech.com/>
Ramesys Hospitality	<http://www.us.ramesys.com/>

For additional hospitality and travel marketing resources, visit our Web site at <http://www.Hospitality-Tourism.delmar.com>.

Guest Accounting

OBJECTIVES

After reading this chapter, you should understand:

- Basic accounting principles
- The two ledgers within guest accounting
- The impact of guest accounting on the front office

INTRODUCTION

As with any business entity, a hotel's overall financial health rests solely on its ability to make and collect money. A hotel must be able to track or account for this revenue. Accounting is the process of tracking and analyzing cost and revenue information. Hotels of all classifications have any number of on-site employees dedicated to the accounting discipline. Certified public accountants (CPAs) are on staff at every chain's corporate office to ensure that all costs and revenues are accounted for. Good accounting practices serve to lessen any potential tax and audit implications. Publicly traded chains have all their accounting documents scrutinized very closely, so accuracy and honesty are paramount. Before looking at hotel accounting concepts, a brief exposure to general accounting basics is warranted.

ACCOUNTING BASICS

Modern accounting principles have developed equations and reports for the dissemination of information. The most basic of these equations is called the **accounting equation**.[1] The accounting equation states:

Assets = Liabilities + Owner's Equity

- An **asset** is an economic resource.
- A **liability** is an economic obligation.
- **Owner's equity** is the level of ownership the owner has in the operation.

The accounting equation must always be in balance. The two sides of the equal sign must themselves be equal. This equation can show at a glance the basic financial state of any business. The accounting equation does not show great detail, but that is not its purpose. Other financial disclosure statements delve more into specifics. Because of the limited detail, the accounting equation is used more often to illustrate details of smaller business entities. Owner-operated hotels would use the accounting equation most often. For example, let's illustrate the accounting equation using a small owner-operated hotel:

Wilson Family Inn

$450,000 − $313,500 = $136,500
(assets) − (liabilities) = (owner's equity)

Here, the Wilson family can claim ownership (or equity) in this operation of $136,500. Should the Wilson family need to raise capital for business or personal use, they can use this equation as a basis for securing a loan. The lack of detail provided by the accounting equation would beg the question, "What exactly are the assets and liabilities"? A bank would surely ask the Wilson family this question. Wall Street would ask the same question of a large publicly traded chain.

(**Note:** The accounting equation changes slightly when looking at a public company. Owner's equity becomes shareholder's equity. The principal does not change though.)

For more financial detail, lenders, investors, shareholders, and others look to a hotel's **balance sheet**. The balance sheet serves to summarize a hotel's financial situation on a given date. It serves as a financial "snapshot" of the current state of assets, liabilities, and equity. Continuing our example, the Wilson family's balance sheet for their inn could look like this:

Wilson Family Inn
Balance Sheet
December 31, 2010

Assets		Liabilities	
Cash	$35,000	Accounts payable	$12,000
Cleaning supplies	$2,500	Salaries payable	$4,500
Linen	$1,100	Taxes payable	$2,000
FF&E (furniture, fixtures, and equipment)	$250,000	Notes payable (mortgages and equipment loans)	$295,000
Land	$55,000	Total liabilities	$313,500
Building	$106,000	**Owner's Equity**	
Office supplies	$400	Wilson, capital	$136,500
Total assets	$450,000	Total equity and liability	$450,000

Looking at this balance sheet, a lender would be able to get a better view of the overall financial position of the Wilson Family Inn. One of the primary factors in determining the amount of money a hotel can borrow is its amount of owner (or shareholder) equity in relation to the liabilities. Here the Wilson family has $136,500 in equity, so that might be the limit of any new borrowing. Lenders also take into consideration the amount of cash on hand a hotel has in relation to its liabilities. If the cash balance is high, the understanding might be that debt service on a new loan would not strain the business cash flow. Other texts devoted to accounting principles and banking will give more in-depth review of these and other financial concepts. It is this starting point from which we continue on to hotel accounting concepts like guest accounting.

"Old accountants never die, they just lose their balance."

—Industry Wisdom

GUEST ACCOUNTING

Most hotels use traditional accounting concepts to organize and track guest information and other data. The tracking of financial transactions within the front office is called **guest accounting**. The accounting term "ledger" is used to identify what information is contained in a certain revenue-tracking vehicle. The vehicles used to track the revenues and charges within the front office are the guest ledger and city ledger. Each of these ledgers serves as an accounting vehicle for a hotel to track who it owes money to and who owes it money. The two primary accounting entries used to track these charges and credits are the **debit** and **credit**. The debit has a positive affect on the total balance of a guest account and the credit has a negative effect. Front office employees deal with these credits and debits on a daily basis.

Guest Ledger

The **guest ledger** is an all encompassing term used to track hotel transactions primarily before and during a guest's or group's stay. The guest ledger is also used to track the daily transactions of each revenue-generating side of the hotel triangle (room, catering, and outlet/ancillary sales). Hotels will create an account within the guest ledger to track this inflow and outflow of revenue. These accounts can be thought of as a place to "house" credit and debit transactions. The types of accounts may vary in name from hotel to hotel, but the functions of each are generally consistent. The most frequently used types of accounts are discussed next.

House Account

The **house account** serves as a perpetual account to track recurring transactions that occur within the hotel. A house account may be created to track the daily dry cleaning service. The charges and credits for each day's dry cleaning must be tracked somewhere. House accounts can be created to track commissions and other obligations. The house account can also serve as a vehicle that "houses" deposits for groups and other financial transactions for future uses.

Guest Account

The guest account is created at some point between the creation of a room reservation, and the actual arrival of a hotel guest. Each individual guest account will track debits and credits incurred prior to and during a stay. Advance deposits for individuals are placed, or posted to the guest account. **Posting** is the act of applying a debit or credit to an account. Room rates and outlet/ancillary charges are also posted to the guest account as they are incurred. The guest account must be created prior to check-in so that the front desk will be prepared for arrival.

Master Account

The **master account** closely mirrors the individual guest account. The main difference is that a master account encompasses registration/accounting information for an entire group, not individual attendees. Individual guest and

GUEST HISTORY ACCOUNT

The guest account often remains in the front office for a day or two after departure to ensure that all appropriate charges are tallied. Once the guest account is "aged" the appropriate length of time, it becomes a **guest history account.** Guest history accounts are stored in the memory of the PMS computer to give hotels a documented record of as many details of each guest's stay as possible. Each guest history account will record room preferences, rates, individual room numbers, posted charges, phone transactions, and so on. As was reviewed in Chapter 8, this guest history information becomes part of a valuable marketing database. Guest history also positively impacts service levels, as hotels can now anticipate requests/preferences prior to arrival of returning guests.

Guest history is stored within the PMS for a limited time because of the memory space used. Depending on the system capacity, once the memory level reaches a critical point, it must be purged. The purged data is then printed out and stored as a document, copied to microfilm and stored, or converted to digital disk storage.

group charges related to a specific group based on billing arrangements (i.e., room/tax, catering, etc.) are routed to the master account as applicable. **Routing** is the process where credits/debits incurred by one account are manually or automatically transferred to another account.

City Ledger

The guest ledger exists for the purpose of tracking hotel transactions primarily before and during a guest's or group's stay. The guest ledger tracks each of the main account types (house account, guest account, and master account). After a guest or group has departed, any outstanding balances are transferred to a different ledger. The **city ledger** is used to track revenues due to the hotel. These revenues are called **receivables**.

Within the accounting department of the hotel, one or more individuals are responsible for the management of the receivables due. This department is called Accounts Receivable. These individuals will manage the city ledger by creating a city ledger account in the accounting menu of the PMS for each guest ledger account that checks out with a balance due the hotel.

Whether a master, house, or guest account, the guest ledger must be cleared of noncurrent accounts in order to make way for new arrivals. A noncurrent account is measured by its departure date. This is directly tied to the

Sample Aging Statement

Name	Current	30	60	90	120
Joe Smith	$240				
AVD Co.		$3000			
123 Heat				$6500	
Jane Doe					$250
Bill's Hair	$950				
XYZ Inc.			$600		
Pets R Us		$400			
K's Hut	$9500				
Totals	**$10690**	**$3400**	**$600**	**$6500**	**$250**
Ave Days Outstanding: **36 Days**					

FIGURE **9-1**

Aging statement

creation of guest history accounts. Once the account in question has "aged," it becomes a history account. At that same time, if a balance is due, a city ledger account is created to track those revenues. Within the city ledger, an **aging statement** tracks how long each receivable has remained uncollected. Hotels (and most other organizations) depend on their receivables to cover operating costs. Mismanagement of the aging statement (e.g., letting receivables age without collection) may result in poor cash flow. Figure 9-1 illustrates what a sample hotel aging statement may resemble.

The city ledger and guest ledger are kept separate inside the PMS in order for the revenues to be properly managed. Some hotels have permanent city ledger accounts for organizations that use the hotel often. Other systems must create a new city ledger account each time. The city ledger is used to manage the receivables and track the hotel's basic financial health. Again, as with every business entity, financial health is dictated by revenues and expenditures. Management of receivables ensures that revenues are indeed collected.

It is for this reason that ensuring proper credit guidelines is stressed in all aspects of front office operations. If the front desk checks in a guest without obtaining a proper method of payment and the guest departs without paying, the balance must be transferred to the city ledger. In summary, the city ledger is comprised of every guest, group, and vendor who has been extended credit.

ACCOUNTING ENTRIES

The process of updating the accounting menu is achieved through a series of **entries**. Each accounting entry must be documented. Within the guest accounting menu, different types of entries are used to track financial trans-

UNCOLLECTED RECEIVABLES

Once a receivable's age has exceeded a certain time frame set by senior management (say, 180+ days), it could be classified as uncollectable. At that point, the hotel might "write-off" this billing as bad debt. This process effectively removes that amount from the aging statement. It is no longer an asset due the hotel. The accounting department may refer these bad debts to a collection company in cases of individual guest nonpayment. For organizations that do not pay, the hotel may notify Dun & Bradstreet and various credit bureaus. The hotel will certainly inform other hotels of the organization's poor payment history if called upon for a reference. The hotel may, in some cases, be able to claim these write-offs as a tax deduction. In the rare circumstances that these written-off debts are eventually paid, they are reclassified as "write-off recovery" funds.

actions. Not unlike journal entries used by other industries, these hotel accounting entries serve specific purposes to accurately document each transaction. Different hotels may use different names, but the basic types of entries will remain the same. The front office accounting formula summarizes how these entries are tallied up:

Beginning Balance + Charges – Credits = Ending Balance

Accounting entries will post either automatically or manually. **Automatic posting** is defined as the transfer of guest charges to an account as they are incurred. Hotels that integrate their outlet/ancillary venues to their PMS system will utilize point-of-sale terminals (POS). A POS terminal in the restaurant, for example, will automatically post a dinner charge to the proper guest account based on the name and room number information provided by the diner. Automatic posting of charges from outlet/ancillary venues can only occur if the guest account has signing privileges. Another common automatic charge is the room/tax posting each night.

Manual posting, as has been reviewed earlier, occurs when an individual must apply a charge to an account by hand. A massage charge incurred may have to be posted manually, for example (see Figure 9-2). Often, as is the case with ancillary services like massage, shoeshine, gift shop, and so on, the hotel does not perform the service itself. These guest services are very often outsourced.

Therefore, the owner/operators of these services must bring these charges up to the desk by hand. A member of the front desk staff usually does the manual posting. Within a manual posting environment, every possible

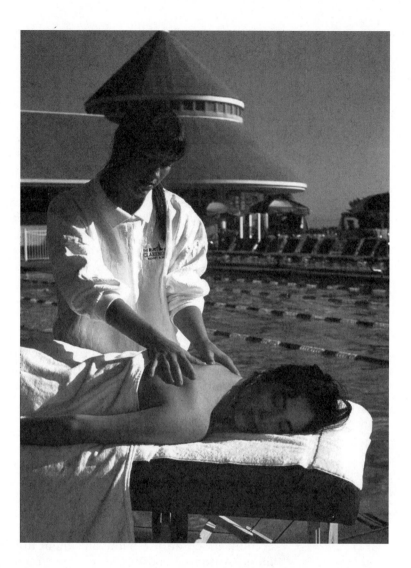

FIGURE **9-2**

Hotel massage *(Courtesy KSL Resorts/Claremont)*

charge will assume a specific code that the individual uses so that the PMS will recognize it. Each outlet and ancillary venue will be assigned a different number. Every conceivable charge (shoeshine, massage, etc.) can be posted in this manner.

As has been reviewed, the two primary accounting entries used are the debit and credit. The debit has a positive effect on the total balance of a guest account, and the credit has a negative effect. This effect of positive and negative can be confusing. The "positive" effect raises the balance, and the "negative" lowers it. This is because as a guest incurs charges, they are owed to the hotel but not yet paid for. As charges are posted to an account, the balance becomes negative. For example, once a guest checks in, the balance is zero. Once he/she incurs a charge, say a $50.00 room service bill, that charge gets posted to the account. At that time, if the charge were posted automatically, that guest would have a negative $50.00 balance. Upon checkout, they would pay what was owed and bring that negative balance back to zero.

The **correction entry** is used to correct a mistake in the posting process. Each time a correction is made, it must "cancel out" the effect of the erroneous first entry. For example, to correct a gift shop charge (debit), the correction must be a credit so that the net effect on the final balance is zeroing. Each time a change is made to an account, it becomes a permanent part of the record even if it was corrected off. This is to ensure that there is a way to go back and determine where any error was made, and provide insights as to where it should have gone in the first place. Although some hotel guests find this confusing, it is vital to ensure that the hotel conforms to these rules, referred to as the **USALI**—uniform system of accounts for the lodging industry. Figure 9-3 illustrates how the debits and credits may look on a PMS screen.

The **accounting transfer** is an entry used when a charge or credit needs to be "sent" elsewhere within the guest ledger. If a charge was posted to a wrong room, a transfer can take that specific charge and post it on the correct account. Instead of correcting it off completely, the transfer posts it somewhere else without eliminating it. A cash deposit posted to the wrong account

Debits and Credits

description	db	cr	total
guest room	**215.00**	**0.00**	**215.00**
telephone	29.10	0.00	29.10
restaurant	98.36	0.00	98.36
lounge	7.75	0.00	7.75
guest laundry	17.75	0.00	17.75
room tax	15.05	0.00	15.05
sales tax	2.07	0.00	2.07
transfer bal.	0.00	0.00	0.00
package	0.00	0.00	0.00
counter sales	23.56	0.00	23.56
commissions	995.34	0.00	995.34
miscellaneous	0.00	0.00	0.00

(Enter) to itemize, (PgUp), (PgDn), (Esc) to exit

FIGURE **9-3**

Debits and credits
(Courtesy TPE Research)

Sample Guest Folio Display

Line #	Date	Room/Acct	Reference	Credit	Debit	Emp.
	Guest Name:	**M/M Jones**	Room Number:		**123**	
	Arrival Date:	**12/1**	Payment Billing Method:		**CA/SRT**	
	Departure Date:	**12/3**	Reservation Status:		**1**	
1	12/1	123	Room Rate		100.00	AI
2	12/1	123	Room Tax		6.00	AI
3	12/2	123	Room Serv.		38.50	JB
4	12/2	123	Movie		8.00	KM
5	12/2	123	Room Rate		100.00	AI
6	12/2	123	Room Tax		6.00	AI
7	12/3	**132**	Gift Shop		12.95	JB
8	12/3	**132**	Gift Shop (132)	12.95 (TR)		JB
9	12/3	123	Bar		10.00	SD
10	12/3	123	Bar	10.00 (CO)		SD
11	12/3	123	Check Out	258.50		
					Balance Due: 0	

FIGURE **9-4**

Guest folio

can be transferred to the correct one. The transfer does not change the net status of the guest ledger. The transferred debit remains a debit; the transferred credit remains a credit. Transfers are used when the debits/credits are valid and not in need of being eliminated (corrected), just moved (transferred).

The actual summary of charges that a guest incurs is called a guest folio. The folio generally refers to the printed summary of charges given to the guest upon departure. It is the information that is included in this folio that eventually becomes guest history information. A guest folio is actually the guest accounting menu printed on paper (see Figure 9-4). A guest folio looks the same as the accounting menu display reviewed in the previous chapter.

ACCOUNTING DOCUMENTATION

Every accounting entry must be "justified" in some way. The justification of every entry is achieved through some sort of documentation. Before posting to an account, a charge must be approved by the guest (gift or restaurant charges, for example). The guest who signs these charges to a room is authorizing the charge by signing the receipt. The document that was signed serves as the validation.

Whether in a manual or automatic posting environment, each time a debit, credit, or correction is made to an account that the guest is unaware of, another method of justification must be used. A manual document is created by the front desk or accounting employee making the adjustment to the account. These documents are called **charge/credit slips**. Front desk employees must understand these documents and their importance.

These slips are used when the entry has a net effect on the overall guest ledger. A transfer, because it does not affect the credit/debit balance of the guest ledger, does not necessarily need documentation. Because every line item on the accounting menu is noted with an employee ID, the transfer can be traced if need be. These slips will explain the entry and be signed by appropriate supervisory personnel. All these forms of justification combine to form the **audit trail**, which is needed to conform to USALI. An audit trail serves as documented history of transactions. This trail may be traced back by auditors when the books are reviewed.

A **paid out slip** is another slip that is used to document a transaction. The paid out slip debits an account (charges) in return for cash paid on the guest's behalf. Paid outs are often used for gratuities or cash advances. A **petty cash slip** is used for non–guest-related expenses incurred by the hotel. Because each front desk clerk has a bank that they must maintain, the petty cash slip is used as documentation to reimburse that person's bank when reconciling at the end of a shift. Although petty cash never shows up in guest accounting, it is important to realize that this can be a recurring part of the hotel clerk's duties.

GUEST ACCOUNTING AND THE FRONT DESK

Understanding the principles behind guest accounting is important for all hotel employees to some degree. Within the rooms division, the areas that deal with guest accounts are the front desk, reservations, and night audit. From a frequency perspective, understanding guest accounting is paramount to the front desk.

Front desk employees may handle cash throughout their day. Guests may choose to pay for their charges with cash even if they put down a credit card at check-in. Most hotels allow their guests to cash personal checks of a certain amount. The front desk must handle these duties as well. Similar to a cashier at the corner store, front desk employees must be able to handle these transactions. The money used is called an individual's bank.

A **bank** is simply a cash reserve assigned to individual front desk employees/managers to handle daily transactions. Each bank is audited by the **general cashier** to ensure that proper accounting procedures are adhered to and to avoid fraud. The general cashier is an accounting employee who maintains the cash supply inside the hotel. In addition to the front desk, outlets and ancillary venues may conduct cash transactions throughout the day. The general cashier ensures that these departments have adequate supplies on hand, and makes bank deposits of excess cash. On weekends or holidays, when a cashier may not be scheduled, the front office manager may maintain a "reserve" bank to replenish individual employee banks as needed.

Banks are counted prior to each shift to ensure that the minimum reserve is there, and at the end of each shift, a "cash out" process is undertaken to match all transactions with what is now in each individual bank. Front desk employees "drop" their excess cash to the general cashier. The general cashier replenishes individual banks that have paid out more than taken in (due to check cashing for example). This "drop" may be itemized in a document resembling the one in Figure 9-5.

Employee Name _____   Date _____

Currency	Dollar	Cent
Hundreds		
Fifties		
Twenties		
Tens		
Fives		
Twos		
Ones		
Silver (Wrapped)		
Dollars		
Half dollars		
Quarters		
Dimes		
Nickels		
Pennies		
Silver (Loose)		
Dollars		
Half dollars		
Quarters		
Dimes		
Nickels		
Pennies		
Foreign Currency*		
Total		

FIGURE **9-5**

Drop sheet

FOREIGN EXCHANGE

If a hotel chooses to convert foreign currency, it must post the exchange rates it is offering clearly in the front office area. Front desk employees must make a note in their drop log of the daily posted exchange rate so that they are replenished with dollars. Foreign currency exchange rates at hotels are generally not as favorable as those at banks because the hotel incurs additional costs in offering this service to guests. Also, with the proliferation of automated teller machines in hotels, the international guest has other options of obtaining U.S. currency.

The process of closing each individual's shift and reconciliation of the bank is analyzed next.

Shift Closing

An important duty for front office managers is to verify the individual banks of desk agents. Each desk agent will run a report from the PMS called an **employee shift closing report**. The employee shift closing report outlines each transaction the agent completed within the guest ledger. All guest registration and guest accounting transactions are noted. Each employee is assigned an identification number within the PMS to track his or her transactions, regardless of the computer terminal. The PMS shift closing will list exactly how much cash, checks, credit card receipts, postings, and paid outs were conducted by the agent based on that identification number. As was reviewed earlier, the employees must submit their banks to the general cashier for audit. Money (cash, checks, credit card receipts) collected in excess of the bank balance are "dropped" to the general cashier for deposit. Because of the amount of money some agents collect in a day, the managers should assist in verifying this dropped amount. A sample shift closing is illustrated in Figure 9-6.

When each agent on a shift has completed his or her own employee shift closing, the manager may conduct an entire shift closing. This report will summarize all the transactions completed by each shift member. Although not as important as employee shift closings, the entire shift closing may help to find errors. Common errors occur when employees complete transactions at various PMS terminals without changing the identification numbers.

Shift Closing

description	db	cr	total
cash/checks	**0.00**	**1288.33**	**−1288.33**
paid-out	**33.45**	**0.00**	**33.45**
total	33.45	1288.33	−1254.88

Deposit Drop. . . I   I

FIGURE **9–6**

Shift closing
(Courtesy TPE Research)

NOTES

1. Bazley, J., and Nikolai, L. (1986). *Financial Accounting.* Boston: Kent Publishing Co.

CHAPTER NINE **REVIEW**

KEY TERMS

accounting equation
asset
liability
owner's equity
balance sheet
guest accounting
debit
credit
guest ledger
house account
posting
master account
guest history account
routing
city ledger

receivables
aging statement
entries
automatic posting
correction entry
USALI
accounting transfer
charge/credit slips
audit trail
paid out slip
petty cash slip
bank
general cashier
employee shift closing report

REVIEW QUESTIONS

1. What are the differences and similarities between the guest account and the master account?

2. How does the guest ledger differ from the city ledger?

3. When should a correction entry be used? In what instances would a transfer be used instead?

4. Define USALI.

5. Why is the audit trail so important?

6. Explain the importance of obtaining proper methods of payment and how that process might impact accounts receivable and the aging statement.

7. Complete the following: The accounting equation of XYZ Hotel shows $250,000 in owner's equity and $675,000 in assets. What are the liabilities?

8. How is the term "ledger" used in guest accounting?

9. What is an aging statement? Why is it important?

10. What is the front office accounting formula?

DISCUSSION QUESTIONS/EXERCISES

1. Obtain an annual report from a large hotel chain. (Many are available online.) What does their balance sheet look like? What other reports are included? Can you make a judgment as to their financial health from this document? What is their cash flow? Compare this report to their current stack price. Can you make any correlation?

2. Hotels rely on PMS's to manage many aspects of operations. What happens if the system crashes? Contact the Front Office Manager of a nearby hotel. Ask what procedure is followed when there is a computer failure and guests are checking out. Answer the following questions:

   a. Is there a set procedure in place for this situation?

   b. What type of backup reports are generated? What are they called?

   c. What is the timeliness of backup reports?

   d. How are additional charges handled?

   e. Did you feel confident that this procedure would work?

   f. Has this ever happened at this property?

   g. Have the front office agents been trained on this procedure?

   h. How quickly could this procedure be implemented?

   i. How are checkouts communicated to Housekeeping?

   j. How are checkouts communicated to PBX?

3. Complete a mock folio for the following guest charges. Compute each charge based on the hotel accounting formula. Determine the current balance chronologically as this guest's account is updated:

- Sent in advance deposit of one night's room and tax.
- Signed Guest Registration at check-in confirming the nightly rate of $149 @ 11.8% state tax and 2.0% occupancy tax.
- The Guest is staying 3 nights.
- Ordered a beverage from the Lobby Bar @ 5:15 p.m. $6.20
- Signed for Dinner in the Restaurant @ 7:30 p.m. $37.91
- Ordered Room Service Breakfast @ 6:30 a.m. $21.48
- Tipped Doorman @ 7:45 a.m. $2.00
- Bought sundry item from Gift Shop @ 5:50 p.m. $7.23
- Ordered a beverage from the Lobby Bar @ 6:10 p.m. $12.40
- Signed for Room Service Dinner @ 8:20 p.m. $45.62
- Ordered Room Service Breakfast @ 6:20 a.m. $23.87
- Tipped Doorman @ 7:25 a.m. $2.00
- Called hotel to ask for late check out one day early. Was advised ½ day rate would apply.
- Bought sundry item from Gift Shop @ 2:15 p.m. $8.53
- Checked out at front desk @ 2:30 p.m.
- Tipped Doorman @ 2:40 p.m. $2.00

Item	Amount	Debit/Credit	Current Balance
Advance Deposit Room	$149.00	Credit	
Advance Deposit Tax	$17.58	Credit	
Advance Deposit Tax	$2.98	Credit	
Lobby Bar Beverage	$6.20	Debit	
Dinner in Restaurant	$37.91	Debit	
Room Charge	$149.00	Debit	
Room Tax State	$17.58	Debit	
Room Tax Occupancy	$2.98	Debit	
Room Service Breakfast	$21.48	Debit	

Item	Amount	Debit/Credit	Current Balance
Gift Shop sundry item	$7.23	Debit	
Lobby Bar Beverage	$12.40	Debit	
Room Service Dinner	$45.62	Debit	
Room Charge	$149.00	Debit	
Room Tax State	$17.58	Debit	
Room Tax Occupancy	$2.98	Debit	
Room Service Breakfast	$23.87	Debit	
Gift Shop sundry item	$8.53	Debit	
Room Charge	$74.50	Debit	
Room Tax State	$8.79	Debit	
Room Tax Occupancy	$1.49	Debit	
Grand Total Due at Checkout		Credit	

INTERNET RESOURCES
Accounting Resources

The following sites offer resources on several different accounting topics. These topics include hotel-specific issues, as well as, generally accepted accounting practices and principles.

American Institute of Certified Public Accountants	<http://www.aicpa.org/index.htm>
American Accounting Association	<http://accounting.rutgers.edu/raw/aaa/index.html>
Hospitality Accounting Group	<http://www.hospitalityaccounting.com/>
Hospitality Accounting Services	<http://www.hotel-accounting.com/>

For additional hospitality and travel marketing resources, visit our Web site at **<http://www.Hospitality-Tourism.delmar.com>.**

CHAPTER 10

Night Audit

OBJECTIVES

After reading this chapter, you should understand:

- What individual reports make up the night audit report
- How the night audit department is deployed
- The hotel performance report
- Manager On Duty responsibilities

INTRODUCTION

As emphasized throughout this text, the nature of hotel operations (24 hours a day, 7 days a week) requires staffing and services continuously. At some point, there exists a need for a daily reconciliation of all the hotel's activities. Therefore, a front office department with access and knowledge of these activities was created to act as the reconciling agent. This mandates a department with a diverse set of responsibilities and skills.

NIGHT AUDIT OVERVIEW

The night audit department of the front office, as defined earlier, is the team that assumes the role of reconciling a hotel's daily activities and transactions. This department compiles a series of reports and data into a report called the **night audit report** for management review.

Because the hotel never stops operating, there exists the need to determine at what point the current day ends and the next day begins. Organizations that close at some point in the day are able to easily establish a change in date. Hotels must designate a certain point in the night, called the **date roll**, to establish this change in date. Because the reconciliation of the hotel's activities may take between four and ten hours, the date roll may not occur at midnight, as one might think. In fact, it is not unusual for the date to roll between 2:00 A.M. and 4:00 A.M. The date roll must occur prior to the earliest of departures to ensure that all applicable charges are posted in the guest ledger. The night audit performs many functions. Depending on the hotel, the night team will:

● Verify daily hotel transactions.

● Generate summary and statistical data for compiling into the night audit report.

● Assume responsibility for certain front office functions, such as front desk and PBX.

● In many cases, have its leader serve as the manager on duty (MOD) in the absence of senior management.

NIGHT AUDIT DEPLOYMENT

The night audit team will vary in makeup and composition depending on the hotel. Generally, the night audit team will consist of:

● The night audit manager

● Two to five auditors (depending on the size of the hotel and the number of ancillary operations)

● One or two food/beverage auditors (depending on the number of outlets)

Hotels of every size, location type, and product type will have a night audit function of some sort. Every hotel must be able to reconcile each day's activities. Night audit may only consist of one person, but there will always be an individual in charge of this reconciliation.

Because of the nature of the work done, the night audit team often falls under the purview of the accounting department. Because night audit is involved in so many activities surrounding the front office, the front office manager will give input and direction as needed. In many cases the night audit team has a dual reporting structure to both accounting and the front office.

It is extremely difficult to pinpoint the characteristics that make up the ideal night auditor. The third-shift nature of the work makes it unattractive for many people. The industry as a whole often experiences difficulty in fully staffing the night audit team. Some of the highest turnover rates within any hotel exist here. Night audit can be attractive to students. Often, individuals interested in management positions within the front office or accounting will spend time learning the night audit.

NIGHT AUDIT REPORTING

The night audit team's primary responsibility is to verify the posting of charges within the guest ledger. All transactions, including room rates, outlet/ancillary postings, banquet charges, and other miscellaneous charges, must be posted correctly in order for the hotel to accurately report financial data. This verification process will vary primarily between manual and automatic posting environments.

As has been reviewed, the profit margin and total revenue contribution of room sales are the primary revenue source for a hotel. Therefore, ensuring that proper rates are charged is vital for maximizing revenue. The night audit team cannot know the reservation or the sales history involved in the creation or quotation of every room rate. The hotel industry uses market codes to serve as reference points for each room rate. The market code is assigned to each reservation as it is made so that it can be properly verified. The market code is assigned within the PMS computer system. Each of the standard rates will have a prearranged market code:

- Weekday/Weekend Rates
- Rack Rates
- Corporate Rates
- Volume Account Rates
- Government Rate
- Seasonal Rates
- AAA/AARP
- Industry Rates
- Walk-in Rate
- Premium Rates
- Advance Purchase Rates
- Package Rates

Within each reservation, the market code does not change. The night auditor can verify that the proper rate is charged by cross-referencing the code with the predetermined rate. This process ensures that no employee has misassigned a rate or has committed fraud by charging lower/higher rates than mandated by management. Each time the group sales department negotiates a new rate for a group booking, a new market code is assigned for that booking to serve the same purpose.

The codes themselves vary greatly. For the sake of discussion, a sample market code for an AAA rate might be AAA/02/C (the name of the rate, the year in effect, and C because it's chainwide in scope). The night audit team will use the market codes to verify the rates in an automatic posting environment. In a manual environment, the night auditors will actually post the room/tax charges based on these market codes.

A **room rate posting report** will be generated for inclusion into the night audit report that verifies the rates for all the rooms within the hotel occupied nightly for management review. A room rate posting report might resemble Figure 10-1.

The posting of outlet/ancillary charges must be verified as well as the room rates. The food/beverage auditors usually do this. Again, in a manual environment, the night audit team may post each charge to the appropriate guest ledger account.

FIGURE **10-1**

Room/tax posting

Date: 8/6/01 Time: 1:55:39		Room and Tax Posted			Golden Bay Star Hotel Page #1 of 15		
Room #	Rm Type	Market Code	Rate	Occupancy Tax	Sales Tax	Total	
427	NSK	AAA/99/c	$89.00	$8.90	$5.05	$102.95	
507	NSK	ARP/01	$89.00	$8.90	$5.05	$102.95	
513	SMD	Joneswed	$99.00	$9.90	$5.61	$114.51	
515	SMD	Joneswed	$99.00	$9.90	$5.61	$114.51	
610	SUITE	Joneswed	$0.00	$0.00	$0.00	$0.00	
726	DDSM	123Corp	$115.00	$11.50	$6.52	$133.02	
789	DDSM	123Corp	$115.00	$11.50	$6.52	$133.02	
819	NSK	123Corp	$115.00	$11.50	$6.52	$133.02	
833	DDSM	42cora	$135.00	$13.50	$7.65	$156.15	
949	SMD	Joneswed	$99.00	$9.90	$5.61	$114.51	
1101	NSK	42cora	$135.00	$13.50	$7.65	$156.15	
1500	SUITE	Walkin	$350.00	$35.00	$19.85	$404.85	
SUB TOTAL:			$1,440.00	$144.00	$81.64	$1,665.64	

In the automatic environment, reconciliation between the total sales report of each outlet/ancillary venue and the total postings to the guest ledger must be completed. As has been reviewed, each posting within the PMS is accompanied with a code. Those codes identify each charge. Each outlet will have a corresponding code. The team will include an **outlet/ancillary reconciliation report** into the night audit report that must match the total sales reports of each outlet/ ancillary venue. A page of that report might resemble Figure 10-2.

In addition to that report, the Food and Beverage (F&B) auditors may conduct analyses of food/beverage cost and labor cost. An additional report they may complete is called the **food and beverage potential report**. F&B potential is defined as the reconciliation of what was sold in the outlets to what price it was sold at. The potential report is used mainly to uncover fraud and poor practices within the F&B outlets. All this information is complied into the **food/beverage audit report**. A similar verification process will be conducted by the night audit team for banquet and A/V charges.

All the accounting entries conducted by the front desk during the course of the day—transfers, corrections, slip postings (charges, credits, and miscellaneous), paid outs, and petty cash entries—are checked. Each employee's bank out and drop are verified and reconciled. A **PMS summary-posting report** of all the posting activities conducted during the course of business at the front desk is verified against individual bank outs and then included into the night

FIGURE **10-2**

Outlet/ancillary posting

Date: 8/6/01 Time: 1:58:39		Outlet/ancillary reconciliation report			Golden Bay Star Hotel Page #1 of 1	
Outlet	Code	Item	Price	Tax	Room #	Total
J Restaurant	11	Breakfst	$12.00	$1.20	525	$13.20
J Restaurant	11	Breakfst	$10.58	$1.06	323	$11.64
J Restaurant	11	Breakfst	$8.95	$0.90	455	$9.85
J Restaurant	12	Lunch	$15.27	$1.53	323	$16.80
J Restaurant	12	Lunch	$6.98	$0.70	122	$7.68
J Restaurant	12	Lunch	$4.35	$0.44	501	$4.79
Gift Shop	22	Sundries	$2.95	$0.30	525	$3.25
Gift Shop	24	Magazines	$5.95	$0.60	122	$6.55
Gift Shop	23	Mints	$0.95	$0.10	606	$1.05
Shoe Shine	66	Shine	$6.00	$0.60	455	$6.60
Pro Shop	73	Clubs	$895.00	$89.50	323	$984.50
Pro Shop	76	Glove	$12.95	$1.30	323	$14.25
SUB TOTAL:			$981.93	$98.23		$1,080.16

audit report. The general cashier provides this information to night audit. A sample PMS shift closing is illustrated in Figure 10-3.

Other reports that the night auditors generate are:

- **Credit Card Transaction Report**—this report is conducted so that accounts receivable can verify the allowances and revenue due from each credit card company on the city ledger.

- **Arrival/Departure Report**—an analysis of the number and names of guests who came and went during the course of the day.

- **No-show Report**—this report is also run for the benefit of the accounts receivable department. The verification of who had a guaranteed reservation and did not show up will assist in determining who needs to be billed.

- **Credit Limit Report**—this report is run to verify that guests within the hotel have not exceeded their credit card limits or cash balances on hand. The information from this report should be shared with accounts receivable and the front office manager.

FIGURE **10-3**

Shift closing

| Date: 8/6/01 | PMS Shift Closing | Golden Bay Star Hotel |
| Time: 2:55:49 | Shift#1 | Page #1 of 1 |

Credit Card	Amount
American Express	$3,254.32
Visa	$5,621.03
Discover	$1,244.75
Diners/CB	$504.69
Credit Card Total:	$10,624.79

Postings	Amount
J Restaurant	$63.93
Gift Shop	$10.85
Shoe Shine	$6.60
Pro Shop	$998.75
Posting Total:	$1,080.13

Adjustments Total:	−$133.65
Paid Out Total:	−$50.00
Corrections:	N/A
Shift Total:	$11,521.27

- **Comp Rooms Report**—the night auditors must verify each room that has no rate posted to it. This report will include a reason for the complimentary status (e.g., per group contract, VIP, distressed guest, etc.).

- **Out of Order Rooms Report**—any room that cannot be sold must be listed. The reason for the OOO status (e.g,, leaky shower, renovation) should be listed and an indication of action taken (notified engineering) should accompany it.

- **In-House Report**—this report lists each and every guest who occupied a room during the night audit process.

- **Message Report**—this report prints out all the reports that were delivered via the PMS message system in the day. It is a backup document that serves as a permanent record.

The verification responsibilities of the night audit represent only a portion of their duties. Overall hotel statistics must be recorded and summary reports generated that conform to the USALI guidelines. The hotel performance report is the most common form of this summary. The average rates, occupancy numbers, and performance of the outlet/ancillary revenue centers are summarized by night audit each night in a hotel performance report. This report may be referred to as the "daily" report, the "flash" report, the "morning" report, or the "gross revenue" report. Each name refers to the same document. Figure 10-4 and Figure 10-5 illustrate examples of this report.

The hotel performance report is reviewed each morning by senior management and department heads throughout the hotel. This very important tool illustrates the revenue and occupancy performance of the entire hotel. It is a document that serves as a tool for future budgets, because it creates a historical record of day-by-day performance. This information is shared with owners, chain management, the IRS, and Wall Street. Accuracy is very important. A chain, for example, combines all their hotels' performance reports into one document, and that document is used to reflect the chain's performance.

These reports are combined with the various verification reports covered earlier into one large night audit report. The night audit report itself is a summary of numerous other reports. The most important of which are the ones we have covered:

- Credit Card Transaction Report

- Arrival/Departure Report

- No-Show Report

- Credit Limit Report

- Comp Rooms Report

XYZ Hotel Performance Report (200 Room Hotel)
Friday the 13th, 2001   Page 1 of 2

Market Segment		Occupancy	Room Revenue
Transient			Transient Avg. Rate = **$150**
Business	50	25%	($150.00 X 90) =
Pleasure	40	20%	Total Trans. Revenue = **$13,500.00**
Sub-total	**90**	**45%**	
Group			Group Average Rate = **$135**
Corporate	50	25%	($135 X 80) =
Assoc.	10	5%	Total Group Revenue = **$10,800.00**
Other	20	10%	
Sub-total	**80**	**40%**	
Other			**N/A**
Comps	5	2.5%	
OOO	0		Total Room Rev. $24,300
Sub-total	**5**	**2.5%**	Gross Avg. Rate **(24300/175)** = **$138.86**
Total	**175**	**87.5%**	Net Avg. Rate **(24300/170)** = **$142.94**

FIGURE **10–4**

Performance Report 1

- Out of Order Rooms Report
- Hotel Performance Report
- PMS Summary-Posting Report
- Outlet/Ancillary Reconciliation Report
- Room Rate Posting Report
- Food/Beverage Audit Report
- Food/Beverage Potential Report

Often, many of the components of the night audit report are never looked at again. In hotels there is an on-going need to prepare as much documentation as possible for an audit trail. However, much of the night audit report (beyond the performance report) is not relevant to management. External auditors, investors, and the IRS find the information contained in the night audit report very useful, though. The report itself is often printed into a large binder and stored. It may also be compiled into a digital or microfilm format for permanent storage.

```
┌────────────────────────────────────────────────────────────────────┐
│            XYZ Hotel Performance Report (200 Room Hotel)             │
│              Friday the 13th, 2001     Page 2 of 2                   │
├────────────────────────────────────────────────────────────────────┤
```

Outlet		Banquets/Catering Revenue	
Mr. Big's Restaurant		Banquet Breakfast Covers	0
Breakfast Covers	30	Banquet Breakfast Avg. Check	0
Breakfast Avg. Check	$8.95	Banquet Lunch Covers	30
Sub-Total Brkfst Revenue	**$268.50**	Banquet Lunch Avg. Check	$20.00
Lunch Covers	50	Banquet Dinner Covers	100
Dinner Avg. Check	$12.95	Banquet Dinner Avg. Check	$45.00
Sub-Total Lunch Revenue	**$647.50**	**Total Banquet Revenue**	**$5,100.00**
Dinner Covers	75		
Lunch Avg. Check	$15.95	**Audio Visual Revenue**	**$6,200.00**
Sub-Total Dinner Revenue	**$1,196.25**		
		Gift Shop Revenue	**$3,200.00**
Total Food Revenue	$2,112.25		
		Game Room Revenue	**$125.00**
Mr. Big's Lounge		**Total Hotel Revenue** (rooms, catering	
Beverage Covers	120	and outlet/ancillary) = **$41,305.75**	
Beverage Avg. Check		**Total Expend. per Occ. Room**	
Sub-Total Beverage Revenue	**$268.50**	(413057/175) = **$236.03**	

FIGURE **10-5**

Performance Report 2

TRIAL BALANCE

The night audit trial balance is the process the team undergoes to ensure that every report, posting, and transaction collected and audited in each report is accounted for. In essence, the trial balance is a test for accuracy. Most PMS's allow for a trial balance function that can be run at the end of the shift. This trial balance is usually run before the night audit report is finalized. Should the trial balance find errors, the night audit team must uncover them and correct them. This process can be lengthy and time-consuming, especially in a larger hotel. Veteran auditors have likened this process to "finding a needle in a haystack," as there can be hundreds of transactions to search through. This is another reason hotels stress accuracy in each activity of the front office.

NIGHT AUDIT CHECKLIST

The night team has a variety of tasks and duties to perform each evening. It is vital that these tasks are completed in a timely manner because some duties are dependent upon the completion of others. The AM front desk shift cannot check out early departures in the morning unless the date has rolled. Most night audit managers utilize a checklist similar to the checklists used by front desk managers. Figure 10-6 illustrates a sample night audit checklist.

ABC Hotel and Towers - Night Audit Checklist

Date: Day:
Night Audit Manager On Duty

11PM
_____ Review pass on log with PM desk manager
_____ Print and file Contingency Report*
_____ Cancel all non-guaranteed reservations
_____ Run preliminary PMS reconciliation report
_____ Disable telephone automatic posting
_____ Run frequent guests awards report
_____ Balance Front Office shift closings
_____ Close out POS systems
_____ Collect shift closings from outlet/ancillary employees
_____ Review and verify credit card postings and reconcile
     with PMS
_____ Complete room and tax audit
_____ Review market code report

1:00AM
_____ Post room and tax via PMS
_____ Post tax adjustments if applicable
_____ Print and file new contingency report
_____ Complete all reports needed for hotel performance
     report
_____ Distribute performance report to departments
_____ Complete second PMS preliminary balance
_____ Run PMS data backup

3:00AM
_____ Run final trial balance
_____ Complete date roll
_____ Verify date roll completion
_____ Verify error free
_____ Authorize PMS to accept new date and postings

FIGURE **10-6**

Night audit checklist

ANCILLARY NIGHT AUDIT DUTIES

Because the hotel never closes, the night auditors may have to assume a variety of responsibilities in conjunction to their primary tasks of preparing the night audit report. Although not hired to work in other departments, the need may arise where sickness or other reasons prevent employees from coming to work. The night auditors often may have to step in to assist.

Some hotels employ their night auditors in a dual role. Some of the individual auditors may also operate the PBX switchboard or front desk. Some even perform security duties as needed.

Guest Security and Incident/Accident Reporting

The night audit manager may be the highest-ranking employee on the premise during the evening. They are often required to assume the role of a manager on duty (**MOD**) in senior management's absence. The duties of the MOD can differ greatly. The primary responsibilities include customer service, guest safety, and accountability. In all cases, the MOD is authorized to speak and act on the general manager's behalf. Even though the night audit manager has the primary responsibility of creating the night audit report, the efficient running of the hotel and the well-being of the guests supercede anything else.

The night audit MOD, because of the scheduled shift time, may become involved with a variety of guest service and security issues. Early morning hours are when lounges and bars close and catered functions end, so intoxicated guests can cause problems. Tired guests arriving to the hotel at those hours may have traveled long and far, so an ability to use guest satisfaction skills is important.

As the acting manager in charge, the night audit manager should be familiar with a variety of security procedures. Although these procedures apply to any manager acting as the MOD, the night audit manager may have more opportunities to put them into practice. In terms of guest security, the MOD is responsible for proper documentation of all incidents and accidents.

The **MOD report** is a summary of activities and guest interaction in a given shift. The MOD should document the condition of the hotel and other relevant data for the executive management team. Walked guests, angry guests, employee problems, equipment malfunctions, and the like are all documented in the MOD report. Loud noises from guest rooms can disturb other guests. If attempts to quite the room fail, the MOD may be called upon to visit the room and request compliance in person. All this information is documented in the MOD report. The MOD report is useful for all hotel managers, because they are not usually present during these hours.

If serious situations occur, they are documented differently. An **incident report** is used to supplement the MOD report. An incident can occur in a variety of ways. An incident often occurs when attempts to resolve a situation by the MOD fail. Severely disorderly guests, for example, may not calm when asked to by the MOD. If continuing conduct results in the summoning of police, an incident has occurred. In fact, any police, fire, or ambulance calls results from an incident. Guest injuries, power outages, fires, and other situations where outside assistance is needed are defined as an incident. The MOD must document everything in detail because these incidents may end up being resolved in a court of law. The MOD may be a witness, and incident reports may become evidence. Insurance companies use these documents to help settle claims as well.

The MOD is also responsible for hotel employees, so when an employee injures himself or herself on the job, this must also be documented. Employee injuries are classified as **accidents**. They are different from incidents because they are not guest related. The same care and concern is taken for accidents as incidents, but the documentation is different. Often, the state Occupational Safety and Health Administration (OSHA) will mandate specific forms to document employee accidents.

In each case, whether incident or accident, the MOD should document everything that is relevant to the situation. To help ensure that all the correct steps are taken by the MOD, he/she might refer to a checklist that contains items similar to these:

- Guest name(s)
- Date and time
- Location inside/outside hotel
- Description of incident/accident
- Participant(s) statements
- Witness(es) statements
- Outside agency contacted (police, fire, etc.)
- Name of hospital, degree of injury

In the most serious of these cases, the general manager would be notified at home. Hotel legal and insurance departments become involved as needed. The MOD who documents an incident/accident well can lessen hotel liability. This documentation may also help set the ground work for learning why something happened and how to avoid it in the future.

ABOUT MY JOB

Night Audit Manager
Lori Harris

I have to tell you all, that despite what you might think, night audit is a fascinating department to work in. Quite literally, on any given shift, night audit performs all hotel functions in addition to the tasks of preparing the performance report. This variety is very appealing to me.

I basically run the hotel while the guests (and senior management) sleep. My goal is to ensure everyone's safety and complete the required reports with my team. Sometime in the early morning (around 2:00 A.M.), once we have all our data ready, we begin the date roll process. What many do not know is that the date roll entails shutting down the entire PMS. In essence, while the date roll is being completed, the hotel must be run manually. For that time (about an hour, if all works out right), we rely on contingency reports we ran prior to the shutdown. These reports list who is currently in the hotel and what rooms we have available. These are important if we were to get any arrivals during this time. We obviously do not want to check anyone into an occupied room!

We work through our checklist diligently in order to complete the date roll and reports before the earliest risers choose to check out. Sometimes we do not complete our tasks until later in the morning. Certainly frustrating for all, this is often outside our control. For example, if a front desk clerk or an F&B outlet made several posting errors during the day, we must try to correct them ourselves. After all, we can't call employees at 3:00 A.M.! Accuracy is paramount.

Night audit is a great way to learn about all hotel operations. For those like me who are eager to move up the ranks, night audit makes a great stepping stone to advancement. The only negative can be the hours. I do have some staff members who love these hours because they have another day job or they go to school. With the right mind-set, anyone can find something they enjoy about this job.

In the end, I gauge the success of my day on one thing: If I can beat the sunrise home, the shift was a success!

CHAPTER TEN **REVIEW**

KEY TERMS

night audit report	no-show report
date roll	credit limit report
room rate posting report	comp rooms report
outlet/ancillary reconciliation	out of order rooms report
report	message report
food and beverage potential report	in-house report
food/beverage audit report	MOD
PMS summary-posting report	MOD report
credit card transaction report	incident report
arrival/departure report	accidents

REVIEW QUESTIONS

1. What makes the night audit department so important to a hotel?

2. What information is collected for the hotel performance report? Why is accuracy so important for this and all night audit reports?

3. When does the date roll typically occur?

4. What is the role of the MOD?

5. What items are listed on the MOD checklist for accident/incident reports?

6. What is a trial balance?

7. What items are included in the MOD report? Who sees this report?

8. What is the PMS summary-posting report?

9. What is the importance of the rate market code?

10. What information is collected for the night audit report?

DISCUSSION QUESTIONS/EXERCISES

1. Some hotels staff a MOD in the daytime as well as night audit. Why would they do that? Could a MOD serve on different shifts? Could the different departments designate their own MODs? What would be the logic in having more than one MOD working at the same time?

2. Complete a sample Hotel Performance Report based on the following information.

Category	Value/Number
Total Rooms	505
Out of Order	5
Vacant	67
ADR	$152.83
F&B Covers	1,292
Average Check	$21.98
Banquet Covers	592
Average Check	$54.27
Over Rooms Revenue Forecast by	$1,454.02
Under F&B Forecast by	$3,895.86
Over Banquets Forecast by	$291.08
Arrivals	278

ABC Hotel

Occupancy %	
Arrivals	
ADR	
Rooms Sold	

Category	Revenue	Forecast	Variance
Rooms Revenue			
F&B Outlet Revenue			
Banquets Revenue			

3. Arrange to interview a night audit manager of a large downtown hotel. Answer the following questions:

   a. What is the name of the hotel you have selected?

   b. What is the location of this property?

   c. What is the size of this property?

   d. What is the name of the night audit manager?

   e. How long has he/she been in this position?

   f. What position did he/she have prior to becoming the night audit manager?

   g. How many auditors are on staff nightly?

   h. Generally, what time does the date roll occur?

   i. Are postings done automatically or manually at this hotel?

  j. Is he/she also the MOD at this hotel?

  k. What does he/she enjoy most about being a night audit manager?

  l. What does he/she enjoy least about being a night audit manager?

  m. Have there ever been any emergency situations during his/her shift?

  n. What is the best advice he/she can give you as a novice to the industry?

  o. What was the most interesting thing you learned from this night audit manager?

4. Complete the following performance report (this is a 1,000-room hotel).

Friday the 13th, 2004

Nice Hotel & Towers
DAILY PERFORMANCE REPORT

Market Segment		Occup. %	Room Revenue	
Transient			Transient Avg. Rate =	_____
Business	150	_____	Total Trans. Revenue =	_____
Pleasure	240	_____		
Subtotal	**390**	_____		
Group				
Corporate	100	_____		
Assoc.	200	_____	Group Average Rate =	_____
Other	75	_____	Total Group Revenue =	_____
Subtotal	**375**	_____		
Other				
Subtotal	**0**			
Comps	25	_____	Total Room Revenue =	_____
OOO	10	_____	Gross Average Rate =	_____
Subtotal	**35**	_____	Net Average Rate =	_____
Total	**800**	_____		

Housekeeping

OBJECTIVES

After reading this chapter, you should understand:

- How rooms are assigned to housekeepers
- Housekeeping standards
- How housekeeping supplies and inventory are managed

INTRODUCTION

The rooms division areas all must function together in order for the hotel to maximize efficiency. As stated earlier, each area needs the other in a symbiotic relationship that mirrors a successful sports team: Each position working together for the benefit of the entire team. Within the rooms division team, there is arguably no more vital a position than housekeeping. Research has shown that a clean guest room is extremely important. In fact, the two most often cited reasons for a guest not returning to a hotel are a dirty guest room and slow check-in. Cleaning and preparing guest rooms for sale to guests enables the entire hotel team to function. Room sales are the most important aspect of a hotel's business. The front office, reservations, and night audit have their "positions," but housekeeping holds the team together. They deliver the hotel product. This interrelationship is illustrated in Figure 11-1.

FIGURE **11-1**

Rooms division team

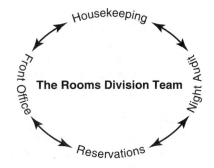

ROOM ASSIGNMENT

Planning is required in order for housekeeping to operate at peak efficiency. The cleaning and maintenance of guest rooms and common areas is very labor-intensive. It is for this reason that housekeeping departments are generally the largest in any hotel. This labor intensity also makes up a large portion of the room cost reviewed earlier. Therefore, management of the housekeeping department must use all the tools at its disposal to limit costs. Proper planning begins with efficient deployment of housekeepers. This deployment begins with a review of reports.

Housekeeping PMS Reports

Each morning, the housekeeping department runs a series of reports from the housekeeping menu of PMS that dictates the expected guest room activity for that day. These reports are the same ones used by the front office: the arrivals report, which lists every guest due to arrive; the departures report, which lists each guest who is due to check out that day; the in-house report, which lists each room that was occupied and not due to check out; the exceptions or out of order report, which lists each room that is being withheld from sale.

The housekeeping manager or director of services uses these reports to direct their staff of housekeepers for that day. The rooms getting first priority to clean are those of departing guests. The departures report is used to direct housekeepers to those rooms first, as they must be prepared for resale as soon as possible. The arrivals report is used to allocate vacant/ready rooms for new guests. Together with the front desk, the housekeeping department finds vacant/ready rooms for the front desk to assign. The in-house report lists the rooms that people are currently occupying. These rooms must be cleaned as well, but they are lower on the list of priority for the housekeepers. The out of order report simply identifies what rooms the housekeepers should avoid, as they are not suitable for sale anyway.

These reports are used by housekeeping to assign the workload of each housekeeper. Rooms are assigned based on their current status code. The understanding is that rooms with departing guests take longer to clean than those rooms currently occupied. Rooms that are vacant and clean obviously do not need to be cleaned again.

Housekeeper Allocation

The director of housekeeping or executive housekeeper begins each morning with a review of these reports. Based on the number of rooms that need cleaning that day, housekeeping management is said to "break out the house." This process divides the rooms to be cleaned into sections. The assignment of rooms to an individual housekeeper is called a **section**. A section of rooms usually consists of 16 to 18 guest rooms. This number is based on an expectation of cleaning two vacant/ready rooms per hour. Housekeeping is said to **turn** a room when it goes through the act of cleaning and preparing it for resale. It is important to assign sections with rooms as close together as possible. A section with rooms on many floors would diminish a housekeeper's ability to turn rooms, because they would spend time traveling between rooms and thus not complete their section in a timely manner.

When possible, housekeepers (sometimes referred to as room attendants; maid is no longer an acceptable term) are given an equal share of occupied rooms and rooms with departing guests to clean each day. Some hotels assign the departing rooms to the better or more senior housekeepers. Housekeepers may be assigned the task of cleaning enhanced rooms or suites based on ability or seniority as well. The vast array of room designs and makeup in the marketplace requires skilled cleaning professionals.

The proper allocation of housekeepers is vital to getting every room ready for occupancy by the stated check-in time. At a typical hotel, check-in time can be anywhere from 3:00 to 5:00 P.M. This is the time the hotel has committed to its guests. In fact, the check-in time is usually printed on the hotel's collateral (registration card and other items), and this is the time usually communicated to guests during the reservation process. Given that the checkout time can be anywhere from 11:00 A.M. to 1:00 P.M., this span of three to four hours is what housekeeping is given to clean every room in the hotel on a given day.

The room status codes are used to gauge which rooms are ready for sale. Should a guest depart earlier than the posted checkout time (say, 9:00 A.M.), that would allow the housekeepers to prepare that room for any new guests known to be arriving early. Because these arrival and departure times are hard to gauge, most hotels cannot guarantee an early arrival time to guests. By the same token, guests are discouraged from checking out late, often with a fee.

Some hotels may offer a late checkout grace period, but that usually does not exceed one hour.

In most hotels, the arrival and departure of guests is not orderly. Often, guests depart without checking out, which would leave the hotel under the assumption that it was still occupied. If a housekeeper was to enter an occupied room to clean it, and it was found to be vacant, a manager would join the housekeeper to verify it. Once verified as vacant, the manager would notify the front desk to check that room out. That room would then change its status code from O/D to V/D.

There are instances where housekeeping and the front desk disagree on the proper status code a room should have. When the two departments have different information on the status of a guest room, a **discrepant code** is said to exist. A discrepant code is created when the states of cleanliness or states of occupancy are inadvertently combined. An occupied/ready status is a discrepant status because that state is not possible. Ready only applies to rooms that are "ready" for sale. An occupied/vacant room is also not possible. Discrepant rooms arise when the guest departs earlier than planned or when the front desk shows the room occupied, but housekeeping finds it empty. A guest who checks out of the room, but does not immediately depart, would cause a discrepant status as well. A manager or supervisor easily solves these challenges with an inspection.

WHEN GUESTS OVERSTAY

Laws in most states prohibit hotels from evicting a guest from a room even if they stay in that room for more nights than was on the original reservation. The hotel has an obligation to provide accommodations to this guest. However, the hotel has every right to charge the room rate as it sees fit. So, if a guest had booked a discounted rate for two nights, and decided to stay an extra night, the hotel can choose to increase the rate. These occurrences, although uncommon, are especially troublesome in sold-out situations. An arriving guest may be without a room if a departing guest chooses to remain.

The only exception to this rule is in cases where the guest has not provided an acceptable method of payment. If a credit card was declined, or if the guest did not provide a cash deposit, the hotel can ask the guest to leave. Again, although they cannot physically remove the guest(s), they can change the lock on the door, which will force the guest to come to the front desk to settle the account. In extreme cases, law enforcement may be called upon to assist.

HOUSEKEEPING OPERATIONS

Once a housekeeper is assigned a section, he/she prepares the equipment needed to clean those rooms. Each housekeeper is assigned a **housekeeper's caddie**. The caddie is a handheld carrying case that can be easily brought into a guest room. Each caddie will consist of:

- Glass cleaner

- Bathroom cleaner

- Multipurpose cleaner

- Bath amenities (shampoo, conditioner, soap, etc.)

For various reasons, today's housekeeping department is staffed with housekeepers with varying levels of knowledge of English. To ensure that the cleaning products in a caddie are used properly, many are color coded with icons or numbers. It is common for these product labels to be printed in English, Spanish, and French.

Each night, the PM housekeeping staff is responsible for restocking each caddie as needed. The housekeeper will place this caddie on a **housekeeping cart**. This cart is what will hold the towels, linens, glasses, vacuum, and miscellaneous items needed to clean a guest room. For the safety and comfort of the housekeepers, the carts are designed to certain specifications:[1]

- Handle heights should be between 30 and 36 inches.

- Handles are rounded, instead of square, for easier grip.

- Eight-inch wheels allow for ease of movement over door thresholds.

- Wheels placed on the farthest edges of a cart allow for stability and ease of movement.

The stocking and resupply of these carts is the responsibility of the housekeeper. However, housekeepers are assisted in restocking by a **houseperson**. The houseperson's role is to support the housekeepers and maintain the cleanliness of guest hallways.

Most hotels have a linen supply room on each guest room floor. The houseperson maintains an inventory of housekeeping supplies, called a **par**, for each housekeeper in this supply room. A par is the amount of items needed to complete the cleaning of an assigned section. The linen supply room is actually filled with one half-par of supplies at a time. The understanding is that the housekeepers will use one half-par in the morning, and go to lunch with the supply room empty. The housepersons are to restock the supply room with another half-par during the lunch break of the housekeepers. Once the housekeepers have completed their assigned section, the houseperson would again stock the supply room with another half-par for the next morning. Par is a term used to describe inventory for other departments as well. The beverage department is said to keep a par of all beverages in stock, based on anticipated usage.

The housepersons are also responsible for checking in on the housekeepers throughout the day to remove dirty linen from their carts and to restock them with cleaning materials and amenities as needed. On average, one houseperson is assigned to 125 rooms, which works out to be one houseperson for every eight housekeepers.

In addition to supporting the housekeepers, the houseperson must maintain the cleanliness of the guest hallways. The houseperson will vacuum the halls twice a day and empty ash urns as needed. They must ensure that room service trays are removed, light fixtures are dusted, elevator entrances and vending areas are clean. Another member of the housekeeping staff, the lobby houseperson, will maintain the cleanliness of the hotel's common areas. These people are responsible for vacuuming the carpets, polishing brass, and buffing marble. In hotels with many group functions, the lobby housepersons may plan their day around the group's agenda. This enables them to clean ash urns and lobby restrooms after scheduled group breaks, when these items need attention most. Most group functions will break at or around 10 A.M. and 2 P.M. (in addition to a lunch break). Because the maintenance of common areas is so important, the lobby housepersons (sometimes also referred to as lobby attendants) are not given the responsibility of supporting housekeepers.

HOUSEKEEPING GUEST ROOM STANDARDS

Housekeepers must have the ability to clean rooms rapidly and thoroughly. Each guest room must meet the cleanliness standards set by management. These standards will differ from hotel to hotel. The cleanliness requirements may differ between room configurations and designations as well. A hotel's guest room cleanliness standard is difficult to list, because standards would differ so greatly. Figure 11-2 represents a sample cleanliness checklist a hotel may require of its housekeepers.

Housekeeping managers train their housekeepers to meet these requirements, but they are not necessarily able to check each and every room to ensure that they are met. Therefore, most hotels incorporate a random room inspection process. A **rooms inspector** is usually assigned to a group of eight housekeepers. The actual number of assigned housekeepers may differ based on hotel size and product type. Of all the rooms that are reported clean, the inspector will pick two rooms at random from each housekeeper's section. The rooms inspector would simply use the housekeeping checklist as a guide. This random inspection becomes a written review of sorts for each housekeeper. The thought process is if a housekeeper is below standard in a certain area, it

Guest Bay Resort and Towers Housekeeping Checklist					

	Yes	No		Yes	No
1. Entry Door			**5. Work Area**		
Door clean in and out	☐	☐	Proper placement of collateral	☐	☐
Frame and weather-stripping	☐	☐	Telephone clean	☐	☐
Do Not Disturb in place	☐	☐	Matches/ashtrays clean and		
Door chain	☐	☐	in place	☐	☐
A/C Vent clean	☐	☐	Chair clean	☐	☐
Door tariff sheet in place	☐	☐	Desktop dusted	☐	☐
Entrance light dusted, bulb			Waste basket clean/liner		
working	☐	☐	in place	☐	☐
Bedroom vent	☐	☐	**6. Drapes/Sheers**		
2. Closet			Open to one foot	☐	☐
Door clean in and out	☐	☐	Windows clean	☐	☐
Hangers	☐	☐	Glass clean	☐	☐
Dusted, free of fingerprints	☐	☐	Window sill	☐	☐
Laundry bags	☐	☐	Valance dusted	☐	☐
Shoe shine bags	☐	☐	**7. Furniture**		
Vacuumed and swept	☐	☐	Cushions placed properly	☐	☐
3. Bathroom			Pictures clean/straight	☐	☐
Mirror/door clean	☐	☐	Lamp cords neat	☐	☐
Floor clean	☐	☐	**8. Beds**		
Shower walls	☐	☐	Sheets/pillows cases changed	☐	☐
Chrome/soap dishes	☐	☐	Pillows clean and in place	☐	☐
Stoppers/overflow/drains	☐	☐	Corners tucked	☐	☐
Tiles/tub clean	☐	☐	Headboard clean	☐	☐
Shower curtain/liner/rod	☐	☐	Bedskirt/ruffles clean	☐	☐
Toilet clean	☐	☐	Under the bed clean	☐	☐
Toilet paper supplied	☐	☐	Bedspread clean and wrinkle free	☐	☐
Soap supplied	☐	☐	**9. Overall Room**		
Amenity Tray clean and supplied	☐	☐	Phone books in nightstand	☐	☐
Bath rug	☐	☐	Alarm clock set at correct time	☐	☐
Waste basket clean/liner in place	☐	☐	Carpet vacuumed/swept	☐	☐
Glasses/coaster clean and			Carpet edges	☐	☐
supplied	☐	☐	Spots treated	☐	☐
Vanity/sink clean	☐	☐	Baseboards clean	☐	☐
Vanity mirror clean	☐	☐	Wallcovering clean	☐	☐
Towel rack chrome	☐	☐	Brass polished	☐	☐
Bath towels, face towels, hand			Room fresh smelling	☐	☐
towels stocked	☐	☐	**10. Maintenance/Safety**		
4. Television/Armoire			All malfunctions reported to		
Dusted	☐	☐	engineering	☐	☐
Proper volume set	☐	☐	Sharp objects/needles reported	☐	☐
Clean inside drawers	☐	☐	Medical waste reported	☐	☐
Ice bucket/tray clean and supplied	☐	☐	Guest entry verified with		
Remote control working and			room key	☐	☐
in place	☐	☐	Injuries reported	☐	☐

Figure **11–2**

Housekeeping checklist

will be repeated in each room they clean. Therefore, a random inspection will be able to identify any recurring problem. The role of rooms inspector is sometimes carried out by senior housekeepers, as they are understood to be the most experienced. Every room that has been blocked for an arriving VIP will also be inspected.

A quality control of the rooms inspectors is also conducted. The executive housekeeper/housekeeping manager or a designate will inspect rooms as well. These individuals will inspect 5 to 10 rooms a day that have been deemed acceptable by the rooms inspectors. This is an important process in that housekeeping management needs to ensure that standards are met by all.

HOUSEKEEPING MANAGEMENT

Each morning in housekeeping begins with the assignment of sections and a general discussion of issues of the day. The managers will discuss with the housekeepers items that may impact them, such as:

- Groups in-house

- Known early arrivals or late departures and VIPs

- Safety procedures

- Chemical-handling guidelines/**MSDS** (a **M**aterial **S**afety **D**ata **S**heet is issued and posted for all chemicals used in a hotel. This sheet lists how to properly use and store the chemicals as well as their possible harmful effects.)

- "Task of the Day" Management often assigns housekeepers a special cleaning project each day. It is nearly impossible to completely clean, also referred to as **deep clean**, every room each day. Managers designate a different cleaning item to pay special attention to. These items may include dust in high areas, rust stains, and so on.

Housekeeping management often utilizes a daily checklist to assist in prioritizing their day. An A.M. and P.M. checklist might resemble those in Figure 11-3.

Turndown Service

Hotels that have been rated four star and/or four diamond or higher are required to offer their guests **turndown service**. Turndown service is a process by which the guest room is made warm and inviting for the evening. Some hotels provide this service automatically; others will perform it only on request for standard configuration rooms and automatically for VIPs and those staying in enhanced or suite rooms. Turndown service is usually conducted between 6:00 P.M. and 9:00 P.M. A turndown attendant should be able to

AM Shift Housekeeping Checklist	
Time Completed	**Task**
6:30	Open department. Run arrivals and in-house reports
6:45	Meet with lobby attendant, review day ahead
7:00	Break out the house
7:00	Conduct back of the house walk through
7:15	Conduct front of house and common area walk through
8:00	Conduct housekeepers meeting, assign task of the day
8:30	Conduct supervisor/houseperson discussion
9:00	Meet with front office leaders
10:00	Review discrepant rooms
11:00	Run departures report
1:00	Ensure VIP room ready and inspected
1:30	Conduct front of house and common area walk through
2:00	Review next day schedules
2:45	Review days activities with PM shift management
PM Shift Housekeeping Checklist	
Time Completed	**Task**
3:00	Run departures report
3:15	Review remaining departures with front office
4:00	Conduct front of house and common area walk through
5:00	Conduct back of the house walk through
6:00	Ensure all V/D and discrepant rooms are cleaned/resolved
9:00	Ensure chemical bottles/housekeeper caddies filled
9:00	Inspect linen par in supply rooms
11:00	Review special projects with right crew as needed
11:00	Review activities with right crew management

FIGURE **11-3**

A.M./P.M. **checklists**

complete 40 turndowns in those three hours. This job is popular with students because its set hours enables them to work part time.

The actual turndown service can entail many things. It can be a very detailed process at the finest hotels. The standards differ from hotel to hotel. Generally, turndown service includes:

- Closing of draperies

- Soft music

- Corner folding of bedspread away from pillow (i.e., turn down the sheets)

- An amenity presentation. This amenity might include chocolates, or mints, fruit, or some other item. In addition to that, a welcome card from the general manager might be included.

- Soft corner lights are lit.

- A "room tidy" is conducted, which is no more than a quick cleaning of the room. The tidy might include removing visibly used linens, arranging pillows, emptying of ashtrays and wastebaskets.

- Some hotels place a breakfast door hanger next to the amenity presentation. This door hanger enables the guest to choose the items and time they want breakfast delivered the next morning. At night, the employees delivering express checkout folios to the floors will pick up the breakfast door hangers and take them to room service.

Staffing

Because of the nature of the work, the housekeeping department generally has a higher turnover rate than the rest of the hotel. In tight labor markets this can be very problematic. Housekeeping managers continually conduct wage surveys of nearby hotels to determine the market average salaries. Hotels seeking to recruit and retain more housekeepers will, among other things, position themselves as the market leader in wages.

The job description of a housekeeper is fairly consistent amongst hotels. A good housekeeper will succeed at any hotel. A sample job description for a housekeeper might resemble this:

ABC Hotel

Housekeeper Job Description

The housekeeper is responsible for the cleanliness and overall appearance of guest rooms. Essential functions include treating guests in a friendly manner; vacuuming/sweeping carpets and floors; mopping floors as needed; dusting/ polishing furniture; cleaning bathroom items—showers, sinks, tubs; making beds according to standard; removal of used/soiled linens; reporting of mechanical problems to engineering; report safety hazards; changing guest room status with management; and other tasks deemed necessary by management.

Performance Standards

Customer satisfaction:	As measured by guest responses, feedback, complaints, and customer survey responses with specific reference to guest room cleanliness and appearance.

(continued)

Work habits:	As measured by appearance, grooming, promptness, attendance and adherence to safety and security standards.
Personal development:	As measured by skill development in position or crosstraining in a new position.
Safety and security:	As measured by adherence to hotel safety, security, and emergency procedures including key control, lifting heavy objects, and using chemicals.
Room cleaning:	As measured by the number of rooms cleaned daily with reference to hotel standards; adherence to cleanliness standards based on visual inspections and housekeeping checklists.

Job Characteristics

- Ability to calm upset guests
- Willing and able to assist coworkers as needed
- Effective follow-through on job duties and assignments
- High level of attention to detail

Staffing issues arise for management daily. In situations where a housekeeper is sick, or can't make it to work for some reason, the remaining housekeeping staff must be able to pick up the additional load. Many hotels have implemented the **guest room buyback process** to encourage other housekeepers to take on a larger load of rooms. The buyback process allows housekeepers to "purchase" guest rooms over and above the number assigned to them in their initial section. For each guest room cleaned beyond the assigned section, the hotel will pay the housekeeper anywhere from $3.00 to $8.00. Housekeepers who "buy" an additional few rooms can essentially increase their average hourly rate for the day by a few dollars or more. This monetary inducement has proven successful in many hotels.

Lost and Found

Because housekeepers often discover items in rooms left behind by guests, a hotel's lost and found area is usually located in the housekeeping manager's office. A manager or supervisor is appointed administrator. A lost and found log is maintained by the administrator that outlines the following information:

- Date found

- Room number or area found

- Description and condition of article

- Name of finder

- Where it is stored

- Eventual disposition

Honesty is a very prized commodity in housekeeping. Housekeepers come into contact with guest valuables daily (wallets, purses, money, etc.). Ensuring that valuables left behind by guests are turned into the lost and found administrator is important. Some hotels impose a waiting period (say, 90 days), after which point the individual may claim whatever it was they turned in as their own. The actual waiting period is subject to state law.

Some hotels involve their loss prevention department in situations where the lost items were of very high value. In addition, the loss prevention department becomes involved in situations where illegal items are found. Unfortunately, illicit drugs and stolen items are sometimes left behind in guest rooms. Housekeeping management should involve the loss prevention staff if they deem the material questionable. In turn, the loss prevention staff will involve law enforcement if the material left behind is determined to be illegal. They assist law enforcement by treating the guest room as a crime scene. All access is restricted, and evidence is quarantined. They may even conduct preliminary interviews of the staff. These steps must be taken to reduce any hotel liability and preserve clues until the appropriate law enforecement personnel arrive to take over.

Supply and Inventory Management

Outside of the food and beverage department, housekeeping is usually the only other department in the hotel that has to maintain significant inventories and continuously order supplies. They are responsible for the physical makeup of the guest room, so linens, towels, bath supplies, and other items must be maintained.

The inventory and supply process can be difficult to quantify. Because guest amenities, linens, and towels are not perishable, the need to exactly measure what is needed by housekeeping may not be of importance to management. In essence, no matter the quantity ordered, eventually the stock will be used. This philosophy, though still practiced at some hotels, is not an efficient use of hotel funds. Hotel managers today are very bottom-line driven. If there is no need to absorb the costs inherent with a large inventory, why do it?

Therefore, a method of determining what supplies housekeeping will require was developed. The theory is based on the usage of all materials in occupied rooms over time. Over a length of time, say a week or a year; an average consumption of in-room items can be determined. Based on occupancy data, the usage of in-room items can be averaged out. The requirements of every item can be averaged by this data over time, and is called the **guest supply usage per occupied room**.

For example, assume that XYZ Hotel has 400 rooms. In a given week that averaged 70 percent occupancy, it is known that XYZ Hotel goes through 2,000 in-room shampoos. This would mean that in a given day each occupied room used 1.02 shampoo bottles. Here is how that was determined:

400 rooms × 7 days in a week = 2,800 room nights

2,800 room nights × 70% occupancy = 1,960 rooms occupied

2,000 shampoos divided by 1,960 occupied rooms =
1.02 bottles per occupied room

Using this determination, the XYZ Hotel could look to future occupancy forecasts to determine how many shampoos it would need to order to meet demand. For example, assume that XYZ Hotel has 400 rooms. The front office states that next week the XYZ Hotel will run an 85 percent occupancy. Based on that figure, a determination of how many room nights will occur is easy:

400 × 7 × 85% = 2,380 room nights

From there, housekeeping management can determine the number of shampoos needed by multiplying the number of room nights by the known usage per occupied room figure for shampoos (1.02). Therefore, XYZ Hotel needs 2,477.6 shampoos on hand to meet demand (2,380 × 1.02).

The same method of calculation can be used to determine the need for other housekeeping items. The usage per occupied room figure ensures that the hotel does not carry too much inventory, while at the same time it ensures that every guest room is supplied appropriately.

The supply of linens and towels is determined a bit differently in that the reserve supply, or par, is much more difficult to calculate. An average hotel will keep 3.5 to 4 par of linens and towels on hand at any given time. Why? The allocation of this par is as follows:

- 1 par of all items is in the rooms at any given time.
- 1 par of all items is being cleaned at any given time.
- 1 par of all items are stocked in the linen supply closet by the houseperson in any given day (½ in the A.M. and ½ in the P.M.).
- ½ par of all items is kept in storage in case of breakage or loss.

Thus, 3.5 par is kept on hand.

Some hotels may choose to keep a larger or smaller par on hand depending on the management philosophy. Those hotels that outsource their laundry may choose to keep a larger par on hand in case of any supply problems. A housekeeping seamstress or tailor on staff is able to repair torn or frayed linens, which may reduce the hotel's loss due to breakage. In those cases, a smaller par may be warranted.

Loss due to guest theft is another reason to increase par. Hotels in the past used to pride themselves on towels emblazoned with the hotel logo. They felt that these towels improved a hotel's image. The problem was that these towels were being taken by hotel guests as souvenirs. Today, very few hotels use logo image towels for this very reason.

INDUSTRY PERSPECTIVE

e-Procurement in Hospitality

Darlyne Freedman
Procurement Associate

e-Procurement and hospitality—the two words together seem like a misnomer because the hospitality industry has historically been "behind the times" in the use of new technologies, especially the Internet. What is e-Procurement? The simplest answer is that e-Procurement is the purchase of goods and services, and making the purchase of those goods and services easier by the use of the Internet. If this is done with preparation and forethought, it can effectively put better and more efficient supply arrangements in place and it can help to manage the supplier's performances. It also can ensure that the purchase-to-pay process is made to be better, faster, and cheaper.

What purchases of goods and services can the hospitality industry perform using e-Procurement and how much money can it really save? These questions are at the forefront of any buyer's mind in any industry. "Deutsche Bank currently estimates a US$60 billion domestic and US$100 billion international market for hospitality e-Procurement, including furniture, fixtures, and equipment (FF&E); renovation and construction; service contracts; operating supplies; and food and beverage (F&B). The current estimates on cost savings because of efficiencies gained in supply chain transactions are US$4 billion in the United States and US$7 billion globally."[2] The current

(continued)

growth of e-Procurement in the hospitality industry is on the cusp of an explosion. If hotels want to remain competitive in this next wave of e-Procurement technologies, they are going to have to plan ahead and respond to the new marketplace. Because of the Internet, buyers will have an abundance of information available to them to identify new potential suppliers of a particular good or service with whom they may want to do business. It will certainly give the buyer the ability to perform better research and to benchmark the industry of that particular good or service (see Figure 11-4).

What are reverse auctions? A reverse auction gives a buyer the ability to prepare the specifications of the items or service to be purchased; research, choose, and invite the potential suppliers to bid in an on-line environment on the items or service in the specifications. The multiple vendors "bid down" against each other in "real time." This can speed up the sometimes long and drawn out paper process of creating the specifications, researching the supply base or sending out Requests for Information (RFI), choosing the supply base based on those RFIs, and sending out formal Requests for Quotation or Proposal (RFQ) or (RFP). Keep in mind that anytime a vendor takes an exception to anything in the specifications or requests clarification of anything in the specifications, all the vendors must be notified of the exceptions and the clarifications. This exception/clarification process during a reverse auction is done instantaneously.

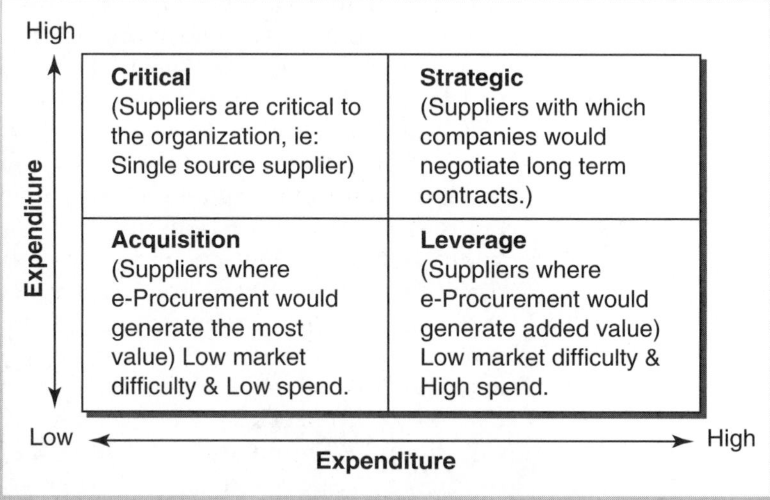

FIGURE **11-4**

e-Procurement

High

Critical
(Suppliers are critical to the organization, ie: Single source supplier)

Strategic
(Suppliers with which companies would negotiate long term contracts.)

Acquisition
(Suppliers where e-Procurement would generate the most value) Low market difficulty & Low spend.

Leverage
(Suppliers where e-Procurement would generate added value) Low market difficulty & High spend.

Expenditure

Low ←———————————————→ High

Expenditure

INDUSTRY PERSPECTIVE
(continued)

When would the hospitality industry use this e-Procurement technology? The potential here is endless. Historically, e-Procurement has been on commodity-based items. However, the trend for the future is anything and everything from acquisition purchases like supplies (pens, paper, stationary, etc.) and linens to contract purchases for services such as security and groundskeeeping. The Portfolio Analysis chart in Figure 11-4 indicates categories of spend.[3] If buyers could place their vendors into one of the four quadrants, it would be easy to decide where the most value would be added in performing an e-Procurement buy. Global expansions of hotel chains will boost supplier accesses to many new markets and will expose the buyers to e-Business. "Although North America will own half of all online sales in 2004," reports Forrester, "e-Business in Western Europe will grow to US$1.5 trillion, followed by Latin America, which is projected to reach US$82 billion in 2004. Developing countries such as Zimbabwe are not projected to have e-Business begin to take off until 2010."[4]

What are the benefits to the hotel chains versus the independents?

Hotel Chains:

- Chains can use their vast knowledge of the industry, experience in purchasing, long-standing supplier relationships, and larger budgets to rework their corporate infrastructure to improve inefficiencies.

- Chains can afford to create safe, secure, and customized Web sites so that staff will be able to buy specific supplier-approved merchandise or services. Then on the "back end" they can manage inventory levels, invoicing, and reporting.

- By having a Centralized Corporate Procurement group within the chains, they are able to control and monitor purchases, control adherence to approved vendor lists, and control of quality levels made by delegated buyers not within the corporate envelope.

Independents:

- These companies will benefit from rebates only given to larger-volume customers.

- Companies outside of the United States will begin to see their influences increase over time and usage of the e-Procurement tool.

(continued)

- In the long run, on-line purchasing can decrease the number of purchasing head count.

What would hinder the hotel industry from utilizing the e-Procurement tool? There will need to be large investments for the future by the hotel industry. There will be issues with training, computer hardware, servers, software, Local Area Networks (LAN), Wide Area Networks (WAN), and a total industry refocus. Some companies within the hotel industry may want to be absolutely certain that all privacy and security issues are completely resolved before even deciding to attempt any type of e-Procurement purchases—privacy in that competitors will not be able to view and steal core business procedures and security from hackers and the scrutiny of the general population outside of the hotel industry.

In conclusion, "To fully realize the benefits of e-Business in general and e-Procurement in particular, hospitality organizations will need to:

- Determine how to integrate their overall business strategy with the e-Business ecosystem
- Identify and weigh the impact on the organization (traditional processes will be affected significantly):
  - How will our traditional "requisition-to-pay" process be affected?
- Ask the following questions to determine how to best integrate e-Business systems/solutions with existing legacy/back-office/front-office systems:
  - What systems are necessary?
  - What skill sets do we need to acquire?
- Ask for answers in key areas as part of evaluating whether to leverage the Application Service Provider model:
  - Does your company have a shortage in internal IT skills?
  - Are there any up-front costs to buyer (subscription fee model)?
  - Will the ASP partner assume responsibility for managing the application?
  - Will the ASP services free resources to be focused on the other areas deemed more critical to your core business?"[5]

INDUSTRY PERSPECTIVE
(concluded)

EXERCISES:

1. You are a buyer at an independent hotel. How would you present to management the business case for performing a reverse auction exercise for the negotiations and renewal of the night security guard contract?

2. You are a purchasing manager for a large hotel chain that is not currently performing any e-Procurement. How would you present to upper management the advantage of spending dollars now for e-Procurement capabilities rather than just keeping the status quo in procurement?

NOTES

1. *Hotel and Motel Management, 216,* 6 (April 16, 2001), Advanstar Publications.
2. Brown, A., Deutsche Bank, "Hospitality B2B Enter the Revolution," May 2000.
3. ADR Consultants, Procurement Workshop Portfolio Analysis Chart, 2001.
4. The Forrester Brief—Global eCommerce Approaches Hypergrowth, Forrester Research, Inc., April 18, 2000.
5. Ngonzi, E., *Hospitality eProcurement.* (Winter 2000). New York: Hospitality Consulting Manager.

CHAPTER ELEVEN **REVIEW**

KEY TERMS

section	rooms inspector
turn	MSDS
discrepant code	deep clean
housekeeper's caddie	turndown service
housekeeping cart	guest room buyback process
houseperson	guest supply usage per occupied
par	room

Review Questions

1. What reports are used to determine a housekeeper's section?
2. What items go into a housekeeper's caddie?
3. Why is the houseperson so vital to the housekeeper?
4. Define MSDS.
5. Explain how the linen/towel par is determined.
6. How is usage per occupied room determined?
7. What processes go into a turndown service?
8. What is meant by the phrase "breaking out the house"?
9. What is a discrepant room status code? How are they rectified?
10. On average, how many housekeepers are assigned to each houseperson?

Discussion Questions/Exercises

1. Could the front desk use the method of "breaking out the house" employed in housekeeping to meet their own staffing needs? With forecasts and historical data at their disposal, couldn't the front desk determine how many check-ins/checkouts a clerk could perform in a given time? What would be the advantages or disadvantages of this method of staffing?

2. Hotels place an emphasis on safety for all employees. What safety concerns would apply specifically to housekeepers? What actions could a housekeeper or hotel take to limit any concerns?

3. A sample 285-room hotel's housekeeping department runs their required reports. Those reports yielded the following information:

   Departures = 90
   Arrivals = 55
   In-House Stay Overs = 160
   Out of Order = 6

   Answer the following questions:

   a. How many rooms MUST be cleaned today?
   b. What is the minimum number of housekeepers needed to staff today?
   c. How many rooms would each attendant be required to clean?
   d. What will be the house status in the morning before any checkouts occur?
   e. What factors may increase cleaning time?

4. Based on the general rule of thumb for par linens and towels, determine the amount of linens needed for the following hotels:

Hotel	# Guest Rooms	Occupancy	Par Required
A	580	87%	
B	730	79%	
C	420	68%	

INTERNET RESOURCES
Web-Based Purchasing

Internet procurement sites are rapidly changing the way hotels secure products and services. At the hotel level, or chainwide, these sites allow for better inventory and quality control of nearly all hotel supplies. The following sites are a few of these resources:

Grainger	<http://www.grainger.com>
Purchase Pro	<http://www.purchasepro.com>
Zoho	<http://www.zoho.com>
hglobe	<http://www.hglobe.com>
Allegiant	<http://www.allegiant.com>

For additional hospitality and travel marketing resources, visit our Web site at <http://www.Hospitality-Tourism.delmar.com>.

12

Reservations and Forecasting

OBJECTIVES

After reading this chapter, you should understand:

- How to determine occupancy
- Overselling and its impact
- The principles of yield management
- Forecasting
- The sales strategy and management techniques used in reservation offices

INTRODUCTION

The reservations department is perhaps the most well-known hotel department to the general public. Most people understand its purpose. If someone wants a room at a hotel, they know that they need to contact the reservations department. Most people do not know how the reservations department actually works. How are rate designations implemented? Why is one rate offered on a given night and another the following week? The first step in understanding what rate designations are offered and when is the determination of availability.

DETERMINING OCCUPANCY AND AVAILABILITY

Perhaps the most fundamental aspect of hotel analysis is the determination of occupancy and availability. Occupancy and availability are mirror opposites of each other. In most cases, what is not occupied is available for sale. Out of order rooms may skew that number somewhat (they are not occupied, but they are not available for sale either). How one looks at occupancy versus availability can be summarized with the old adage "Is the glass half empty or half full?"

Within the world of reservations, the interplay between occupancy and availability is crucial. The goal of reservations, in conjunction with group sales, is to fill all the sleeping rooms. The first step in achieving that goal is to determine how many rooms are available for sale. There are many factors that go into determining availability. Availability is never constant; it is always in a state of flux. On any given night, reservations are being made, and others are cancelled. People who initially checked in for multiple nights leave early; others stay longer than expected. Availability can literally change from minute to minute. Determining availability requires both hard data analysis and a level of instinctual guesswork. It is the ever-evolving nature of availability that makes its determination both a skill and an art.

Assigned the task of determining availability is the reservations department. It is they who use the levels of availability and occupancy in implementing the rate structure. Determining availability should not be confused with forecasting. Forecasting, which is covered later in this chapter, is a much more detailed analysis of the future. Availability, though similar to forecasting, looks at the present moment in time. In the modern hotel, property management computer systems assist the director of transient sales in determining the levels of availability and occupancy. Although computers are useful, one should know what factors the computer considers in making these determinations.

Availability Factors

Current Number of Reservations

Often referred to as the number of rooms "on the books", the number of currently reserved rooms is the starting point of availability determination.

Historical Factors

One of the best ways to predict future outcomes is to look to the past. The term **history** is used in both group and transient room analysis. History is defined as the documented record of historical data. Looking at how a hotel performed in the past is a good way of predicting how it may perform on a given night in the future. History can apply to many things. The group sales-people look to a group's history in determining how many rooms will actual-ly be used in relation to how many they have committed to. A group's outlet usage history gives a restaurant manager an idea of how many covers to expect. With determining availability, history can guide decision-makers in limiting the pure guesswork. Sometimes referred to as "wash factors," his-torical factors are vital to an accurate determination of availability. Without history, the following historical factors would be unsubstantiated guesses:

- Early arrivals—Making an allowance for guests who check in before they are due helps ensure that availability is as accurate as it can be.

- Early departures—Along the same lines as early arrivals, allowing for a certain number of guests who check out earlier than expected is important in determining accurate availability.

- Cancellations—Guests may cancel a reservation for many reasons. No hotel can say with absolute certainty how many reservations will be cancelled, but a good historical record of past years can give a fair-ly good determination.

- "No-shows"—Within transient room sales, there are two types of ways a reservation is held for a guest. (1) A reservation can be held on an arrival-time basis. This means that the hotel and guest have agreed that if after a certain time the guest has not arrived, the reser-vation is released. Typically, these types of reservations are held until 4:00 to 6:00 P.M. Once that reservation is cancelled, the guest assumes no liability. The hotel is then free to sell that room to another guest. (2) A guaranteed reservation is held for a guest the entire night. The guest will guarantee arrival by providing a credit card number when the reservation is made. Both the hotel and guest understand that the credit card will be charged, whether it is occu-pied or not. A guaranteed reservation that is not occupied is called a **guaranteed no-show (GNS)**. Because these reservations actually charge the guest, they are counted as occupied rooms even though no one slept in the room. Whatever type of reservation it is, avail-ability is affected by these "no-shows."

- Stayovers—Guests who stay longer than planned must be accounted for in some way. History is the only good way of predicting how many may do so.

- Out of order rooms—Rooms that are held out of inventory for any reason diminish the number of rooms available for sale. Again, they do not affect occupancy calculations because no guests actually stay in them.

● Walk-ins—At any given time, a guest may arrive unannounced looking for a room. Although history can shed some light on how many walk-ins to expect, the many variables that affect this number make their prediction difficult. Market factors such as compression of demand, weather, transportation disruptions, and others can affect the number of walk-ins.

Each of these factors will affect the determination of availability at any given point in time. Some of these factors have a positive effect on the number of rooms available, others have a negative effect. Figure 12-1 illustrates this positive/negative effect on availability.

Figure 12-2 uses this positive/negative relationship in an example. In this example, the XYZ hotel has 100 rooms and the director of transient sales has been assigned the task of determining occupancy.

FIGURE **12-1**

Determining availability factors

Determining Availability Factors
(Counted at the time of determining availability)
Each of these availability factors combine to positively
or negatively affect the number of available rooms.

Factor	Affect
• Early Arrivals	Plus
• Cancellations	Minus
• No-Shows	Minus
• Early Departures	Minus
• Stayovers	Plus
• Other Factors	
Out of Order	Minus
Compression	Plus *or* Minus

FIGURE **12-2**

Availability exercise

XYZ Hotel
Starting Point: On the Books 50 Rooms

Availability Factor		Resulting Effect
Projected Early Arrivals:	10	(add 10)
Cancellations:	12	(minus 12)
Projected No-Shows:	8	(minus 8)
Projected Early Departures:	5	(minus 5)
Projected Stayovers:	10	(add 10)
Other Factors:		
No out of order rooms, city	6	(add 6)
is not busy, but history		
shows that an average of 6	51	Projected Occupancy
walk-ins occur		
Therefore, availability is:	**49**	**(100-51)**

HOUSE COUNT

The hotel **house count** is similar to the availability determination but differs in a few fundamental ways. The house count does not take into consideration historical factors, market factors, or any unknowns. The house count is an actual quantifiable number. The house count looks at how many rooms are in-house, how many are due to arrive and how many are due to check out. That number, less any OOO rooms, yields a house count. The house count does not use any projections. The house count is used in many ways as the starting point of determining availability.

OVERSELLING

Based on the availability on any given night, a hotel may sell more rooms than are actually in inventory. This practice is called **overselling**. Using the historical record, a hotel may oversell in order to offset the effect of the minus (or negative) factors that determine availability. Though some consider overselling an undue gamble, many hotel managers strive to fully sell out the hotel using this practice. There are drawbacks to overselling. The most obvious of which is not having enough rooms for guests with reservations. When a hotel aggressively oversells and does not have enough rooms for confirmed reservations, it must "walk" the guest. A **walked reservation** is a guest who must stay somewhere other than where they were initially booked to be. A confirmed reservation refers to guaranteed reservations, not those held on a time-of-arrival basis. The hotel that walked the guest must honor its obligations by compensating them in some way. There are no hard and fast rules as to how the hotel must compensate the guest, but most reputable hotels will:

- Pay for the room at another facility of the same or better quality.

- Pay for a phone call so that the individual can notify others of the change in accommodations.

- Provide transportation to the new facility, and back if applicable. A guest who is part of a group will want to return in the morning to attend group functions. A transient guest who has more than a one-night stay should be allowed to return to the original hotel to complete the stay if they wish.

- Other incentives can include a free breakfast, an upgrade upon return, an in-room amenity, an apology from management, and even some type of direct monetary compensation.

It is up to the reservations department to monitor the extent to which a hotel may oversell. A hotel that is oversold many days in the future may find that wash factors have reduced the number of reservations as the date approaches. Had that hotel not oversold in the first place, it would find itself with too few reservations. Upper management largely dictates the extent to which a hotel may oversell. Some hotel managers feel the risk of walking guests does not justify the potential return of a sold-out hotel. After all, a guest who is upset about being walked may never return.

The determination of how far to oversell differs from hotel to hotel. The criteria used will differ as well. Figure 12-3 illustrates what factors a director of transient sales may consider in determining how far to oversell a hotel.

- Line 1 lists the number of rooms currently on the books for that date.

- Line 2 lists the number of guests due to arrive on that date.

- Line 3 lists the number of nonguaranteed reservations for that date. Nonguaranteed reservations play a role in overselling because they often do not arrive.

- Line 4 lists the estimated number of guests who will not arrive even though they have guaranteed reservations. History may provide a percentage by which the number of the no-shows can be estimated. In this example, the hotel has a historical 5 percent rate of no-shows with guaranteed reservations.

- Line 5 lists the number of guests who may depart earlier than their reservations dictate. Again, history can be a guide. In this example, the hotel uses a different percentage for each day of the week.

FIGURE **12-3**

- Line 6 lists the estimated number of guests who will stay longer than expected. The percentage used here to calculate this figure is unique.

Overselling

OVERALL ANALYSIS
(This Sample Hotel has 420 Rooms)

Day	WED	THU	FRI	SAT	SUN	MON	TUE
Date	7/1/01	7/2/01	7/3/01	7/4/01	7/5/01	7/6/01	7/7/01
Rooms on the Books	331	247	126	211	200	290	422
Due to Arrive	123	121	67	107	134	183	282
Non Gtd Reservations	2	0	6	12	1	3	15
Est. No Shows	6	6	3	5	7	9	14
Est. Early Departures	10	11	9	8	8	6	9
Est. Stayovers	4	4	4	2	3	4	5
Due to Depart	206	203	212	38	117	78	148
Revised on Books	317	234	111	188	188	276	389
Variance	14	13	15	23	12	14	33
#Rooms to Fill	103	186	309	232	232	144	31
Oversell #	434	433	435	443	432	434	453

This hotel has determined that their number of stayovers often resembles 60 percent of the no-shows of the previous night. Again, there are no hard and fast rules; each hotel will tailor their analysis to suit its own needs.

- Line 7 lists the number of guests who are due to depart.

- Line 8 reflects an adjusted figure of what the hotel estimates will be their actual number of rooms on the books by using the positive/ negative effects of the availability factors. It takes the original on-the-books figure and subtracts the nonguaranteed number, no-show number, and the early departing number. It then adds the stayover number because that has a positive effect on the number of rooms.

- Line 9 shows the difference between the original on-the-books number and the revised figure.

- Line 10 subtracts the revised on-the-books figure from the total number of rooms the hotel has (in this case 420). This yields how many rooms the hotel needs to fill.

- Line 11 determines the oversell target, which this hotel should try to reach by adding the number of rooms to fill to the original on-the-books number.

If a hotel managed its overselling perfectly, it is said to have achieved a **perfect sell**. A perfect sell is reached when every room is occupied and no guest was walked. Some conservative hotel managers have lowered the level at which they consider the hotel perfectly sold. To reduce the risk of walking, some managers accept a 95 to 98 percent occupied hotel as fully sold. Wherever the threshold is set, the reservations department always prides itself on achieving a perfectly sold hotel.

YIELD MANAGEMENT

As was mentioned earlier, the combination of group and transient rooms makes up the hotel's occupancy, or overall room demand. The reservations department must understand the nature of the group base and the individual booking cycle. The interplay between group and transient must be managed in order for room revenue to be maximized. The group base is known before the individual booking cycle becomes a factor. Because a hotel has a group base before the booking cycle starts, the reservations department can charge room rates based on how many rooms are available. Understanding opportunity cost and the simple laws of supply and demand, reservations must maximize the room revenue for the remaining rooms. This pricing strategy is called **yield management**.

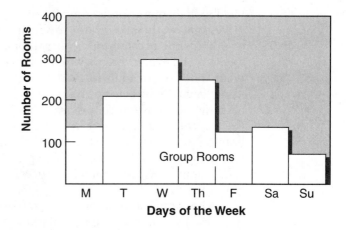

FIGURE **12-4**

Sample group base

For example, Figure 12-4 shows a fictitious hotel's group base for a specific week. Imagine that the individual booking cycle for this hotel is 1 week out. The hotel has 400 rooms for sale each night. In this example, the group base differs throughout the week as different groups come and go. Although it comes close at times, the hotel never sells out based solely on group demand. This is where transient rooms become a factor. Transient rooms, as managed by the reservations department, fill the voids left by the group base in the hotel inventory (Figure 12-5). Using yield management, hotel salespeople try to come as close to full occupancy as possible each night while maximizing the hotel's revenue potential. How exactly does yield management work?

Yield management is a flexible tool that directors of transient sales use to maximize revenue. Its flexibility allows for continual adjustments as business factors change. As we know, availability can evolve from minute to minute.

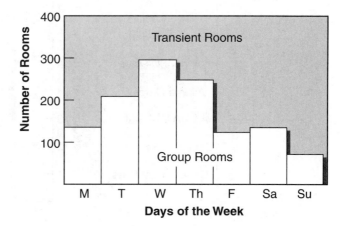

FIGURE **12-5**

Transient versus group

Yield management can be thought of as an automobile engine. Sometimes, the driver pushes the accelerator to speed up. Other times, the driver may let up or pull off the accelerator to coast along. At still other times, a brake may be applied. The ever-changing circumstances of the roadway dictate to the driver what tools are needed to manage the car. Yield management works in the same way. The director of transient sales can "accelerate" or "put the brakes" on how the transient rooms are sold.

In the hotel industry, the engine from this analogy is replaced with the hotel's rate structure. Lower rates, which are cheaper to buy, act as the accelerator by making it more attractive to book. Higher rates (and their higher price) slow down the booking process as more guests are presumably priced out of the market.

The simplest way of understanding yield management is to assign a numerical value to all the rates within the rate structure. If one were to assign the rates a number (say 1 through 7) corresponding to their value, the practice of yield management becomes easier to understand. Figure 12-6 illustrates the concept of assigning a numerical value to room rates. As each rate nears rack rate, its number value goes up. A target rate is thus created for the reservations staff to quote for each remaining room. The manager would assign a higher number to each night as the hotel neared sold-out status. Figure 12-7 illustrates what numerical value would be quoted based on how many rooms are on the books. Today, many smaller hotels use this numerical pricing strategy in their application of yield management because of its simplicity.

Large and mega-size hotels need more tools to best maximize their room revenue. Due to the complexity of managing the inventory of hundreds of sleeping rooms, directors of transient sales in larger hotels can expand their yield

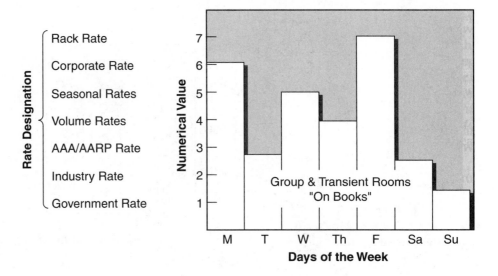

FIGURE **12-6**

Numerical value rates

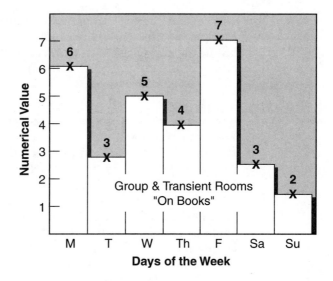

FIGURE **12-7**

Numerical quotes

management tools. These hotels use limiting criteria called **rate restrictions** to manage inventory. These hotels incorporate two main restrictions into their yield strategy: rate availability and length of stay.

Rate Availability Restrictions

Rate restrictions are the most widely used type of restriction. This practice is similar to the numerical value strategy reviewed earlier. The difference here is that the manager actively manages the availability of each rate. As availability changes, the director of transient sales may input certain **rate triggers** that alter what rates are to be quoted. A rate trigger is a signal programmed into the reservation computer system that instructs it to change the rate based on preset criteria. As rooms are booked and others cancelled, different rate triggers become active or inactive. This active rate management approach highlights the difference between rate restrictions and the more basic numerical pricing method.

In situations where demand is thought to be forthcoming, but the time frame hasn't entered the traditional booking cycle, the director of transient sales may restrict a rate before any rooms are booked. The manager is said to have "turned off" these rates. Normally, once occupancy reaches a prespecified number, discounted rates are turned off. However, there are cases where a large citywide convention or major sporting event is known to be coming long before any transient reservations are made. Here the manager becomes proactive by turning off discounted rates early. In some cases, the hotel may have never sold discounted rates, and thus may have them restricted from the start. This practice is called **driving rate** because it attempts to maximize the rate revenue early. This approach must be made carefully. If too many rates are restricted too early, the hotel may find itself empty when it had hoped to fill. In those situations, the director of transient sales may have to "open up" all rate restrictions at the last minute to try to gain occupancy.

Length of Stay Restrictions

Rate restrictions are not the only yield management tools available to a hotel. Lengths of stay restrictions attempt to limit imbalances in occupancy during the week. Situations can occur where one night, for whatever reason, has a higher demand than others do. An availability "spike" is said to occur. A spike can be problematic for hotels. If a spike occurs to such an extent that one night becomes sold out, but the following night is wide open, no new reservation could be taken for both nights. The spike precludes any additional occupancy on the night the hotel really needs it. The same spike can affect the various hotel types in different ways. Based on the traditional demand levels, a spike on a Wednesday is not as big a problem for a resort as it is for an airport hotel. A Friday night spike may not be an issue for that same airport hotel because Friday is a traditionally low-demand night. But a Friday spike for the resort would preclude two night stays, and weekend nights are in high demand for resorts in season.

The opposite of a spike is called a "hole." Periods of low demand resulting in low occupancy also create problems for a hotel. A hotel that has spikes and holes in succession must take another look at their yield management strategy, because that situation is very difficult to rectify. Figure 12-8 illustrates how spikes and holes result in a hotel's availability that resembles peaks and valleys.

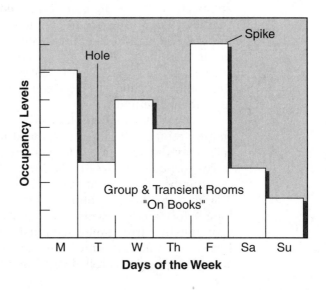

FIGURE **12-8**

Spikes and holes

There are three types of length of stay restrictions a hotel may employ to avoid and rectify spikes, based on the situation.

Closed to Arrival Restrictions

A **closed to arrival (CTA)** restriction is useful in slowing demand on one night while increasing demand on the prior night. A CTA restriction won't allow any new reservations for check-in on that night, but does allow for stay-overs. Literally, it closes new arrivals. A CTA encourages reservations on the night before where it is needed. For example, if Tuesday were already spiking for a particular week while Monday resembles a hole, a CTA on the Tuesday night would be a good option to even out the demand.

Minimum Length Stay Restrictions

The **minimum length stay (MLS)** restriction mandates that all new reservations stay at the hotel for a minimum number of nights. This restriction is effective when demand is known ahead of time to be strong on certain nights but less so on others. The MLS is very effective when used over holidays, for special events, or for citywides. For example, if an event falls on a Sunday, with the primary demand Saturday and Sunday, an MLS on the Friday would mandate staying all three nights. That will help bring the occupancy up on a date not otherwise affected by the event. The term MLS is usually followed by the number of nights it affects. For example, an MLS-3 equates to a minimum three-night stay on a given day. The MLS is also referred to as a "must stay," as in "must stay three" restriction. Restrictions can be used in combinations as well. Using the previous example, a MLS on that Friday, coupled with a CTA on Saturday, will ensure that the Friday doesn't become a hole. The MLS on Friday does not preclude one-night stays, which are also desirable in this situation. In this example, with these restrictions in place, a new reservation could be for one night or three nights, not two.

Modified Length Stay Restrictions

The modified length stay (also called Min/Max) restriction takes longer stays into consideration. It is a hybrid of the MLS and the CTA. It is similar to MLS in that it requires a certain number of nights and resembles the CTA in that new arrivals are restricted. The differences are that it focuses on lengthening a reservation as well as limiting the length of stay. For example:

Assume that a hotel is full on Tuesday, Wednesday, and Saturday. A Min/Max will restrict Tuesday arrivals unless the guest is staying more than two nights. This way, the hotel will also receive demand on Thursday night, which might be needed. But, that same Min/Max will not allow that reservation to extend past Friday night because Saturday night is sold out. In this example, the Min/Max becomes a "must stay three, but no more than four" night reservation.

Rate Averaging

A yield management tool used less frequently than the restrictions already presented is **rate averaging**. Rate averaging simply averages the target rates for any multiple-night reservation. Averaging rates may be easier than applying the other restrictions. A drawback, of course, is that averaging does not apply to one-night stays. For example, a guest wishing to stay at a hotel Wednesday, Thursday, and Friday nights may be quoted the average of the available transient rates (see Figure 12-9).

$$\$130 + \$120 + \$150 \div 3 = \$133 \text{ (average rate)}$$

Yield Management for Groups

It is generally understood that groups are booked in advance of the transient booking cycle. Using the three sides of the hotel success triangle, groups are evaluated on their total impact to the hotel. That is, groups are measured not only by their sleeping room impact but also by their catering contribution and their anticipated outlet/ancillary usage. What happens when group booking opportunities come up within the transient booking cycle? As can happen, depending on the hotel, groups may find themselves in need of sleeping rooms and meeting space at the last minute. At times like these, the group salespeople must consult with the reservations department.

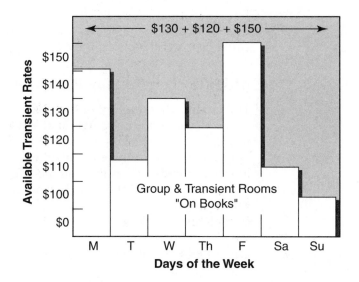

FIGURE **12-9**

Rate averaging

If the reservations department has begun to implement yield management strategies, the group sales effort should mirror them. Group bookings of a short-term nature should be quoted target rates supplied by the director. It is understood that room rates are higher within the transient booking cycle. Due to opportunity cost considerations, hotels must maximize the room revenue of each remaining room. Group bookings should not be lower than transient available rates for this reason. **Displacement** occurs when lower-rated group rooms are booked in place of higher-rated transient rooms. Hotels try to minimize displacement whenever possible. Ideally, the last-minute group booking will achieve a rate comparable, if not higher than, the rate being quoted for transient rooms.

There are situations, though, where the hotel may forgo the higher room revenue. If the group in question is providing an extremely high amount of revenue to the other two sides of the hotel success triangle (namely, catering and outlet/ancillary revenue), an argument could be made to book it. If a group is able to shift their arrival/departure pattern, it may become more attractive as well. Displacement can be minimized if the group is providing rooms on one or more dates with holes. Groups who book several programs at one time, called **series groups**, might merit an exemption from yield management as well. A series group may need to bring their lower-rated business over one or two dates of expected high occupancy. But their remaining sets of dates may be over periods of low occupancy. These situations mandate "looking at the big picture."

In the modern hotel, computer programs can determine profitability and assist in booking decisions. These programs take the proposed group's revenue impact and compare those figures to expected transient revenue. Using historical data and forthcoming yield management restrictions, these programs then provide a detailed displacement analysis. Together with the director of group sales, a director of transient sales can make a decision based on what is best for the hotel using this information.

RESERVATIONS MANAGEMENT

The discussions regarding availability and yield management shed light on the foundations of the reservations department. Laying the groundwork on why the reservations department does what it does makes it easier to understand how it does it. The reservations department (referred to simply as "reservations" inside hotels) is responsible for two important functions: making all transient bookings and supplying the rest of the hotel with occupancy data. The director of transient sales must monitor and manage a staff of reservations agents. He or she must also collect, analyze, and distribute occupancy information to the rest of the hotel. This dual role makes the director of transient sales extremely important. Within reservations, these roles are called forecasting and sales management.

Forecasting

"To guess is cheap.... To guess wrongly is expensive."

—Confucius

The impact of the data reservations supplies to the rest of the hotel is vital. Providing information on what occupancy levels are forthcoming, in essence how busy the hotel will be, is called **forecasting**. The reservations forecast incorporates group and transient data to provide the hotel with an overall picture of the sleeping room activity. As with many industries, estimates on future demand dictate how resources will be used. Within a hotel, the various departments depend on reservations to forecast what will be required of them. The reservations forecast may impact:

- Asset allocation—hotels can predict from the forecast what demands may be placed on its infrastructure. How the depreciation of high occupancy will affect the renovation cycle of sleeping rooms is one example. Engineering can use forecasts to schedule repairs as well as predict what the costs of heat, light, and power will be. Forecasts also provide data to the group sales department notifying them well in advance of low occupancy-need periods. This enables the group sales effort to allocate resources in filling those need periods.

- Staffing levels—the front desk, the bellstand, the outlets, and ancillary venues in a hotel use the reservations forecast to determine future demand. The forecast aids in anticipating required staffing levels to meet this demand. A fully staffed front desk may not be necessary when the hotel is only half full. The forecast will note the arrivals and departures on a given day so that housekeeping and the bellstand will be aware and ready ahead of time. The health club and golf course know from history how many people they can expect based on these forecasts as well. Human resources can step up recruitment efforts if the forecast shows a large increase in demand.

- Inventory availability—in addition to asset allocation and staffing, forecasts aid in determining what inventory each of the departments must keep on hand. The restaurants and lounges can order the requisite food and beverage based on the forecasted occupancy levels. Again, based on history, the outlets can calculate how many guests (called "covers") they can expect from the forecast. Housekeeping will know how many sheets and towels they would need.

Any major swings in a forecast must be communicated to all levels as soon as the data is verified. An unforeseen group cancellation two days out will impact bellstaff, front desk staff, housekeeping, and others for the duration of the group pattern. Timely notification of these changes allows the affected departments to alter personnel schedules and withhold pending inventory orders as needed. The further out either a potential area of low occupancy or a need period is identified, the sooner yield management tools can be applied to attempt to rectify the situation. With this in mind, continuous accurate forecasting is the key to a successful hotel operation.

In forecasting hotel occupancy, the reservations department determines how many rooms of the available inventory will be sold on a particular night. This number is then divided by the total room inventory to produce the occupancy percentage.

$$\frac{\text{Rooms sold}}{\text{Rooms available}} \times 100 = \text{Occupancy percentage}$$

Perhaps the most fundamental forecast, the occupancy forecast affects the asset allocation, staffing, and inventory requirements of many departments. Because all hotels are in the business of filling sleeping rooms, occupancy forecasts look at the core of the hotel business.

The reservations forecast incorporates other factors as well as occupancy. Hotel owners and investors also want to know forthcoming room revenue data. Because the forecast combines both group and transient rooms, it allows for a detailed breakdown of each segment. The groups on the books will yield their own average rate. Transient rooms will do the same. Each segment will also encompass its own portion of the overall occupancy. By determining occupancy by segment and applying the correct average rate per segment, the hotel can then calculate total room revenue. We know that ADR (average daily rate) is simply total rooms revenue divided by occupied rooms. Rev-par, (revenue per available room) can also be obtained by multiplying occupancy by ADR. Rev-par, addressed in detail in another chapter, simply put, is the universal method of comparing hotel productivity regardless of product type, location, and size.

The last primary component of a forecast is to determine arrivals and departures. Forecasting arrivals and departures is close to the process of determining availability. Arrivals are based on reservations already on the books, plus anticipated walk-ins and early arrivals, less early departures and "no-shows." Forecasting departures is a little different. The hotel's house count, which was reviewed earlier, now comes into play. Departures can be forecasted based on the following formula:

Previous night's house count
plus
Current day's arrivals
minus
Current night's house count
equals
Current day's departures

(This formula can be applied to any date in the future once the house count and arrivals have been determined.)

Forecasting Factors

Forecasting is a time-sensitive process. Forecasting in reservations is analogous to weather forecasting. With predicting weather, the farther out the forecast, the less accurate it becomes. This is due to the many variables in weather patterns. Hard, quantifiable data become less prevalent. The same can be said about reservations forecasts. The reservations forecast is quite accurate in the short term, and less so in the long term. Weather forecasts also use history in much the same way reservations forecasts do. Looking back at weather patterns for the same date in past years can be a good starting point for future forecasts. Reservations historical data can be viewed in the same way.

History in Forecasting. History plays a big part in forecasting future occupancies. The quality of historic data is critical. Having the ability to look back in time and see how many corporate rates were typically booked on a Tuesday in March will be very helpful. Also, knowing that this same date last year had the biggest snowstorm of the year will help the manager know not to view the data as typical. Historical transient data is best reflected in the transient booking cycle. Questions like "How far out from arrival are transient rates booked?" and "Is the hotel in that window of opportunity now, or was it already missed?" are mirrored in the transient booking cycle. Figure 12-10 illustrates a transient booking cycle analysis for a sample hotel. The number of rooms booked was low 60 or more days before arrival, but it increased dramatically within a 30-day window. But close analysis shows that not every month was the same. Each month had a slightly different booking cycle. Some reflected a farther out cycle, whereas others were more short term.

History, of course, cannot be used as a forecasting tool for newly built hotels. Although new hotel managers make use of some tools at their disposal (namely, citywide convention calendar of events, call around shopping, and future group bookings), the benefits of history do not come into play. It is for

	Actual	Days From Arrival					
		15 Days	**30 Days**	**45 Days**	**60 Days**	**75 Days**	**90 Days**
January	723	592	402	319	200	97	79
February	1772	1451	1044	551	347	219	175
March	3324	3304	2706	2035	1602	1109	779
April	2912	2992	3010	2577	1723	1350	1009
May	2383	2415	2292	1670	1176	831	545
June	2465	2356	1998	1920	1489	956	815
July	4425	4479	4472	3384	2391	1386	1193
August	4039	4060	3621	3054	2585	1940	1567
September	1624	1601	1697	1475	1050	766	602
October	1899	1842	1601	1221	873	625	466
November	1796	1699	1385	581	307	199	92
December	1286	1201	1051	599	420	186	101
Total	28648	27992	25279	19386	14163	9664	7423

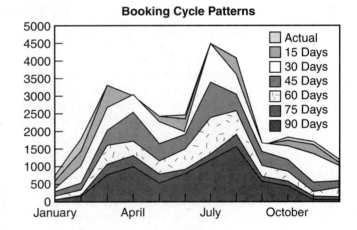

FIGURE **12-10**

Transient booking cycle

this reason that new hotel forecasts are generally not very accurate for the first 12 months of operation.

There are several factors to consider when forecasting occupied rooms. The rooms-on-the-books figure is the best place to start. This is a combination of group and transient rooms. Booking cycle analysis provides the transient data. The group data are forecasted a little differently. With group history, the data are specific to each group. That means that unless the hotel books the exact same groups, on the exact same dates, and for the exact same number of rooms, the data won't be accurate enough to use in a forecast. Group history can be an aid to the forecast, but it cannot stand alone. History for specific groups is useful for the group salespeople in their booking analyses (e.g., how many sleeping rooms are typically contributed by the group). But for a forecast, the director of transient sales must complete a group rooms worksheet.

Group Rooms Worksheet. The **group rooms worksheet** is a tool the reservations department uses to aid in forecasting. It breaks down each booked group's characteristics. Figure 12-11 shows a sample worksheet.

A tremendous amount of information is contained within the group worksheet. For a given week, each group is listed, and the information relevant to a forecast is highlighted. The first column lists basic information such as the group name, market code, the start date, the reservation method, and responsible salesperson:

Worksheet Example		Information Provided
Group:	**Sunny Tours**	Group name
Code:	**Sun**	Market code
Start Date:	**4/17**	The date the group arrives
Res Meth:	**List**	Reservation method
Salesp.	**John**	Group salesperson responsible for the booking

The reservation method is a very important piece of information. There are three primary ways a group can make reservations. (1) Rooming list—simply a list of names provided by the group indicating who and how many will require sleeping rooms. Typically, hotels will require a rooming list before the **cutoff date**. The cutoff date is the last possible date the hotel can hold contracted rooms for a group before releasing them. The cutoff date is required to give the hotel advance notice of how many rooms the group will utilize. If a group will not need as many rooms as contracted, the hotel still has time to fill them using the yield management strategies available to reservations. Therefore, the cutoff date often mirrors a hotel's transient booking cycle. A resort may impose a cutoff date of up to 60 days in advance, whereas an airport hotel may require a 30-day cutoff. (2) Individual call in—another way group guests can make reservations is by calling directly into the hotel reservations department. The reservations staff is made aware of the group booking by the sales department and inputs into their computer system how many rooms are being held and what the rate is. The same requirements regarding adherence to cutoff dates apply here as well. Some hotels feel the call-in method puts undue demands on the reservations staff, by taking them away from transient reservations. Other hotels think they get a better "feel" for the nature of a group by speaking to the members directly. (3) Reservation cards—the least used method of reserving group rooms is by mailing in **reservation cards**. A reservation card is a preprinted form that group guests would fill out to make reservations. The guest would supply name, arrival/departure dates, and any special requests. This method is time-consuming, and the cards risk getting lost in the mail.

FIGURE **12-11**

Group rooms worksheet

ABC Hotel Group Worksheet
Week of 4/17/00

Group Info	Type	Sat. 4/17 Rooms	4/17 GST	Sun. 4/18 Rooms	4/18 GST	Mon. 4/19 Rooms	4/19 GST	Tue. 4/20 Rooms	4/20 GST	Wed. 4/21 Rooms	4/21 GST	Thu. 4/22 Rooms	4/22 GST	Fri. 4/23 Rooms	4/23 GST	Revenue	Comments
Group: **Sunny Tours**	Blocked	10		10		10										Total Rooms: 24	Series group.
Code: **Sun**	Booked	8		8		8										Avg. Rate: $99.00	Double Occ.
Start Date: **4/17**	Forecast	7	14	7	14	7	14									Total Revenue: $2,376	
Res Meth: **List**	Actual		14														
Salesp: **John**	Arrivals	7															
Group: **123 Tools**	Blocked			30		30										Total Rooms: 60	Repeat
Code: **Tool**	Booked			30		30										Avg. Rate: $125.00	group.
Start Date: **4/18**	Forecast			28	28	28	28									Total Revenue: $7,500	
Res Meth: **Ind**	Actual			28	28												
Salesp: **Sally**	Arrivals			28													
Group: **Model Club**	Blocked			10												Total Rooms: 5	SMERF
Code: **Mdl**	Booked			5												Avg. Rate: $89.00	Group. high
Start Date: **4/18**	Forecast			5	10											Total Revenue: $445.00	no-show
Res Meth: **List**	Actual			5	10												factor
Salesp: **John**	Arrivals																
Group: **Smith Gears**	Blocked							125		125		125				Total Rooms: 360	High outlet
Code: **Smth**	Booked							120		120		120				Avg. Rate: $109.00	usage
Start Date: **4/20**	Forecast							120	135	120	135	120	135			Total Revenue: $39,240	
Res Meth: **Ind**	Actual																
Salesp: **Sally**	Arrivals							120	135								
Group: **Math Assoc.**	Blocked											55		55		Total Rooms: 110	Group of
Code: **Mth**	Booked											55		55		Avg. Rate: $118.00	teachers
Start Date: **4/22**	Forecast											35	35	35	35	Total Revenue: $12,980	
Res Meth: **Ind**	Actual											35	35				
Salesp: **Bill**	Arrivals																
Group: **Jones Wedding**	Blocked													15		Total Rooms: 7	Wedding on
Code: **Jns**	Booked													7		Avg. Rate: $79.00	Saturday
Start Date: **4/23**	Forecast													6	12	Total Revenue: $553	
Res Meth: **Ind**	Actual													6	12		
Salesp: **John**	Arrivals																

Worksheet Example	Information Provided
Blocked	Number of rooms set aside for group
Booked	Number of rooms actually booked
Forecast	Hotel's estimate on actual usage
Actual	Actual numbers are completed after the group departs. It will become the foundation of history for future bookings of the group.
Arrivals	How many of the group are due to arrive that day

The second column lists information pertaining to the number of rooms being held for the group. A **group block** is the number of rooms the hotel is contractually required to provide a group. (The group base of rooms at any one time is made up of all the group blocks.) The blocked number in the worksheet reflects the group block. The booked number shows how many actual group reservations were made. This figure may be lower or higher than the blocked number due to the demand of the group participants. If the group demand or "pick up" exceeds the block, it is up to the director of transient sales to decide if and how far over their block the group can go. The forecasted number takes several factors into consideration. First it looks at the group's specific history (if applicable). Knowing how many rooms this specific group utilized in the past gives a good indication of how they might do in the future. Second, it looks at the slippage factor. **Slippage** is the term used when analyzing the group room performance. It is the difference between what is contracted and what actually arrives. Often, what is contracted for is not realized. Hotels know this, and they make forecasts that reflect it. Slippage is actually the group equivalent to the transient wash factors discussed earlier. The reservation method can be a good indicator of potential slippage. The rooming list is a very good indicator of how many rooms the group will bring in. Because the attendees are "prescreened" (i.e., committed verbally or in writing to the meeting planner) before they are placed on the rooming list, they are more likely to arrive. The individual call-in method tends to "slip" more than the rooming list method because control is taken out of the planner's hands. In this method, individuals must be counted on to make their own reservations. The reservation card methods tend to have slippage factors even greater than the call in method. Filling out a card and mailing it in takes more time than calling in does. As a general rule, the following figures apply when determining slippage based on the reservation method:

Reservation Method	Slippage Percentage
Individual call in	10 to 15
Rooming list	5 to 10
Reservation cards	15 to 20

Slippage is an important factor to consider when determining yield strategy. The reservations department must accurately determine group slippage if it is to engage in overselling. Mismanagement of group room performance can adversely affect yield management results.

			Sat. Rooms	4/17 GST
Group:	**Sunny Tours**	Blocked	10	
Code:	**Sun**	Booked	8	
Start Date:	**4/17**	Forecast	7	14
Res Meth:	**List**	Actual		
Salesp.	**John**	Arrivals	7	14

In this example, the group "Sunny Tours" has contracted for 10 rooms, but actually reserved 8. The hotel forecasts 7 actually used based on the criteria discussed earlier. The GST figure is how many people are expected. This group shows that there will be twice as many guests as there are rooms, so obviously all the rooms are double occupancy. The number of guests is important to the forecast because the outlets and other areas of the hotel need to know what the potential demand may be.

Revenue		Comments
Total Rooms:	24	
Avg. Rate:	$99.00	Series group.
Total Revenue:	$2,376	Double Occ.

Each group is summarized at the end by tallying the total number of rooms and the total revenue generated by the group (rooms multiplied by average rate). Comments from the salesperson are included that may help in the forecast. Here, "Sunny Tours" was noted as a series group. That knowledge may provide solid history, assuming that the group has been there several times in the past.

Contract Rooms. A variation of the group booking is called the contract room. Airlines, for example, have certain cities they fly to most frequently (called hubs). These cities often become the final leg for a certain flight crew. The flight crew (pilots and flight attendants) fly together throughout the day on various flights. The Federal Aviation Administration puts strict limits on the length and duration of flights a crew may undertake in a day. Hotels in these hub cities are needed for overnight accommodations.

Airport location types are the most obvious first choice for these accommodations. Flight crews aboard long-distance flights or long-haul flights (e.g., Asia to Europe) may be mandated a certain number of days between shifts. They may prefer to have their accommodations in areas with several dining and recreational options, thus downtown and suburban location types may be options as well.

Because the flight schedules are known far in advance, the airline will negotiate with a hotel in that hub city for a certain amount of rooms each night. This block of rooms, called **contract rooms**, are set aside for the airline each and every night, whether they are occupied or not. The airline benefits in that they have guaranteed accommodations that do not require reservations. No rooming list is needed; the airline manages the assignment of rooms instead of the hotel.

Each night the flight crews may be different, but the number of rooms needed will remain the same. This is because airlines schedule flights based on the demand to certain cities. This demand equates to a specific number of seats. Knowing this, airlines schedule specific types of aircraft for each flight that can accommodate the required number of seats. These aircraft will each have a specific number of personnel in the flight crew. It is that number that the airline uses to determine the number of contract rooms needed.

The airline is billed directly for the rooms, so the flight crews do not have to pay for the rooms out of pocket. The hotel benefits in that the airline pays for all these rooms each night. In exchange for this guaranteed occupancy, the airline will receive a drastically reduced rate. Often, that rate is marginally above room cost. In some states, contract rooms are exempt from certain taxes because they are considered a form of housing, not lodging. Occupancy taxes, which are added to a room rate by the state or local government, do not apply to long-term, temporary housing, such as apartments. Contract rooms can be viewed as long-term temporary housing as well. Those tax savings are passed on to the airlines. Other organizations, such as overnight delivery companies, bus companies, and cruise lines may use contract rooms.

In regards to forecasting, contract rooms must be accounted for. Because these rooms are set aside each night, they have the effect of removing that number of rooms from inventory at the hotel. In essence, contract rooms shrink the size of a hotel. They are included in the forecast a little differently than regular groups. Because they are guaranteed and paid for, the hotel cannot release any unused rooms. Therefore, there is no reduction in what is forecast. The number of contracted rooms must be listed as occupied. The group rooms worksheet will reflect contract rooms as illustrated in Figure 12-12.

ABC Hotel Group Worksheet
Week of 4/17/00

Contract	Status	Sat. 4/17 Rooms	4/17 GST	Sun. 4/18 Rooms	4/18 GST	Mon. 4/19 Rooms	4/19 GST	Tue. 4/20 Rooms	4/20 GST	Wed. 4/21 Rooms	4/21 GST	Thu. 4/22 Rooms	4/22 GST	Fri. 4/23 Rooms	4/23 GST	Revenue	Comments
	Blocked	10		10		10		10		10		10		10		**Total Rooms: 70**	
	Booked	10		10		10		10		10		10		10		**Avg. Rate: $49.00**	
Group: **Sunny Tours**	Blocked															Total Rooms: 24	Series group.
Code: **Sun**	Booked	8		8		8										Avg. Rate: $99.00	Double Occ.
Start Date: **4/17**	Forecast	7	14	7	14	7	14									Total Revenue: $2,376	
Res Meth: **List**	Actual	7	14														
Salesp: **John**	Arrivals	7	14														
Group: **123 Tools**	Blocked			30		30										Total Rooms: 60	Repeat
Code: **Tool**	Booked			30		30										Avg. Rate: $125.00	group.
Start Date: **4/18**	Forecast			28	28	28	28									Total Revenue: $7,500	
Res Meth: **Ind**	Actual			28	28												
Salesp: **Sally**	Arrivals			28	28												
Group: **Model Club**	Blocked			10												Total Rooms: 5	SMERF
Code: **Mdl**	Booked			5												Avg. Rate: $89.00	Group. high
Start Date: **4/18**	Forecast			5	10											Total Revenue: $445.00	no-show
Res Meth: **List**	Actual			5													factor
Salesp: **John**	Arrivals			5	10												
Group: **Smith Gears**	Blocked							125		125		125				Total Rooms: 360	High outlet
Code: **Smth**	Booked							120		120		120				Avg. Rate: $109.00	usage
Start Date: **4/20**	Forecast							120	135	120	135	120	135			Total Revenue: $39,240	
Res Meth: **Ind**	Actual							120	135								
Salesp: **Sally**	Arrivals							120	135								
Group: **Math Assoc.**	Blocked											55		55		Total Rooms: 110	Group of
Code: **Mth**	Booked											55		55		Avg. Rate: $118.00	teachers
Start Date: **4/22**	Forecast											35	35	35	35	Total Revenue: $12,980	
Res Meth: **Ind**	Actual											35	35				
Salesp: **Bill**	Arrivals																
Group: **Jones Wedding**	Blocked													15		Total Rooms: 7	Wedding on
Code: **Jns**	Booked													7		Avg. Rate: $79.00	Saturday
Start Date: **4/23**	Forecast													6	12	Total Revenue: $553	
Res Meth: **Ind**	Actual													6			
Salesp: **John**	Arrivals													6	12		

FIGURE **12-12**

Contract rooms

Completing Forecasts

Once the group data are gathered, it is combined with transient data to create the reservations forecast. There are several types of forecast; each is generated based on a specific time period. As was discussed earlier, the best forecasts are short-term. The farther out the forecast, the less accurate it becomes. Hotels differ as to which time periods they forecast, but most commonly, forecasts are broken into two types: short-term and long-term.

Because short-term forecasts are understood to be the most accurate, they are the most widely used within the hotel. Crucial staffing and inventory decisions are based on these short-term forecasts. The most common time periods used in short-term forecasts are:

- 3 day
- 7 day
- 10 day
- 14 day

Figure 12-13 illustrates what a short-term 10 day forecast may look like. At a glance, this forecast supplies all the relevant group, contract, and transient data. Each department can glean from this document valuable information of the future.

10 Day Forecast
Week of 4/17/00

Day: Date:	Sat. 4/17	Sun. 4/18	Mon. 4/19	Tues. 4/20	Wed. 4/21	Thur. 4/22	Fri. 4/23	Sat. 4/24	Sun. 4/25	Mon. 4/26
Occupancy %	99%	73%	34%	39%	41%	69%	78%	90%	90%	70%
Rooms Occupied	454	336	157	179	190	319	358	414	415	318
Comp. Rooms	3	5	7	7	4	1	1	1	1	1
Guest Count	498	389	230	279	257	366	381	454	483	355
Arrivals	271	165	114	99	103	222	227	233	258	210
Departures	227	284	292	77	92	83	108	177	257	265
Group Rooms	55	20	65	100	115	93	52	35	19	79
Contract Rooms	10	10	10	10	10	10	10	10	10	10
Transient Rooms	386	301	75	62	61	215	295	368	385	228
Total Rooms Sold	451	331	150	172	186	318	357	413	414	317
Group Guests	69	32	110	150	175	105	63	45	30	99
Transient Guests	429	357	120	129	82	261	318	409	453	256

Total Revenue: $379,512.09   Average Occupancy = 73%   Rooms Sold = 3109

FIGURE **12-13**

10-day forecast

Long-term forecasts are not as useful for other departments but can be beneficial to the group and transient sales teams. Long-term forecasts are used to shed light on preliminary yield management strategies. Reservation departments use these to prepare for upcoming events. The group sales effort can see how their production is compared to expectations. There are three main types of long-term forecasts:

- 30 day (or comparable cutoff date)
- 90 day
- 12-Month Rolling-Annual Budget/Marketing Plan

The 30-day forecast is used primarily to monitor individual group pickup. At this point (assuming that 30 days is the cutoff date used), all groups should have their rooming lists in or have made all their reservations via call in or reservation cards. Groups that do not have their information in can be in danger of losing their allotted rooms. Due to the transient booking cycle, it may be difficult to rebook rooms left unused. The 30-day forecast is used by the director of transient sales often to remind the group salespeople to follow up with their group(s).

The 90-day forecast is the primary yield management indicator. It is at this point that the reservations department makes their first estimate of group usage. Using the slippage and historical factors reviewed earlier, the reservations department can estimate the total number of group rooms needed. He/she can then begin to tailor yield management based on what is left to sell. If there seems to be few available rooms, the rate triggers may be set high. Too low, and no restrictions may be placed on transient booking at all. Again, in order to maximize total room revenue, the reservations and group sales departments must communicate.

FORECASTING FREQUENCY

The 30- and 90-day forecasts may be prepared more often than their time frames indicate. The 30-day forecast may been completed weekly, and the 90-day forecast may be done monthly. This will cause obvious overlaps in the days being forecast, but that is beneficial. This overlap allows for continual monitoring and revision. Trends not seen in one forecast may be picked up in another. Waiting 30 to 90 days between forecasts may cause the hotel to miss recent developments (e.g., a group cancellation or new booking). Continual revisions also allow for checks of the competition and their pricing strategies. Adjustments to a hotel's yield management may be warranted if it is known that competitors are sold out in advance. A hotel can certainly "drive rate" in those circumstances.

FORECASTING IMPORTANCE

Forecasting can have an impact on more than just the hotel. Hotels in a chain, for example, will forward their forecasts to their regional controllers for compilation. These controllers, in turn, combine their forecasts into one complete chainwide forecast. That forecast reflects how the chain as a whole will perform. Publicly traded companies, like Hilton and Starwood, report these forecasts to Wall Street. Industry analysts with organizations such as Morgan Stanley, Solomon Smith Barney, and FirstCall Financial will make recommendations on the chain's stock based on these forecasts. Chains that do not meet projections based on forecasted numbers may see their stock price drop as a result. Therefore, the hotel forecast must always be as accurate as possible.

The last-long range forecast goes by many names. Its primary use is to assist in planning for the annual budget, or **marketing plan**. A marketing plan is a document put together by a hotel's senior management to chart a course for the next year. It summarizes departmental goals, advertising schedules, financial targets, and market conditions. Also referred to as the "budget," the marketing plan is created each year at the same time to determine how the hotel will perform in the coming year. This can be done on a fiscal or annual year basis. This forecast helps lay the groundwork for the sleeping room portion of the budget. Using historical data and other tools, this forecast provides management with a starting point for the marketing plan.

RESERVATION SALES MANAGEMENT

The data collection and analysis role of the director of transient sales is important to any hotel. The other crucial role he or she plays is managing the reservations sales team. A properly managed reservations department will maximize transient room revenue using the tools reviewed earlier. Managing the transient sales effort requires proper staffing, training, call management, and sales strategy.

Staffing

Staffing and scheduling are critical in reservations. Within the reservations department, the director is the leader. In large and mega-hotels, a reservations manager may also be on staff. Reporting to these managers are staff reservations agents, also called "reservationists." The agents must implement all the yield management strategies laid out by management. The reservations staff may consist of just two or three agents, or a few dozen. This is one of the few departments where the daily occupancy of the hotel does not effect staffing levels. The reservations department is proactively booking rooms, so they are not affected by occupancy as are the reactive departments (i.e., housekeeping, outlets, and ancillary revenue sources). These departments rely on the forecasts generated by reservations to determine their staffing levels.

Hours of operation in reservations must be reflective of the hotel's calling audience. A missed call equates to missed revenues. If the hotel is physically located on the west coast but has a large east coast customer base, the time zone difference must be taken into consideration. The general "rule of thumb" for reservations staffing is to adhere to prime selling time. **Prime selling time** is defined as the specific hours during the day when the transient guests are most likely to call in for a reservation. Figure 12-14 illustrates the traditional peak-demand hours. Prime selling time will differ from hotel to hotel based on their group versus transient mix and traditional booking cycle. Weekends and evenings may require reservations staff because those are also times when transient reservations are made. Another factor to consider in staffing is the hotel's advertising schedules. Special packages, discounts, and other promotions may increase volume during their runs.

The number of agents required is dependent on these call volumes. Reservation calls are routed to available agents via an **automated call distributor (ACD)**. The ACD monitors the available and busy extensions and routes the calls accordingly. All good ACD systems produce call volume reports at regular intervals. The director of transient sales or the reservations manager will review those reports frequently, as often as every hour. The data in those reports identifies how long calls are kept waiting, among other things. Armed with this data, proper staffing and scheduling will fall into place.

FIGURE **12-14**

Prime selling time

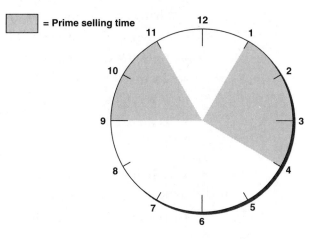

Training

The reservations department is often viewed as an extension of the sales department. Each call is a sales opportunity. Not long ago, reservation agents were viewed as nothing more than operators or order takers. Those days are long gone. The amount of transient revenue that is produced in reservations is unquestionable. When hiring for reservations, a sales or customer service background is preferred. People can be taught software systems, but it is much harder to teach someone to be enthusiastic, friendly, and eager to please. A good phone voice is also important for a reservations agent. Proper grammar usage is vital. In some markets, bilingual agents can be very valuable.

In any sales capacity, knowledge of the product is vital. Because reservations agents sell the hotel, knowledge of the facility is paramount. The ability to describe all aspects of the guest experience is needed. The agent is often the first hotel employee a guest comes in contact with. This first contact must begin the process of satisfying the guest. This time honored adage applies: "You can only make one first impression."

Firsthand product knowledge (refreshed on a regular basis) will help the agent sell the property on every call. Each agent should compile a fact sheet or computer file listing as much hotel information as needed. Some questions will come up again and again, still others may be very unique. The information for this fact sheet should include, but not be limited to, answers to the following common questions:

Food and Beverage Outlet Information

- Has the local food critic commented about the restaurant?
- Does the hotel offer buffets at set times, or based strictly on occupancy levels?
- What are the hours of operation for each outlet? Do these times change during the week or during seasonal shifts?
- Is there a dress code? What is the average cost for each meal?
- Does the Chef prepare daily specials?
- Do holiday hours differ from normal hours of operation?
- Is room service available 24 hours a day?
- Is there a happy hour?

General Hotel Information

- When was the hotel last renovated?
- Is the hotel ADA (Americans with Disabilities Act) compliant?
- Does the hotel offer automatic checkout?

- Is there a business center on site?

- Are there coffeemakers, fax machines, data ports in the rooms?

- What TV channels are available in the rooms?

- What are the hours of operation for the fitness center?

- Are children's activities available?

- Is there an airport shuttle service?

- Does the hotel participate in frequent stay programs and airline/car rental tie-ins?

- What major airlines service the local airport?

- What are the in-room amenities?

- What are the costs for roll-away beds and cribs?

- Are there any nearby restaurants or attractions and what are their costs and hours of operation?

- Who owns the hotel? What are the names of the executive committee members?

- What are the directions to the hotel from major thoroughfares?

- What is the average cab fare to downtown or the airport?

- What are the phone numbers for other nearby hotels (in case of a sold-out situation)?

RESERVATION EVALUATIONS

Employing an evaluation system via mystery callers is an excellent way to provide objective feedback to reservations agents. Sometimes called "shops," these test calls can be made at various times over a given period. The agents are evaluated on how they handled the call, and other criteria deemed appropriate by the director. Need areas or weaknesses can be identified based on these test calls. Constructive retraining may be required if the need is identified. As part of the hotel's training program, agents are made aware of the existence of these test calls and are told to always expect them. These test calls are sometimes made by other managers in the hotel, or by a professional outside evaluator. The agents are made aware of their individual evaluations after results have been tabulated. Team scores can be shared and used as part of an incentive program.

The training of reservations agents should be ongoing. Some progressive hotels allow their agents to work in other departments from time to time. The ability to learn other jobs within the hotel can be rewarding to the employee and valuable to the hotel. Referred to as **crosstraining**, this allows the agents to learn and grow professionally, at the same time expanding their hotel knowledge. Crosstraining is also valuable to the hotel because it creates a pool of multiskilled employees who can be used in other departments as needed. Reservations agents, simply by the nature of their work and their familiarity with PMS's, often serve as backup staff to the front desk. The reservations department can also crosstrain other employees in transient sales.

Call Management

The ACD system aids the director of transient sales in managing call volume, but it also can aid in other measurements. Reservations agents are measured in their ability to make a reservation on every call. The ACD system can provide data specific to each phone extension, thus each agent. The ACD data are limited to the length and scope of the call, but it cannot measure what is said on each call. These ACD data, coupled with other tools, are used to measure the productivity and efficiency of the agents.

The ACD data most useful to the director of transient sales are call length, wait time, and dropped calls. Call length is important because long calls preclude agents from taking other incoming calls. It is for that reason that agents are taught to keep calls as short as possible, without rushing the guest. Wait time is a good measurement of demand versus staffing. If people are waiting a long time to reach an agent, then more staff might be necessary. Wait time can also related to call length. If it is determined that staffing levels are appropriate based on historical data, but wait time is going up, it is a logical assumption that the staff are taking longer with each call. Dropped calls (sometimes referred to as abandoned calls) are the number of people who simply got tired of waiting and hung up. This obviously is detrimental to any hotel. As a percentage of all calls, most hotels strive to reach a dropped call level of 2.5 percent or less.

Some hotels try to make use of the wait time. Hotels may incorporate a recorded message into their ACD system. Recorded messages that inform the guest of the hotel's products and services begins the sales process before they ever speak to an agent. They can be a good way of creating interest in the outlets and ancillary services. Messages that ask the caller to "please wait" and that reinforce that "your call is important to the hotel" are common. Other hotels have moved away from these recorded messages. Data from several customer focus groups have revealed that guests feel that the messages are redundant and somewhat intrusive. Many people do not want to be "sold to" while on hold. Hotels run the risk of increasing their dropped call volume as well with messages because once a message repeats, the caller senses that they have been on hold longer than the hotel may have intended.

Although the ACD data are useful, they do not provide a complete picture of the agents' productivity and efficiency. The primary measurement for all reservations agents is called the **conversion ratio**. The conversion ratio is defined as the number of transient bookings made versus the number of calls received. The conversion ratio is sometimes referred to as the "closure rate." Because the ACD can list how many calls came in to an agent's extension, and the PMS computer can list each reservation made, a simple calculation can be made to determine conversion. A good agent has an average closure rate of 45 percent or more. An agent's ability to close every call with a booking is paramount to their success. Another important measurement is the agent's ability to upsell. **Upselling** is the ability to move a guest from a lower-priced product to a higher-priced product. The ability to convince a guest to reserve a suite versus a regular room is a good example. Upselling is difficult to measure. Because so much is done verbally on a reservations call, it is hard to document the act of upselling. The best way to track upselling is to measure the number of "regular" rooms available at the time of the call. If lower-priced rooms are available, but the agent convinced the caller to buy a higher-priced room, then a good job of upselling was done. Upselling is not done when the only remaining available room is a high-priced suite. The director of transient sales will use a **reservations map** to determine what types of rooms are available and when they are available. These maps can show specific room numbers and their availability for specific dates. The agents themselves also use other types of reservations maps to check availability of certain room types, designations, and configurations. Figure 12-15 illustrates what a room number reservations map may look like.

MOTIVATION

Motivating reservations agents goes beyond effective training and strong leadership. Some type of incentive compensates the group sales department within every hotel in part, or in whole. Just as the sales managers sell group rooms, reservations agents sell transient rooms. As stated before, the transient sales effort is viewed as an extension of the group sales effort. Therefore, reservation agents should be given some type of incentive to sell transient rooms. Incentive programs run the gamut from upsell programs, to conversion programs, to revenue production programs. Return on investment should be measured with any incentive program. Although cash is usually the number one incentive for most people, other "soft dollar incentives" can be appreciated. Soft dollar incentives are those goods or services the hotel itself can offer. Those can include a weekend stay at the hotel, a membership in the health club, dinner in the restaurant, or something similar.

ABC Hotel Reservations Map
(room number specific)

Room Number	Date							
	2/4/01	2/5/01	2/6/01	2/7/01	2/8/01	2/9/01	2/10/01	2/11/01
100	..	..	..	..	..	..	..	..
101	IN	**	**	..	..	..	..	..
102	..	..	IN	**	**	**	**	
103	..	..	..	..	..	..	..	..
104	..	IN	**	**	..	..	..	..
105	..	..	..	..	..	..	..	..
106	..	..	##	##	##	##	##	..
107	..	..	##	##	##	##	##	..
108	..	..	##	##	##	##	##	..
109	..	..	##	##	##	##	##	..
110	..	..	..	..	..	..	..	..

Screen Icon	Meaning
..	Indicates the room is not reserved for anyone, thus it is available
IN	Indicates the room is being checked into that day
**	Indicates the room is occupied on that day
##	Indicates the room is out of inventory for that day (out of order)

Figure **12-15**

Reservations map

Proper call management includes knowing what to say on the phone. The phone call is the primary transient avenue to any hotel. Although faxes play a minor role and the Internet is arguably growing in its role as a transient avenue, the phone remains the dominant method of making a reservation. It is for that reason that the agents must have a good speaking voice and know how to speak eloquently. A reservations agent must be able to communicate and use a computer at the same time. A quality call results when the agent communicates with the guest and uses the computer seamlessly.

There are a few rules most successful agents follow to ensure a quality call. Certain words and questions help ensure conversion and limit call length. The mannerisms and tone of the agent can literally "make or break" the call. The actual words used will differ from agent to agent and hotel to hotel. It is important to allow differing personalities to show through. There are, however, certain basic qualifying questions each agent should cover and a few "do's and don'ts" all agents should remember.

The purpose of asking qualifying questions is to ensure that the agent understands the guest's needs. The agent needs to ask the proper questions to give the front desk and other front office departments as much information as possible. The check-in process will be smoother for the guest if relevant data are accurate. Proper qualifying questions also limit call length because they immediately get to the needed information and avoid pointless questions. Basic qualifying questions include:

- *"Are you attending a group or convention?"* The purpose of this question is to ensure that the caller receives the appropriate rate and that the group gets credited with the reservation. If the reservation is not credited to the group, it may affect the hotel's forecast. The group rooms worksheet must reflect accurate group pickup.

- *"How many people in your party?"* This question alerts the agent to quote a rate based on the room occupancy. The proper rate designation that applies to doubles, triples, and quads can be quoted accurately.

- *"Are you a member of our frequent stay program?"* This question may remind the caller that there are other benefits to staying with this particular hotel.

- *"Have you stayed with us before?"* Most PMS's store previous guest information. Called guest history, this information, if managed properly, can alert the hotel to guest preferences. By asking this question, the agent may be able to check on a favorite room, or know ahead of time that the guest will require a crib, and other special needs.

- *"Do you prefer smoking or nonsmoking?"* Again, a question to provide a better sleeping room experience.

- *"What is your estimated time of arrival?"* This question is asked on behalf of other departments within the front office. The front desk can allocate the first vacant/ready rooms to the guests arriving earlier than others. The bellstand will need to know arrival times to staff properly.

- *"What credit card would you like to use?"* This question serves two purposes: (1) It makes each reservation a guaranteed reservation. This is the preferred type of reservation because it is confirmed. The agent should follow this question with a notice of the hotel's guaranteed reservation policy. (2. Providing a credit card during the reservation process makes the check-in process quicker because guests do not have to produce the card. They can simply leave their charges on the card number provided.

- *"Let me reverify this information for you."* Though not actually a qualifying question per se, this statement allows the agent to go back and verify the accuracy of each of the other questions. This statement also begins the closure process by cementing the sale in the mind of the guest.

Over time, most agents develop unique ways of asking qualifying questions. Individual style helps to keep the process more human and less structured. Throughout a reservations call, the agents may find themselves answering questions instead of asking them. This is an important part of the reservations agent's role. It is why hotels spend so much time on training and educating agents on the facility itself. This is again where individual personality and style enhance the guest experience. There are, however, certain phrases that agents should avoid. Some "do's and don'ts":

Don't Say	Do Say
I don't know.	*I'll be happy to check on that for you.*
We are oversold.	*We are sold to capacity.*
I can't confirm a king bed room.	*I would be happy to request a king for you.*
This computer system is new, and I don't know it well.	*My computer is down right now, please bear with me.*
We still have many rooms available.	*We are filling up, but I am confident we have a room for you.*
Bye.	*Thank you for calling the ABC Hotel.*

Other "rules of thumb" include avoidance of silence. Dead air can lead to confusion and hesitancy in the guest. Agents should make conversation as best they can. The only time silence is acceptable is after a rate quote. Once a rate is quoted, the guest may need time to consider it. Inexperienced agents perceive this silence as reluctance and quickly jump in with a lower rate. This should be avoided. Another tool for agents is to quickly give their first name upon greeting the caller. This begins a rapport-building process that will make the rest of the call much easier.

A canned-speech type of selling is quickly picked up on by callers. A conversational tone adds a personal touch and allows the agent to tailor his or her approach to each caller's needs. The best way to tailor a sell is to begin by asking open-ended questions. Open-ended questions are those that require more than a one-word answer. "What brings you to the hotel?" is an open-ended question that will also alert the agent to the guest's goal. The guest may be attending a convention or might be looking for a romantic anniversary getaway. The proper group rate or "honeymoon" package would be appropriate rate quotes in those cases. These qualifying questions help zero in on what the caller wants, reduce call length, and improve the conversion ratio.

Recapping the reservation with the caller is a step the agent never wants to skip. Verifying the name spelling, restating the arrival and departure day and date, repeating the room type and room rate, and confirming the method of guarantee can avoid customer service issues down the road. A caller may initially state a need for a two-night stay, but when recapping with day and date, the guest may find his/her own error. Misspelling a name is also a common way to create problems. An example of this might occur on a sold-out night when a guest is turned away as not holding a reservation, when in fact the agent simply misspelled it.

Arguably the most important point in a reservation call comes at the end. This is the time where a decision must be made. The reservations agent must always ask for the business. Many times, the caller is ready to make a decision, but the agent either doesn't ask for the booking or offers another option or a lower rate. A caller's silence doesn't always mean they do not want to book a room. Agents must give callers the time to absorb the information provided, and then ask for the booking. When objections do arise, savvy agents come armed with useful answers. "Do your rooms have Jacuzzi's?" could be answered with "No, unfortunately none of the hotels in our area have them. We do have a hot tub in the pool area however." This reply has provided the guest with both a reason to stay at the hotel even though there were no Jacuzzis and a reason not to bother calling the competition. Directors of transient sales should implement role-playing exercises into ongoing training sessions. Making agents aware of different types of objections is a great way to get accustomed to them. Overcoming objections virtually ensures a high closure rate.

Sales Strategy

By providing reservations agents the tools of training and education, and enhancing that with motivation techniques, the director of transient sales can be confident that the hotel's vision is being implemented. Proper call management allows the director to verify that each agent shares the vision. That vision, the primary driver of all activities in reservations, is the transient sales strategy. The transient sales strategy embodies all the aspects of reservations management learned in this chapter, from determining availability and over-selling, to yield management and forecasting. The implementation of all these concepts in an effort to maximize transient room revenue is the primary goal.

There are several different selling strategies when it comes to reservation sales. The "top down" strategy is the most widely used. This strategy has the agent quoting a rate for the hotel's best room type (i.e., most expensive) and moving down to a lower rate if not accepted. This strategy is used in situations where the hotel wants to drive rate. It is not successful in a highly competitive market with low guest room demand. It is successful, though, when buyer confidence is high. **Buyer confidence** is defined as a hotel guest's predetermined desire to book a room at a hotel at almost any cost. Buyer confidence prepares the caller to expect a higher price because of preconceived notions about the hotel. Hotels with a reputation for high quality and service invoke buyer confidence.

The "bottom up" strategy is just the opposite of the "top down" strategy. The agent begins by quoting a rate corresponding to the lowest room type (least attractive or least expensive of the available rooms). The agent then lets the caller know that better rooms (i.e., more expensive) are also available. The agents inform the guest of the incremental rate increases corresponding to the next level of guest room. This bottom-up strategy is also called "menu quoting" because it gives the caller a choice of different rate options. This strategy is the best way for agents to upsell. As each successive rate is quoted, the agents have another opportunity to convince the caller that this is the room type or configuration best suited for them. The bottom-up strategy is also successful when buyer confidence is low. Guests who do not feel a specific need to stay at any hotel may have low buyer confidence. Guests simply looking for the lowest rate, called rate shopping, may not give an agent the time to upsell to the next level of rooms. Agents using this method must be careful not to convey any room type as inferior, as can happen in aggressive attempts to upsell.

The "mid-range" strategy suggests that the agent quote a rate from middle room type, going either up or down a tier based on acceptance or opposition of the guest. Agents using this strategy have the flexibility to tailor their approach to the guest and the progress of the call. Experienced agents are best suited for this strategy, because it requires experience and the ability to implement either the top-down or bottom-up strategy as needed.

Different agents may have varying success with each strategy. It is usually best to allow the latitude to find the selling method best suited for each agent. This would not apply, of course, if the hotel's yield management strategy dictated a specific course of action (e.g., drive rate or increase occupancy). The director of transient sales should make every effort to inform the reservations agents when changes in strategy will occur. If new rate triggers are to be imposed, agents should be informed—to avoid surprises.

INDUSTRY PERSPECTIVE

Yield Management in Practice

Glenda Arnold
Director of Reservations
Indianapolis Marriott North

Supply versus demand is the basic discipline behind yield management. To take the fixed amount of inventory (supply) and to determine the guests' needs to utilize that inventory (demand) is the objective of yield management. To exhaust the maximum amount of inventory available and to realize maximize dollar value of that inventory is the goal.

We use all pertinent information at hand, such as current pace trends, historical data, group activity, city events, competitors' rates, and availability—are all valuable tools in determining whether there is a need to yield the available supply. For example, if there is a slow demand time and inventory is abundant, every opportunity should be left open for the guest to book rooms at a rate that is "market friendly"—in other words, open your doors to allow everyone in you can! If there is a high demand time and inventory is limited, it then becomes beneficial to sell rooms based on more rigid guidelines such as minimum length stays and at more lucrative rates such as concierge or rack. Most hotels offer a variety of rates to accommodate the budgetary needs of various customers. Groups may offer a discounted rate based on a volume booking; negotiated rates are offered to corporations based on estimated yearly volume; special interest groups such as government employees and special member organizations may also have a preferred rate. In addition, there is typically a general population rate or corporate rate offered. Deciding which rates to offer, and on which days of the week, is all part of the yield process. There are occasions when it may be necessary to actually slow down the booking process because of a "peak night" situation. Typically, in a corporate environment hotel, Tuesday and Wednesday nights are considered peak nights. Those are the most often utilized nights for business travelers. To prevent filling only those nights and to prevent guests who want to arrive prior and depart after those nights, it may be necessary to put restrictions on the Tuesday and/or Wednesday to accept only multiple-night stays and at a higher rate. This method of yield management helps to even out the pattern of arrivals and departures, thus increasing revenues and occupancy.

(continued)

Watching the trends, booking pace, and nonprice turndowns is critical in understanding whether the restrictions for booking are too aggressive or too lenient. Changes to the booking guidelines and/or rates may need to be made daily to achieve optimal revenues.

Yielding inventory for special events such as the Indianapolis 500 Race, Brickyard 400, and Formula One is typically managed a little differently than day-to-day reservations. Where there may be an offering of multiple rates on an average day, there may be only one rate offered during a special event. Whether the reservation is booked as part of a group or as an individual, the criteria for booking are the same.

There is greater opportunity to increase revenues during special events because the basic principle is the same—supply versus demand. Special events draw attention, so the demand for inventory is greater. Much more rigid booking requirements such as prepay/nonrefundable packages and multiple-night stays may be put into place to guarantee the anticipated or even budgeted revenues.

Knowing your competitors' rates, booking requirements, and availability is important in helping to decide if your rates and requirements are "in line" with what the market will bear. Historical data, as well as current trends, are valuable in making an informed decision. Of course, it is important to balance that information with the profitability margin expected at your hotel to set the rate.

The simplest (but not necessarily the easiest) way to secure sales is to contract group bookings, which meet the predetermined requirements such as minimum stays and nonrefundable advance payments. Utilizing minimum stays ensures that throughout the event time frame, maximum revenues will be realized. Requiring nonrefundable prepayments helps to guarantee the guests' intent. During non–special event times, a reservation may be guaranteed but not prepaid. The guest simply has to call within a certain time frame to cancel without fear of penalty. During special events, and in many cases, because higher revenues have been budgeted, there is a need to prevent a mass cancellation effort and lost revenues.

For overall successful yield management, the balance between group sales and individual sales is critical. The interplay and understanding of both entities make the process of yield strategies ever changing. Being flexible and quick to react to the current trends helps to increase revenues and occupancy at an immediate

INDUSTRY PERSPECTIVE
(concluded)

level. Using all the aforementioned tools to see how future demand is trending helps in making proactive decisions for long-term growth in both revenues and occupancy. Know the market, shop the competition, watch the trends, and be flexible. Yield management can definitely make a difference to drive occupancy and increase profitability, which are the ultimate goals.

CHAPTER TWELVE **REVIEW**

KEY TERMS

history	forecasting
guaranteed no-show (GNS)	group rooms worksheet
house count	cutoff date
overselling	reservation cards
walked reservation	group block
perfect sell	slippage
yield management	contract rooms
rate restrictions	marketing plan
rate triggers	prime selling time
driving rate	automated call distributor (ACD)
closed to arrival (CTA)	crosstraining
minimum length stay (MLS)	conversion ratio
rate averaging	upselling
displacement	reservations map
series groups	buyer confidence

REVIEW QUESTIONS

1. What are the main types of length of stay restrictions? How do they work?

2. What is call management? What tools are available to the director of transient sales to aid in call management?

3. What should be done to compensate a "walked" guest?

4. What type of sell strategy should be used to drive rate?

5. What factors go into determining availability?

6. What is a house count?

7. What happens when a hotel achieves a perfect sell? How might a conservative hotel manager alter the parameters of a perfect sell?

8. Explain rate averaging. When does rate averaging not work?

9. Explain the concept of displacement.

10. How are departures calculated?

11. What are the three methods groups use to reserve rooms? What are the slippage factors historically applied to each?

12. What are the most common short-term forecasts? What are the most common long-term forecasts?

13. Explain the importance of the marketing plan.

14. Define ACD.

15. Define transient conversion ratio.

DISCUSSION QUESTIONS/EXERCISES

1. Visit any one of the major chain Web sites. Choose a location/hotel. Choose a date and check the available rates. Compare those rates to rates offered for the same hotel/date at the hotel's 800 number (central reservations). Complete the exercise by calling the hotel directly. How easy are each of these reservation avenues to use? What would cause any discrepancies in availability or rate?

2. Hotels today routinely convene meetings to review room sales strategy. The general manager, director of transient sales, director of group sales, and/or director of marketing gather weekly to review forecasts and availability. How important are meetings like this? What issues might arise?

CASE STUDY

Rooms Inventory and Forecasting #1

You are the Director of Transient Sales in the XYZ Hotel. Your property has 400 guest rooms. Engineering has taken out 2 rooms to replace faucets, 1 room to replace the carpet, and 2 rooms for general PM (preventive maintenance).

Sales has booked four groups over this night. The Association of Ironworkers has a block of 85. Their rate is $158. The Fraternal Order group has a block of 30 rooms. Their rate is $173. The Brady and Hill group is in at 72 rooms. Their rate is $163. The Red Gold Corporation has 58 rooms. Red Gold's rate is $169. You had a cancellation on a group earlier in the week that would have given you another 25 rooms at $182.

You are still 14 days out. You are expecting 197 arrivals. Your average transient rate will be $192. You are forecasting 388 rooms the night prior to this.

CASE STUDY | Rooms Inventory and Forecasting #1 *(continued)*

History tells you your groups will wash 2 percent, and you will have a 5 percent no-show factor. Count on 3 early departures, 5 stayovers, and 4 walk-ins.

You had 10 transient rooms booked, but half of those cancelled. You should expect to pick up 19 per day for the next five days, then 7 per day for the next five, and then 3 per day for the remaining days.

Fill in the chart:

Total Inventory	
Available Inventory	
Group Block	
Transient Available	
Transient Booked	
Transient Pickup	
Transient Forecast	
Arrivals	
No-shows	
Early Departures	
Stayovers	
Walk-ins	
Group Slippage	
House Count	
Vacant Rooms	
Group Revenue	
Transient Revenue	
Total Revenue	
ADR	
Occupancy Percentage	

(continued)

CASE STUDY

Rooms Inventory and Forecasting #1 *(concluded)*

Based on this data, please answer the following:

1. How many transient rooms will you forecast on this day?
2. What is the Group Revenue forecast?
3. How many departures will you have?
4. What is your ADR?
5. How many group rooms will slip?
6. What is your overall occupancy percentage?
7. What is your total rooms revenue?
8. How many more rooms do you need to fill?
9. If you filled those rooms with transient, how much more revenue would you bring in?
10. If your cost per room is $33.80, what is your profit for this night?
11. If you charge attrition on the group that cancelled, and they had an allowance of 5 percent, how much will they be charged?

CASE STUDY

Rooms Inventory and Forecasting #2

You are looking at your available inventory for the next several weeks. During a particular two-day period, you have a group base of 85/100. Your 300-room hotel historically carries transient numbers of 150/200. You have 25/45 transient rooms already on the books.

What type of rate control will you employ?

Group		
Transient		
Total		
Variance		
Rate Control		

Rooms Inventory and Forecasting #3

Labor Day weekend is still several months away. Historically you fill on Friday and Saturday, with a sharp decline on Sunday night. You have forecasted a fill all three nights this year. How do you help ensure that you meet your forecast?

Rooms Inventory and Forecasting #4

You are three weeks out, in your prime transient booking window. You are forecasting a fill over the Mon-Wed pattern. You are selling Corporate rate $169 only. A Group Sales Manager wants to put in a 30-room group at $135. This group has not been to your hotel previously, has breakfast meetings each day and off-site manufacturing plant tours each afternoon and into the evening.

What do you do?

Measuring Hotel Performance

OBJECTIVES

After reading this chapter, you should understand:

- Rev-par and market share analysis
- The differences between qualifiable and quantifiable analysis

INTRODUCTION

How can one hotel be measured against another based on the varying sizes, product types, location types, and service levels in the industry? This question has plagued hospitality professionals for years. Measuring performance is important for investors, owners, and managers. Investors need to be able to measure an individual hotel's performance in relation to the industry as a whole for many reasons—not the least of which is financial viability. Owners need to know if the hotels in their portfolio are performing up to expectations. Managers use hotel performance measurements as a yardstick of their own professional ability.

Each of the groups of people interested in measuring performance will view the information in different ways. The investors and owners may prefer to look at "hard data" (i.e., documented numbers). This is a quantifiable approach. Managers may look at other factors. Good quantifiable data may be a goal for managers as well, but how they get there is less quantifiable. The approach they use is qualifiable—that is, an approach that leaves room for interpretation.

In the end, accurate measurement of hotels involves both quantifiable and qualifiable analyses. There are two accepted forms of quantifiable analyses: rev-par and market share. The qualifiable analyses are based on the goals of management. How will a hotel's management achieve reasonable results? Because a hotel derives most of its profit and revenue from room sales, the qualifiable approaches center on filling the sleeping rooms. These managers are said to be either rate driven or occupancy driven.

QUANTIFIABLE ANALYSES

Rev-Par

Chapter 1's analysis of room cost and profit margin illustrated how the room sales component of hotels can be measured. These analyses, though tailored to the hospitality industry, are not exclusive to the industry. Cost analysis, as well as profit and loss, apply to almost every industry. The hospitality industry has developed further tools for the analysis of room sales that are exclusive to the industry. A method of comparing the room revenue from hotel to hotel is called rev-par.

Rev-par is defined as revenue per available room. This analysis allows hotels of different sizes to compare the revenue generated by the sale of sleeping rooms. Rev-par divides the total sleeping room revenue generated for a predetermined time frame by the total number of hotel rooms. Rev-par goes beyond occupancy analysis because it factors in average daily rate.

Rev-par is unique to hospitality. Because of the differing sizes of hotels, the need to compare performance on an even playing field arose. Factoring in the size of a hotel allows any hotel in a specific market mix to compare itself to another. It will be helpful to review again the common hotel-size classifications.

Common Hotel Size Classifications

Classification	Number of Sleeping Rooms
Small	1 to 150
Medium	151 to 400
Large	401 to 1,500
Mega	1,501 and over

The hotel size classification is helpful in describing the relative size of a property. Understanding that hotels of all sizes seek to compare quantifiable data, the need for rev-par analysis becomes apparent. The following example shows how rev-par is calculated.

Assume that the ABC Hotel sells a room for an average of $150.00 a night. In this example, assume that this hotel has 350 rooms.

Rev-par attempts to factor both average daily rate (ADR) and occupancy into one figure. If the ABC hotel had a 76 percent occupancy on a given night, the rev-par calculation would begin with these steps:

Step 1—Collection of data

ABC hotel has 350 rooms, an ADR of $150, and an occupancy of 76 percent.

Step 2—Revenue calculation

76 percent occupancy at a 350-room hotel translates into the sale of 266 rooms.

266 rooms multiplied by the ADR of $150 equals total room revenue of $39,900.

Step 3—Rev-par

Total room revenue of $39,900 divided by the total number of available rooms (350) equals $114.

Rev-par = $114

Rev-par = (Occupancy × ADR) ÷ Total number of rooms

The ABC Hotel in this example had a rev-par of $114 on this particular night. Rev-par can analyze the performance of a hotel over any time frame (nightly, weekly, monthly, or yearly). Rev-par analysis is useful because of the aforementioned flexibility of comparing different size hotels and their respective rates. Another example:

Step 1—Collection of data

● ABC Hotel has 350 rooms, an ADR of $150, and an occupancy of 76 percent.

● XYZ Hotel has 500 rooms, runs an ADR of $120, and a 76 percent occupancy, which results in a total of 380 rooms being sold.

Step 2—Revenue calculation

● The total room revenue for the ABC Hotel is $39,000 ($150 × 266).

● The total room revenue for the XYZ Hotel is $45,600 ($120 × 380).

At first glance, a novice may look at the higher room revenue of XYZ and make the incorrect assumption that it outperformed ABC.

Step 3—Rev-par

The rev-par comparison would show that the rev-par for ABC ($114) is higher than the rev-par for XYZ of $91.20 ($45,600 divided by 500).

This example shows that with what it had to work with, ABC outperformed XYZ when ADR and occupancy were factored in.

Market Share

Rev-par is a useful quantifiable tool in measuring hotel performance. It uses both occupancy and rate information in its calculation. In a competitive environment, sharing rate information is frowned upon due to antitrust concerns. In those cases, how can hotels be compared? Market share allows for quantifiable analysis without rate information. **Market share** is defined as a hotel's occupancy performance in relation to other hotels within a predetermined competitive set. Market share analysis reveals how a hotel performed based on how it "should have done." It also reveals how much business a hotel "took" from competitors.

The first step in determining market share is to determine which nearby hotels fall within the competitive set (refer to Chapter 9). The competitive set should include hotels of similar product type, location type, and service level. The competitive set does not have to include hotels of the same size. Hotel management will determine a competitive set based on these and other market factors, but the main determinant is "Where will people stay, if not with us?"

Once the competitive set is determined, the **total market potential** is calculated. The total market potential is the total number of available hotel rooms within the competitive set. Adding all the sleeping rooms that each member of the set has will determine potential. Because market share is often determined on a weekly, monthly, or yearly basis, the market potential should then be multiplied by the number of nights in consideration.

To illustrate the calculation of market share, let's use the following example. Assume that four hotels are within one competitive set:

Hotel	# of Rooms
A	100
B	200
C	300
D	400
Total Market Potential	1,000 Rooms

The next step in determining a hotel's market share is to determine its **individual market potential**. The individual market potential is defined as the number of rooms a hotel has for sale within a give time frame. On any given night, each hotel has the potential to sell all its rooms. Factors such as OOO rooms may reduce a hotel's individual potential, but that is not considered in market share analysis. Decisions to list a number of rooms as OOO for renovation or other reasons are risks the hotel is taking, and it must face any consequences. Reducing the number of rooms available for sale is directly related to opportunity cost. From the ongoing example, the following is each hotel's individual potential:

Hotel	# of Rooms	Individual Potential
A	100	100
B	200	200
C	300	300
D	400	400

Market share requires one more piece of information prior to analyzing actual data. A hotel's **rightful market share** reveals how much of the total market potential is made up by its own individual potential. In other words, if all the rooms at a hotel are sold within a given time frame, what percentage of the total market does it take up? Using the example, on any given night, each hotel's rightful share is determined by dividing its number of rooms by the total market potential:

Hotel	# of Rooms	÷	Total Mrkt. Potential	= Rightful Shr.
A	100	/	1,000	**10%**
B	200	/	1,000	**20%**
C	300	/	1,000	**30%**
D	400	/	1,000	**40%**

Once the individual and total market potentials are determined and the rightful share of each hotel is known, actual occupancy data are used to calculate market share. As has been stated before, most hotels will share occupancy data with each other, but they cannot share rate information. Most hotels are interested in how they performed in relation to others in their competitive set, so sharing of occupancy is common. There are private companies in many major markets that collect this data and share it with hotels for a fee. Occupancy data that is gathered on a monthly basis is the generally accepted format.

In the ongoing example, assume that the four hotels within the competitive set have sold the following number of rooms in a 30-day month:

$$A = 2,850; B = 4,950; C = 6,300; D = 7,200$$

Now calculate how the competitive set as a whole performed in relation to the total market potential:

(A)	2,850	3,000 (100 × 30)
(B)	4,950	6,000 (200 × 30)
(C)	6,300	9,000 (300 × 30)
(D)	7,200	12,000 (400 × 30)
	21,300 (Actual)	**30,000 (Potential)**

Dividing the actual by the potential, one can see how the competitive set performed in relation to its potential:

21,300/30,000 = 71% occupancy

In this example, the entire set achieved 71 percent of its potential.

Determining how the whole set performed is useful in understanding the market, but the essence of market share analysis is used to determine how an individual hotel did in relation to the rest. Now, instead of using the total market potential figure, one would use the actual total market results. So, using the example, dividing each hotel's actual data by the total actual market data yields how each hotel performed versus the others:

A = 2,850/21,300 = 13.38%
B = 4,950/21,300 = 23.24%
C = 6,300/21,300 = 29.58%
D = 7,200/21,300 = 33.80%
100%

(***Note:*** The sum total performance figure of each hotel in the competitive set must equal 100%.)

The final step in this process is to compare how the actual occupancy data from each hotel relates to its rightful share (also referred to as "fair share").

Actual	Rightful Share	Difference + or (−)
A = 13.38%	10%	+3.38%
B = 23.24%	20%	+3.24%
C = 29.58%	30%	**(.42%)**
D = 33.80%	40%	**(6.2%)**

In the example, hotels A and B gained market share over hotels C and D. Within the competitive set, these hotels outperformed the others despite their size difference. As with rev-par, market share endeavors to make all participants equal. Even though a hotel is smaller, given the pool of business, market share indicates how much of that occupancy was taken from the larger hotels.

This study of quantifiable measurements only covers half of the ways hotel performance is reviewed. The qualifiable measurement, that a bit more difficult to understand, is widely used. What exactly is a qualifiable measurement?

> *"Ninety-five percent of this game is half mental."*
>
> —Yogi Berra

QUALIFIABLE ANALYSES

Qualifiable analyses are based on the goals of hotel managers. What path they will take down the road to prosperity can differ. That road to prosperity will fork, one path goes down the road of rate driven and the other goes down the path of occupancy driven. As seen in Figure 13-1, both end up with a successful hotel.

FIGURE **13-1**

Qualifiable analysis

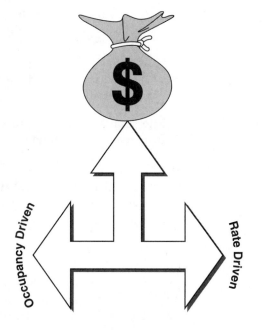

Rate driven management goals may forgo occupancy levels for a higher average rate. The **occupancy driven** goals are simply the opposite, they forgo a higher average rate for greater occupancy.

Each of the qualifiable goals actually uses one of the quantifiable analyses to support its point of view. The occupancy driven managers will use data from market share analysis to support their argument. The results of market share, after all, focus on occupancy. The goal of filling sleeping rooms at the cost of a higher rate is sometimes referred to as a "heads on beds" philosophy.

The rate driven managers will use rev-par to show how the higher rates are making better use of each sold room. They will forgo full occupancy for a better overall revenue picture.

Occupancy driven managers claim that due to opportunity cost, an unsold room costs the hotel money. Any room sold above room cost generates some profit. Another benefit to high occupancy, these managers claim, is that a hotel running at full capacity all the time is more efficient. Employees become better at their jobs because they get more practice. Material and supplies can be purchased in greater bulk, which results in volume cost savings.

Rate driven managers claim that reducing sleeping room wear and tear saves the hotel money in renovation and repair costs. They also claim that the ROI (return on investment) is better when labor and other costs are compared to higher average rate performance.

In the end, there is no absolute approach. Neither is right or wrong, each goal is simply in the "eye of the beholder."

INDUSTRY PERSPECTIVE

Economic Impact of Hotels

John V. Pohl
Sales Manager
Lexington Convention and Visitors Bureau

The convention and visitors bureau works with hotels in a partnership for promoting community tourism and meetings. The economic benefits of these visitors and attendees can be gauged in the dollars and cents of the industry. One hundred single occupancy sleeping rooms could be viewed as having the following potential economic value:

- $10,000 (based on an average room rate of $100 × 100 room nights)

(continued)

INDUSTRY PERSPECTIVE
(concluded)

- $3,000 (based on an average person spending $30 on food and beverage each day)
- $2,500 (based on a discretionary spending of $25 per person per day)
- Total estimated economic value in this simple example would be $15,500

The economic impact of the visitors/meeting attendees to a community should never be underestimated, because the absence of just one large annual event or annual convention can have drastic short-term effects on hotels, restaurants, entertainment areas, and shopping venues. National political conventions, large national associations, and large professional games/activities are examples of events that many cities' convention and visitors bureaus will spend large sums of money to attract to their area. The cities can reap the economic benefits as well as the national exposure in television and print media.

Many convention and visitor bureaus derive much of their funding from the occupancy taxes collected on the community hotel/motel rooms. A portion of the collected tax is budgeted to fund the activities of the convention and visitors bureau, and other portions have been used to fund projects such as airport expansions and construction of new sports stadiums.

CHAPTER THIRTEEN **REVIEW**

KEY TERMS

rev-par
market share
total market potential
individual market potential
rightful market share
rate driven
occupancy driven

REVIEW QUESTIONS

1. Using the hotels in the market share example, calculate market gain or loss using the following occupancy data for a 30-day month:

$$A = 1,750; B = 5,150; C = 6,100; D = 9,500$$

2. What are the arguments that support rate driven management goals?

3. What is needed to calculate rev-par that is not needed in market share analysis?

4. Why is rev-par useful in comparing different hotels?

5. If it wasn't considered illegal, could hotels share rate data and calculate rate market share the same way as occupancy?

6. What is a competitive set?

7. Define rightful market share. What term is also used to express the same concept?

8. Managers with a "heads in beds" philosophy have what qualifiable goal in mind?

9. Define rev-par.

10. What arguments support occupancy driven goals?

DISCUSSION QUESTIONS/EXERCISES

1. The health of the hotel industry as a whole is often measured by rev-par. Statistical information is routinely collected from across the globe to compare rev-par from previous years and to compare rev-par performance between metro regions. Using some of the Internet sites listed at the end of this chapter, or other resources, collect rev-par data from two metro regions. Compare and contrast the two. How do they perform against each other? How are they doing now versus last year? What factors could affect rev-par performance?

2. Why are the performance goals of hotel managers different? Why would some prefer occupancy to rate? What ownership goals could affect the goals of managers? Would a rate driven manager be happy selling only a handful of rooms at rack rate? Why or why not? Would an occupancy driven manager be happy filling all his/her guest rooms with employee or industry rates? Why or why not?

CASE STUDY

Rev-par

In an area under analysis, three hotels are within a competitive set:

    a. 550-room property (Property A)

    b. 800-room property (Property B)

    c. 125-room property (Property C)

Calculate the Rev-par:

1. Property A had an annual occupancy percentage of 83.1% with total guest room revenue of $24,843,318.

2. Property B had an annual occupancy percentage of 79.8% with total guest room revenue of $32,044,360.

3. Property C had an annual occupancy percentage of 71.9% with total guest room revenue of $5,978,270.

4. Based on the rev-par calculation, which hotel had the best performance within the competitive set?

5. Calculate annual fair market share for these three properties.

6. Knowing what each property had in annual occupancy percentage, how did each property do in regards to its market share?

7. What assumptions can you make about these properties knowing their rev-par and market share?

INTERNET RESOURCES
Measuring Hotel Performance

Each of the following Web sites reflects a known and respected industry source for up-to-date industry statistics and trends:

Smith Travel Research	<http://www.wwstar.com/>
Lodging Forecast	<http://www.lodgingforecast.com/>
National Business Travel Association	<http://www.nbta.org/industry/stats_index.htm>
Pricewaterhouse Coopers	<http://www.pwcglobal.com/ca/eng/about/ind/svcs_hosp-os.html>

Guest Service

OBJECTIVES

After reading this chapter, you should understand:

- The visual and verbal methods of communicating guest service
- How to resolve guest conflicts
- The principle of empowerment and its role in guest service
- Working with international guests

INTRODUCTION

Perhaps no duty of the rooms division is more vital than that of guest service. Guest satisfaction is crucial in maintaining loyalty. Guest loyalty ensures repeat business. With the myriad hotel choices in the market today, repeat business ensures a steady revenue stream. All rooms division employees, and others considered front of the house, must be cognizant of their impact on guest satisfaction.

SERVICE STANDARDS

Hotels wishing to foster an atmosphere of quality guest service must establish parameters. Employees in any industry need to have expectations made clear to them. A hotel that clearly defines its guest service guidelines will be able to hold employees accountable. That accountability helps management guide and evaluate employees. An environment like this translates into superior levels of guest service.

Many hotel chains have developed and implemented their own guest service standards. The names for these programs differ, but the overriding theme is consistent amongst all of them: "Guest service is paramount to hotel success."

Establishing guest service guidelines begins with a breakdown of guest interaction. Guest interaction can be verbal or it can be visual. Rooms division employees use those two methods of conveying a message to guests. Guest service is accomplished when the employee conveys the message using both visual and verbal means.

Verbal Means

Speaking, as a method of communication, can reveal much about a person. Verbal communication allows for gaining insight into a guest. Granted, these conversations may not be lengthy, but the aware employees can glean much about a guest's personality in the course of a conversation.

Perhaps the most important verbal tools in ensuring guest satisfaction are the simplest. Often overlooked by rooms division employees deeply involved in other tasks, the basic rules for effective verbal communications are:

- Use an appropriate greeting
- Personalize the conversation (use the customer's name)
- Thank the guest
- Listen
- Avoid jargon

Whether communicating in person or over the phone, employees should greet every guest appropriately. Identify the time of day by saying "good morning" or "good evening." The employee who greets a guest over the phone should also include his or her name and department and offer assistance in the greeting. "Good morning, front desk, this is John. How may I help you?" Phone departmental identification is important, as guests who call need to be reassured that they have reached the appropriate department.

Personalizing the conversation sets a relaxed tone in conversation. Using the appropriate title (i.e., Mr. or Ms.) is important. During check-in or checkout, the guest account will let the front desk employee know the guest's name. In many hotels, the phone system is equipped with a caller I.D. display that will identify the guest room number and guest name when a guest calls. In outlets, many POS systems identify the guest account as well. These tools enable employees to use the appropriate personalized greeting often. When the guest name is not known, sir or ma'am would suffice. Personalizing the greeting also invokes a feeling of appreciation for a guest. Guests greeted by name are subtly reminded that the hotel values their business.

Thanking guests in a sincere manner is also very important. Employees may conduct a variety of guest services in a day. Each of these transactions should be concluded with a "thank you." Thanking a guest for staying at a hotel also implies that the hotel appreciates their business.

Listening is the only way a receiver can hear the message the transmitter is sending. Employees can listen for subtle hints and signals a guest gives out during communication. The employee creates a comfort level when they listen. Letting the guest initiate the tone of the conversation also puts him/her at ease. Failure to listen correctly can cause problems. The seven common listening errors are:[1]

- Failure to concentrate
- Listening too hard
- "Jumping the gun"
- Lagging behind the conversation
- Focusing too much on delivery or appearance
- Omitting
- Adding

Let the guest know that you are giving him/her your undivided attention. Keeping the mind clear of other duties or concerns helps focus attention. Employees who think they know what the guest is going to say are often embarrassed to find out they were wrong. Employees should always keep an open mind when listening. They should be prepared to hear things they may not want to hear. Asking questions helps the guest feel that the employee is actually listening.

Hotel employees should avoid using industry jargon when they communicate with guests. Using hotel terms in conversation may not convey the intended message. For example, "Don't worry, Mr. Smith, I blocked you into a double/double."

Although the employee here is trying to tell Mr. Smith that he is indeed reserved for a room he chose, Mr. Smith might not understand exactly what was said. A better way of saying the same thing would be, "Don't worry, Mr. Smith, I reserved your preferred room type, a room with two beds."

Visual Means

Communicating visually is as important as communicating verbally. Visual communication can reinforce what is being said verbally. The complete delivery of guest service can be accomplished by incorporating both means. The rules for effective visual communication are:

- Communicate with a smile.

- Be cognizant of body language.

- Observe appropriate grooming standards.

The smile is an underappreciated method of conveying hospitality. A genuine smile that accompanies a greeting or thank you reinforces the message. Smiling at guests helps create an atmosphere of comfort. At the front desk, for example, a smile incorporated into the 10x10 rule will greatly increase guest satisfaction. The 10x10 rule, to review, has two parts. The first part states that a guest's perception of the entire stay is, in large measure, instilled in the first 10 minutes upon arrival. The other part states that the front desk must greet a guest 10 feet before they approach the front desk. An employee who begins a conversation with a guest at least 10 feet away from the front desk creates a favorable impression. This makes the guest feel welcome by encouraging their approach. Add to this a smile and the impact is ever more heightened.

Body language can be an important visual marker for rooms division employees. Observing guest body language is like listening with eyes. Observation of guest body language can give the employee clues on how to communicate with the guest. Common body language signals include the following:

- Crossed arms may indicate a defensive posture.

- A guest who leans across the front desk during conversation may be aggressive.

- Strong and consistent eye contact may indicate confidence.

- Strong firm handshakes may also indicate confidence.

- Red eyes may indicate fatigue.

Another often overlooked aspect of visual communications is guest perception. Hotel employees are viewed as an extension of the hotel itself. How a guest perceives an employee often contributes to the guest's overall perception of a hotel. The first and often most lasting perception a guest makes on an employee is the employee's appearance. It is for that reason most hotels have instituted employee grooming standards.

All rooms division employees, whether front of the house or back of the house, should take pride in their appearance. Those in uniform should ensure that the uniform is clean and properly pressed. No buttons or trim should be missing. Footwear should match the uniform and be appropriate for the job duty. Management personnel and other employees not in issued uniforms should also observe these rules. For departments not regularly in physical contact with guests (e.g., PBX), their clothes should be comfortable but still presentable. Employees may walk through a hotel on breaks or en route to accomplishing other duties, so guest observance is always possible.

Another part of the employee's attire is the name tag. The employee name tag usually includes the name, title, and/or department the employee works in. Beyond identification, it lets guests know who the employee is and what his or her area of expertise is. Some hotels include other information on the name tags. A name tag that is identified with a flag of another nation is one way of identifying this employee as one who knows a foreign language. Some hotels list employee hometowns on name tags with the thought that this may spark conversation with guests.

Hair length, jewelry, makeup, beards, and other grooming standards vary greatly from hotel to hotel. What may be acceptable in one hotel may not be in another. Regardless of hotel standard, employees who meet preset grooming standards ensure consistency throughout the hotel. Employees who take care of their appearance let guests know that they take care of the job they do. The guest will perceive that "if an employee takes care of the job they do, they take care of me as well."

Guest service continues with basic duties. A front office employee must have a good working knowledge of phone etiquette. The common expectation is that all calls to the front desk are answered within three rings. Because of the vast number of questions guests may have of a hotel, front desk employees must have a good knowledge of hotel facilities, outlets, activities, and policies. An awareness of their surroundings (local events, directions, and activities) is also helpful to other departments like concierge and PBX. Because the front office is the focal point of the hotel, emergency procedures and policies should be memorized.

GUEST CONFLICT RESOLUTION

Not every guest experience is problem-free. The hotel industry is a service industry that relies on people and infrastructure to deliver a product. Service received from employees is one part. In addition, many physical aspects of the hotel must function well (everything in working order) to ensure that the guest receives the whole product. Unfortunately, one or both of these parts may break down at some point. When that happens, it is important to implement a resolution. Resolving a conflict to a guest's satisfaction can "turn around" an unhappy guest and make him/her a satisfied guest.

"Customers don't expect you to be perfect.
They do expect you to fix things when they go wrong."

—Donald Porter
Senior VP, British Airways

This resolution is best accomplished by adhering to the visual and verbal rules of guest service. Many hotel employees, in their sincere desire to correct a conflict, forget to take the time to listen first. They might also become defensive and inadvertently express that in body language. If it is assumed that the employee is fully trained, the following rules should be followed to meet or exceed a guest's expectations:

- Listen first. Using the rules of visual communication, allow the guest to fully express the problem. Making eye contact and avoiding the crossing of arms at this point keeps the atmosphere open. Interruptions or excuses only make matters worse.

- Summarize and restate the problem. The employee should next reply back to the guest what his/her understanding of the problem is. This summary should also include a restatement of the guest's reaction to the problem. Without condescension, expressing back to the guest that anger or disappointment is an understood reaction validates those feelings. This also lets the guest know that the employee fully appreciates the scope and breadth of the conflict.

- Make no excuses. A guest who is dissatisfied with the guest room shower temperature will be dissatisfied whether the hotel water heater was working or not. Employees should take this opportunity to sincerely apologize on behalf of the entire hotel. Using words like "us" and "we" instead of "they" invokes a team approach to conflict resolution. If a mistake occurred that was the fault of the hotel, it should be admitted. Being up-front and honest, without making excuses, again validates the guest's feelings.

- Resolve the problem. If the conflict is something that can be fixed, it should be done immediately. If it can't, the guest should be compensated in some way. Methods of resolution are dictated by empowerment, which is covered next in this chapter.

- Document the conflict. Hotels seeking to continually improve guest service seek to ensure that conflicts do not reoccur. Documenting the problem will create a record for future changes in training or policy. Hotel managers often use real-life scenarios as teaching tools.

EMPOWERMENT

Guest service is often a focal point of hotel management. Training, experience, personality, and other things contribute to an individual employee's ability to satisfy a guest. Hotel management must support that effort. One way management supports an employee's ability to satisfy a guest is by integrating empowerment in all duties.

A trend in many hotels today is to empower the employees to make guest service decisions. No where is that more vital than the rooms division. **Empowerment** is defined as the ability and authority to satisfy guest complaints/requests within preset parameters. Whenever issues arise, an empowered employee is able to take whatever action is deemed appropriate to solve the problem. Guests are more satisfied when an employee takes care of the situation instead of saying, "I have to ask my manager." Employees gain a greater sense of self-worth as well.

Employees learn to implement empowerment techniques in how they communicate with guests as well. Certain words and phrases should be avoided whenever possible. There are other ways of communicating the same message. For example:

Phrase to Avoid	Phrase to Use Instead
"I don't know."	*"That is a good question, let me find out for you."*
"We can't do that."	*"Well, I haven't encountered this before, let me research it and find a resolution that you are happy with."*
"You have to." or *"This is hotel policy."*	*"Next time, here is how you can avoid this situation."* or *"I think the best way to handle this would be . . ."*
"No."	*"We are not able to reduce your room rate, but I am able to upgrade your room."*
"That's not my job."	*"The person who handles that is (name). Please let me get her/him."*

DIVERSITY AWARENESS

Guest service goes beyond empowerment. Guest service also entails knowledge and understanding of people. The diversity of guests makes it vital that all hotel employees appreciate the differences in people. Most reputable hotels put all their employees through **diversity training**. Diversity training teaches employees that they must understand and appreciate the differences in people. The U.S. Department of Labor predicts that minority groups will compromise nearly half of the U.S. population by 2050.[2] Helping employees overcome stereotypes ensures that no guests perceive a difference in treatment. In the past, racism, sexism, ethnocentrism, and other stereotypes created uncomfortable environments for guests and employees alike. Today, hotel managers teach employees to celebrate these differences. Hotel managers often lead by example by hiring a diverse front desk staff. A front office that is operated by people of various races, genders, ages, and ethnic backgrounds reflect management's understanding of diversity. A diverse guest pool inevitably feels more welcome at a diverse front desk.

INTERNATIONAL GUESTS

Customer service skills are valued across the globe. Many texts have been written on international business protocol and service. Protocol comes from the Greek meaning "the first glue."[3] Proper protocol can be seen as the glue that cements a good business relationship. In the hotel industry, understanding the customer service skills needed in dealing with international guests can be very important. A hotel, by its nature, is the "home away from home" for international guests. Traveling in a foreign land can be intimidating for some people. Using good customer service will help put these visitors at ease. These skills are important for all hotel types, but those hotels located in gateway cities will require those skills most often.

Even before an international reservation is ever made, a hotel must prepare for the guest's arrival. If possible, hotels should share a list of multilingual staff with front office managers. This list should encompass the entire hotel. An engineer who is fluent in French or a chef who speaks Japanese should be documented on this list as well. Should translation assistance be needed, the front office staff can call on other hotel employees. As was stated earlier, some hotels identify their multilingual staff by marking each employee's name tag with the flag of the country the language is spoken in. A guest can easily identify the employee who shares his/her language.

The amount of accommodation a hotel should provide to international guests depends greatly on the volume of visitors. An airport hotel in San Francisco might have a steady stream of Japanese visitors. In that case, everything from welcome letters, itineraries, and travel information to menu selections and amenity descriptions should be translated into the guest's native tongue. This hotel may even create special menu items to cater to the traditional cuisine of the country. A suburban hotel in Omaha may not have the same international volume, so the expense of translating in-house collateral probably isn't warranted. However, they too should have a plan of action in case an international visitor does arrive.

Upon arrival, front office employees need to realize that verbal communication may be a challenge. Even though many international visitors have some knowledge of English, their grasp of the language may be limited. Long and complex sentences often pose problems. An international guest with some knowledge of English may comprehend the written word better than the spoken word. However, even when the sentence is written down, that guest may have a hard time understanding. Keeping sentences short is an easy way to keep a nonfluent English speaker engaged.

Colloquial expressions can also be a problem, because those words are not usually taught in other countries. English dictionaries are usually not much help when it comes to colloquial expressions. Do not make the mistake of speaking more loudly or more slowly, as that can be perceived as a sign of condescension.

Nonverbal information such as one's appearance, tone of voice, facial expression, and body language all provide extra information that enrich understanding. However, when cultural difference is involved, this can cause additional misunderstanding. For example, body language is an integral part of greeting in Japan. Japanese bow as they utter their greetings. Americans extend their arms for handshakes. Americans familiar with each other may even hug. Most Japanese who are familiar with the American culture are accustomed to handshakes, but when it comes to hugs, few Japanese know the rules and manners involved.[4] It this type of difference that front office employees need to be aware of.

It is often best to err on the side of caution. Most cultures are not offended by too much formality; too little, and an employee runs the risk of insult, which would result in a poor hotel experience. Front desk employees should make a special effort to use complete titles. Use of earned titles like "Dr." or "Professor" are a sign of respect. Bellstand staff should always ask permission to assist with baggage. With an international guest, that is even more important They should never assume that they can simply pick up a bag—that invasion of personal space can be perceived as rude in some cultures. In general, front office employees should maintain a respectful distance and take their cues from the guest.

MANAGEMENT'S ROLE IN GUEST SERVICE

Communication is perhaps the most important function of any front desk or front office manager. Communication both with guests and staff is vital. In terms of guest communication, these managers should become involved in guest complaints only after an empowered desk agent attempted to resolve the issue first. Managers who involve themselves in any situation before the agent has had a chance to resolve it successfully on his/her own defeat the purpose behind empowerment. Managers need to be a resource for employees, giving advice only if asked. Of course, proper implementation of empowerment requires evaluation of any action taken by the employee after the fact, if the preset parameters were exceeded in some way.

Some guests may simply prefer to address complaints to a manager. Guest complaints must be viewed as opportunities to improve hotel services, not a "burden" of any kind. Managers must lead by example here. Reactions to guest complaints must be done in a timely, positive, and caring manner. Not every complaint may be valid in the mind of management, but it is valid in the mind of the guest. All complaints should be investigated, evaluated, and responded to. If the front office manager is unable to resolve the situation, it should be passed along to more senior management. The escalation of an issue can and often should go all the way to the general manager.

"Do what you said you would do. Keep the service promise."

—Dr. Leonard Berry
Texas A&M University

GUEST SERVICE TRAINING

Proper training of employees can minimize the role management must play in guest service. The guest service philosophy of a hotel should be communicated constantly and consistently. This communication should begin with the first day of new employee orientation. Hotels should begin the guest service training process immediately. During orientation, new employees (of all departments) should be given the hotel's service philosophy. This message is often best delivered by a member of the executive committee. The impact of a senior manager stating the importance of guest service can be memorable.

Service Mission Statement

A hotel's guest service message can be summarized succinctly in the hotel's **service mission statement**. A service mission statement serves as the rule and/or goal of the guest service philosophy. A sample mission statement might read:

"We, as the staff and management of the Golden Bay Star Hotel, pledge to consistently meet or exceed our guest's expectations in order to ensure complete customer satisfaction."

The mission statement should be posted in all employee break areas, in the cafeteria, and in the changing rooms. The management must continually reinforce this philosophy in both words and deeds. Managers exhibiting ownership of the service mission statement motivate their employees by example. Some hotels choose to post their service mission statement in areas visible to guests. This is advisable only in operations where the goals of the mission statement are being met. Unhappy guests will not take comfort in empty words or promises.

Guest service training continues beyond orientation and introduction of the service mission statement. Guest service training should be constant. New and experienced employees alike should continually refresh their skills. Larger hotel chains have complete divisions at a corporate level dedicated to creating and implementing guest service programs. Smaller chains and independent hotels can take advantage of other resources, for example:

- On-the-job training/reinforcement
- Role-playing
- Commercial videos
- Guest speakers
- Continuing education/distance learning

An excellent way to promote superior guest service is to share examples of actual employee successes. When a manager is made aware of an example of superior guest service, he/she should share it with other members of the department. If appropriate, the example can be shared with the entire hotel. Employees are often motivated by "real life" examples. When it comes to guest service, motivation is very important.

Motivating for Guest Service

Keeping the "service fire alive" in the hearts of hotel employees is as important as effective training. Motivating employees to embody the service mission statement in their day-to-day duties helps ensure guest satisfaction. Motivation is difficult without some method of quantifying results. When an employee has a clearly defined goal, the task of achieving it is much easier. Hotels that dictate "good customer service" can have a hard time relaying that premise to employees. After all, what does good customer service mean?

Quantifying customer service is best achieved from guest feedback. Most hotels have some version of a comment card in guest rooms. These cards encourage guests to rate and/or rank the services received during his/her stay. They also solicit the names of employees the guest feels made an impact on his/her stay. The completed cards are mailed by the guest in business reply envelopes to management. A sample comment card is illustrated in Figure 14-1.

Golden Bay Star Hotel			
Guest Comment Card			

Date of Stay _____ Room Occupied _____

Name/Address (Optional) _____

_____

Please rate your stay: (Please circle one)	**Poor**	**Average**	**Good**	**Excellent**
Reservation Accuracy	1	2	3	4
Check-in Speed	1	2	3	4
Checkout Speed	1	2	3	4
Accuracy of Bill	1	2	3	4
Guestroom Cleanliness	1	2	3	4
Room Service Quality	1	2	3	4
Restaurant Quality	1	2	3	4
Pool/Spa Quality	1	2	3	4
Are You Likely to Return?	1	2	3	4

If we did not live up to your expectations, please let us know:

_____

_____

_____

If we exceeded your expectations, please let us know:

_____

_____

_____

Please share the name(s) of employees who helped make your stay memorable:

_____

_____

FIGURE **14-1**

Comment card

The comment cards are then tallied and the rankings/scores of each department are readily apparent. Hotel management should have in place guest service target goals based on these rankings/scores. Employees or departments that achieve these goals should be rewarded or recognized in some way. Some chains recognize their employees by changing the look of their name tags. Employees named in a comment card, for example, can be awarded points. After a predetermined number of points is achieved, the employee's name tag receives a star or stripe indicating they embody superior customer service skills. Hotel management can take pride in the number of employees achieving these ranks. The employees themselves are proud to wear a name tag that sets them apart. A healthy competition can ensue to see which employees can get the most stars/stripes.

Other motivators include bringing the skilled employees into new hire orientation. Real-life testimonials are powerful learning tools, and setting the tone for new hires in this fashion helps establish good practices. Monetary rewards from the hotel are also good motivators. In-kind rewards such as a free dinner for two or a complimentary stay at another hotel also serve as incentives.

NOTES

1. Anderson, K., and Zemke, R. (1998). *Delivering Knock Your Socks Off Service.* New York: AMACOM.
2. *Hotel and Motel Management, 216,* 1 (January 15, 2001), Advanstar Publications.
3. <http://www.secretary.state.nc.us/international/protocol.htm>
4. <http://virtualtimes.com>

INDUSTRY PERSPECTIVE

Six Sigma and Customer Loyalty

Pete Van Overwalle
Director of Six Sigma, Black Belt
The Westin Indianapolis

Whereas most hotel companies today spend considerable effort measuring the worth of a company and the business it represents, Starwood Hotels and Resorts seeks to understand the value of a single customer over a lifetime. They seek to measure the value of loyalty. To this end, the most significant tool recently deployed is the Six Sigma initiative. Begun in January 2001, Starwood Hotels and Resorts is the first hotel company to embrace this tool that seeks to earn the loyalty of every customer through improved customer service.

(continued)

My role as Black Belt situates me within a single hotel property, namely the Westin Indianapolis. My responsibility includes the planning and execution of three to four projects per year to improve the various processes that impact customer service. Loyalty of a customer is earned when his/her expectation is met, not only once, but every time. In a dynamic environment such as a hotel, this consistency in service delivery is a challenge. Although it is every employee's responsibility to seek improvements, until now there has never been a single dedicated resource to ensure that this occurs on a daily basis.

Consider the front desk, where our customer has a significant opportunity to assess a hotel's service ability. If our typical guest has the expectation of being checked in to the hotel within two minutes, the goal of Six Sigma is to first measure the process of how we check in a guest. This measure, typically called a baseline measurement, is then compared to the customer expectation. The difference is variation. We often find that our check-in times vary from five minutes, to seven minutes, and at times, to as much as ten minutes. Simply stated, our current check-in process is not capable of meeting our customer's expectation. Their loyalty is at risk.

Sigma is the Greek word for *variation*. A sigma rating of 6 represents the amount of variation in 1,000,000 opportunities. Based on our front desk example, if we were to improve the check-in process dramatically, to give us a sigma rating of 6, there would only be 3.4 customers out of 1,000,000 who experience a check-in time greater than two minutes. Admittedly, this is near perfection and probably not realistic in real life. However, the purpose of Six Sigma is to know how much variation there is in your current process and reduce that variation as much as possible. A company's overall sigma rating of 3 or 4 would be far above that of the current industry performance levels.

In today's environment where customers have so many options (discounted Internet fares, double points, hundreds of brand names), we fail to recognize that value is created when we give the customer exactly what they want every time they do business with us.

CHAPTER FOURTEEN **REVIEW**

KEY TERMS

empowerment
diversity training
service mission statement

REVIEW QUESTIONS

1. Explain the importance of setting service standards.
2. What are the verbal and visual means of communication? What is their impact on guest service?
3. Define empowerment.
4. In what ways can management support an employee in guest conflict resolution?
5. What are some common body language signals?
6. Define diversity training.
7. Define the service mission statement.
8. How might a small chain or independent hotel maintain guest service training?
9. Name two of the commonly used employee guest service motivators.
10. Why is maintaining grooming standards so important?

DISCUSSION QUESTIONS/EXERCISES

1. The opportunities to exemplify superior guest service are frequent within the front office. The frequent guest contact offers repeated opportunities to make a guest feel good about the hotel. How can these skills be applied to "real life" situations? For example, assume that you are the swing shift desk clerk on duty. Your hotel has three arrivals left to come in, and only two rooms. Suddenly, you look up from your PMS workstation and see all three guests arriving at the same time. You know one person will not have a room with you tonight. What do you do?

2. You are an employee working a very busy front desk. Phones are ringing off the hook. Guests are beginning to line up in front of you. You must make a decision; do you answer the phone, or let them ring in order to help the guests in line?

3. Make the following phone call to four different hotels. You are looking for directions to the hotel by car. Say only the statement here, answer additional questions if asked: "I am supposed to be at this for a meeting, but I don't know where you are located."

Fill in the table. Answer the following questions:

#	Response Notes
1.	
2.	
3.	
4.	

a. Which hotel gave you the most appropriate response?

b. Were you ever transferred at any hotel?

c. If you were transferred, was it handled appropriately?

d. Were you asked additional questions to clarify your statement at any hotel?

e. If you were driving to these hotels, would you feel confident that you would find them with these directions?

f. Were you thanked for your call at any hotel?

g. Which hotel did you like the most? Why?

h. Which hotel did you like the least? Why?

i. Rank the hotels in order of your preference high to low.

j. If you were to be a guest at these hotels, what impressions have your already formed from this single phone call?

k. If you were the manager of the PBX department at these hotels, how would you feel?

l. What would you say to the employee that you spoke with if you were the general manager of these hotels?

m. Do you think single phone calls like this by guests are important? Why or why not?

4. Arrange to interview a human resources manager of a large hotel property. Answer the following questions:

a. What is the name of the hotel you selected?

b. What is the location of this property?

c. What is the name of the human resources manager?

d. How long has he/she worked at this property?

e. How many employees are there at this property?

f. What type of guest service training is provided for new employees?

g. Who provides the guest service training?

h. Is there any formal process for regular guest service training for existing employees?

i. Does this hotel have a turnover goal?

j. What steps are utilized to control voluntary turnover?

k. What is the "cost" of hiring and training a new employee?

l. How many open positions are currently available at this hotel?

m. What is the main reason for turnover at this hotel?

n. What is the best advice this manager can give you as a novice to the industry?

o. What was the most interesting thing you learned from this manager?

EXERCISE

Guest Service Role-Playing

Guest service skills are best highlighted when practiced. Role-playing exercises help illustrate the principles of guest service and allow for honest critique of individual understanding. This role-playing exercise can be modified to suit any number of guest service aspects. These exercises are best accomplished in groups no larger than three or four participants.

Step 1—Setting: As a class or group, create the background for a fictitious hotel. Begin with determining size, location, and product type. Next determine the rooms division area to be examined. Try looking at different areas such as PBX and bellstand as well as front desk.

Step 2—Create the Scenario: Now create situations that would require implementation of the guest service skills learned in this chapter. Perhaps you have had experiences you could share. Some ideas for scenarios might include:

Guest Interaction

- Walk-in reservation
- Guest inquiring on the surrounding area
- Guest looking for another area within the hotel

Conflicts

- Guest package/fax or message lost
- Guest room equipment malfunction
- Room preferences not met
- Bill inaccurate

Step 3—Script the Dialog: Once the setting and scenario are determined, begin scripting the words to the role-playing exercise. Create the script for both the guest and employee. For each scenario write a script that allows guest service principles to be practiced as well as a script that illustrates the "wrong" way to do it.

Step 4—Action: In front of the class or group, each team should present its guest service scenario. Taking turns in the different roles, the members of each team should act out both the "right" and "wrong" scripts for each scenario. Observers should write down their observations.

Step 5—Critique: When all the teams are finished, the group should discuss each scenario and script. The group should first determine which was the "right" and "wrong" script. Next, analysis of the visual and verbal communication skills is conducted. How well was eye contact maintained? Were some participants sending signals with body language? Was there always a smile?

Constructive comments are welcome on how each team resolved a conflict. If possible, teams could exchange scenarios they created and write new scripts for other scenarios. Again, finish with the acting and critique steps. For smaller groups, a videotape of each script is helpful for allowing participants to critique themselves.

Internet Resources
Hotel Training Web Sites and International Resources

Customer service resources are plentiful on the Web. The following sites are hotel-specific and offer resources and links to customer service and training programs.

HotelTraining.com	<http://www.hoteltraining.com/>
American Hotel & Lodging Association— Educational Institute	<http://www.ei-ahma.org/ei1/index.htm>
CustomerService.com	<http://www.customerservice.com/public/Article5.asp>

For more information on International protocol and service standards, please visit the following sites:

U.S. Department of State	<http://www.state.gov/>
Foreign Embassy Resources	<http://www.embassy.org/>
CIA World Fact Book	<http://www.odci.gov/cia/publications/factbook/>

Glossary

A

AAA—American Automobile Association.

AARP—American Association of Retired Persons.

accident—term used to describe employee injuries.

accounting equation—Assets = Liabilities + Owner's Equity.

accounting transfer—used when a charge or credit needs to be "sent" elsewhere within the guest ledger.

aging statement—within the city ledger, the aging statement tracks how long each receivable has remained uncollected.

all suite—hotel type that offers suites as the primary room type.

ancillary—hotel revenue sources outside of sleeping rooms or food/beverage.

anticipated usage amount—cash deposit required covering the estimated use of hotel facilities and services (e.g., in-room phones, in-room movies, room service, etc.).

arrival chronology—the term used to categorize the stages a transient or group guest go through upon arrival to a hotel.

arrival/departure report—a night audit report that summarizes all the check-ins and checkouts that occurred in the course of a day.

arrivals report—a front office report that lists every guest due to arrive that day; a front office report that lists only those check-ins yet due to arrive at that specific time. This report can be run at anytime during the day.

asset—an economic resource.

audit trail—serves as documented history of transactions.

automated call distributor (ACD)—routes reservations calls to available agents.

automatic posting—the transfer of guest charges to an account as they are incurred.

average daily rate (ADR)—an average of all the rates sold at a hotel on a given night.

B

back of the house—hotel departments with traditionally low amounts of guest contact.

bag delivery—term used when a group's luggage is delivered to individual rooms at some point after the group has checked into the hotel.

bag pull—at a predetermined time in the day (usually when all group attendees are in session), the bellstaff go into each room and "pull" each attendee's luggage. This luggage is then stored until the group is ready to depart.

balance sheet—serves to summarize a hotel's financial situation on a given date.

bank—a cash reserve assigned to individual front desk employees/managers to handle daily transactions.

bellcaptain—the leader of the bellstaff.

bellcart—a large metal cart on rollers that bellstaff use to carry luggage to and from a guest room.

blocking—process of holding or reserving a specific room based on room preferences and other factors.

brand loyalty—the institutionalized preferences of a consumer for a product or service based on a brand name or logo.

bundling—the process of combining one or more hotel products or services together to make the new entity more attractive; most commonly used with package rates.

business transient—transient market subset comprised of guests traveling on business.

buyer confidence—a hotel guest's predetermined desire to book a room at a hotel at almost any cost.

C

captive audience—customers who are staying at the hotel and will, for convenience and lack of other options, partake in the outlets the hotel has to offer.

card approval—process to ensure that each credit card is valid and that a sufficient amount of credit is available on the card.

central reservations system (CRS)—provides the consumer with an avenue to locate a hotel of choice in a certain location.

charge/credit slips—used when the entry in the guest account menu has a net effect on the overall guest ledger.

chief engineer—coordinates the day-to-day maintenance of the hotel's physical structure.

city ledger—tracks revenues due to the hotel.

closed to arrival (CTA)—a useful restriction in slowing demand on one night while increasing demand on the prior night.

commission—(usually 10 percent of the rate for hotels) paid to travel agents by hotels, airlines, and other travel related suppliers to induce further bookings.

common areas—hotel spaces where most, if not all, guests may walk through.

comp rooms report—the night auditors must verify each room that has no rate posted to it. This report will include a reason for the complimentary status (e.g., per group contract, VIP, distressed guest, etc.).

competitive set—hotels of similar product type, location type, and size.

compression of demand—the theory that the need for hotel rooms in a city or geographical region will remain static and fairly constant in spite of what the occupancy level is. In effect, if one part of an area is sold out, the demand for rooms will compress in such a way as to drive those looking for rooms elsewhere.

connecting rooms—have doors between them that can be opened.

contract rooms—a block of rooms set aside for an organization each and every night, whether they are occupied or not.

controller—person in charge of the hotel's financial reporting and cash flow management.

convention center—a locally funded, or privately owned structure that caters to large groups and conventions for meetings of all kinds.

conversion ratio—the number of transient bookings made versus the number of calls received.

core competency—an organizations' strengths.

correction entry—is used to correct a mistake in the posting process.

cost rate formula—method of determining initial hotel rates based on construction costs. This formula determines the average room rate by allocating $1 towards the rate for each $1,000 spent in construction.

credit—has a negative effect on the total balance of a guest account.

credit card transaction report—conducted so that accounts receivable can verify the allowances and revenue due from each credit card company on the city ledger.

credit limit report—This report is run to verify that guests within the hotel have not exceeded their credit card limits or cash balances on hand. The information from this report should be shared with accounts receivable and the front office manager.

credit risk—credit extended to an individual or organization that may be unable to pay.

crosstraining—employees' learning other jobs within the hotel.

cutoff date—the last possible date the hotel can hold contracted rooms for a group before releasing them.

D

date roll—hotels must designate a certain point in the night to establish a change in date.

debit—has a positive effect on the total balance of a guest account.

deep clean—the process of completely cleaning a room.

department heads—managers who are most directly involved in an area's day-to-day operations.

departures report—a front office report that lists each guest who is due to check out that day; a front office report that lists only those checkouts yet due to leave the hotel at that specific time. This report can be run at anytime during the day.

direct billing—a process in which payment of a portion or all of a group's or guest's charges are deferred in some way.

direct billing application—a form requesting some level of credit from a hotel.

director of catering—responsible for the catering side of the hotel sales effort.

director of engineering—involved in the physical aspects of the hotel's operation.

director of food and beverage—runs each department that sells, buys, or prepares food and beverage products for hotel guests.

director of grounds—unique to the resort hotel, the director of grounds is in charge of landscape and the surrounding area.

director of human resources—in charge of all hotel personnel.

director of loss prevention—main priority is the safety and security of all hotel guests and employees.

director of marketing—oversees the hotel's sales and marketing operation, directing the group and transient sales efforts to maximize room revenue.

director of operations—is in charge of the fundamental operational functions of the hotel in a revenue-based deployment structure.

director of recreation—is in charge of a resort's signature attraction.

director of services—responsible for the hotel's housekeeping and laundry operations.

disabled access configuration—sleeping rooms that are ADA (Americans with Disabilities Act) compliant.

discrepant code—exists when housekeeping and the front desk have different information on the status of a guest room.

displacement—occurs when lower-rated group rooms are booked in place of higher-rated transient rooms.

diversity training—teaches employees that they must understand and appreciate the differences in people.

double occupancy—two occupants in a guest room.

driving rate—when demand dictates, a hotel may never even begin selling discounted rates, and thus have them restricted from the start. This practice attempts to maximize revenue when demand is known to be forthcoming.

E

employee shift closing report—outlines each transaction a front desk agent completed within the guest ledger.

empowerment—the ability and authority to satisfy guest complaints/requests within preset parameters.

enhanced configuration—understood to include more amenities and/or services than the standard guest room configuration.

entries—update the guest accounting menu.

executive chef—responsible for the hotel's overall food production.

extended stay—hotels that provide their guests with services, amenities, and facilities that they want or need to facilitate a long-term stay in one location.

F

FF&E—furniture, fixtures, and equipment.

food and beverage potential report—reconciliation of what was sold in the outlets to what price it was sold at.

food/beverage audit report—a night audit report that summarizes the outlet/ancillary report and the F&B potential report.

food cost—the cost of a particular food item in relation to the price for which it is sold.

forecasting—the task reservations performs of providing information on forthcoming occupancy levels.

franchise company—acts as an agent on behalf of the owner and implements the franchise agreement between the owner (franchisee) and the hotel chain (franchiser).

franchised—hotels that are independently owned hotels and affiliate themselves with a chain. In a franchise agreement, the owner (franchisee) pays a franchise fee to the chain (franchiser) in exchange for the rights to use their name.

front—term used to alert the bellstaff that a guest is ready to be escorted to the room.

front log sheet—record kept at the bellstand of all activity by each bellperson; used to ensure parity in all assignments.

front office manager—responsible for a large portion of the most visible aspects of a hotel's day-to-day operations. He or she directs the day-to-day activities of the front desk, the bellstand, and the concierge staff.

front of the house—hotel departments with traditionally high amounts of guest contact.

full service—hotels that by definition provide their guests with services, amenities, and facilities that they want or need to complete a total hotel experience.

G

gateway cities—traditionally those located in an area that makes them the first practical stop for an international flight coming in to a country.

general cashier—an accounting employee who maintains the cash supply inside the hotel. The cashier audits each bank to ensure that proper accounting procedures are adhered to and to avoid fraud.

general manager—the person ultimately responsible for the hotel.

group arrival—occurs when a large number of guests from the same group arrive at once.

group base—the measurement of how many group rooms are "on the books" on a given night.

group block—the number of rooms the hotel is contractually required to provide a group.

group catering—functions such as meetings, events, and meal functions tied to a block of group guest rooms.

group catering contribution—defined as the catering business acquired by a hotel that has all, or a major portion of, the attendees staying at the hotel itself.

group function—can be a meeting, meal, dance, or any other gathering of more than one person. In addition, a group function must have at least 10 sleeping rooms per night associated with it.

group rooms—originate from reservations that are made to bring more than one guest into the hotel (usually 10 or more rooms per night).

group rooms worksheet—a tool the reservations department uses to aid in forecasting.

group résumé—a hotel document that communicates to all vital departments any aspect of a group that may affect them.

guaranteed no-show (GNS)—guaranteed reservation that is not occupied.

guest account—tracks all the data that pertains to an individual guest in a PMS system.

guest accounting—the tracking of debits and credits within the front office.

guest accounting menu—a PMS menu used to track all credit/debit transactions related to a guest's stay.

guest history account—records details of a hotel guest's stay. Room preferences, rates paid, outlet and ancillary usage, and other details are tracked for future marketing and guest service uses.

guest ledger—an all encompassing term used to track hotel transactions primarily before and during a guest's or group's stay.

guest registration menu—a PMS menu that contains all the pertinent information garnered from the initial reservation—i.e., name, arrival/departure, room preferences, method of payment, and other miscellaneous information.

guest room buyback process—allows housekeepers to "purchase" guest rooms over and above the number assigned to them in their initial section.

guest supply usage per occupied room—the measurement of housekeeping supplies used in a guest room averaged over time.

H

hard goods—guest room items that are difficult or expensive to replace, such as TVs or furniture.

history—the documented record of historical data.

house account—serves as a perpetual account to track recurring transactions that occur within the hotel.

house count—looks at how many rooms are in-house, how many are due to arrive, and how many are due to check out. That number, less any OOO rooms, yields a house count.

housekeeper's caddie—a handheld carrying case that can be easily brought into a guest room. Each caddie will consist of glass cleaner, bathroom cleaner, multipurpose cleaner, bath amenities (shampoo, conditioner, soap, etc.).

housekeeping cart—cart that holds the caddie, towels, linens, glasses, vacuum, and miscellaneous items needed to clean a guest room.

houseperson—the houseperson's role is to support the housekeepers and maintain the cleanliness of guest hallways.

hybrid markets—combined target markets.

I

IATA—International Association of Travel Agents.

incident report—report used to make documentation of any calls made to police, fire, or ambulance services and a summary of the circumstances surrounding said incident.

incidentals—nonroom and tax charges.

independent—In these hotels, the owner has no role in management or day-to-day operations. An independent group of managers are responsible to the owner for the hotel's performance.

individual booking cycle—the time between when an individual reservation is made and when that reservation is due to arrive.

individual market potential—the number of rooms a hotel has for sale within a give time frame.

in-house report—a front office report that lists each room that was occupied and not due to check out.

intermediary—person or entity that acts as a liaison between a guest and the hotel.

J

journey segment—is the maximum reasonable distance traveled in one day along trade or travel routes using the transportation of the day.

junction points—Areas where different trading routes intersected also became favored stopping points.

K

key control systems—ensure guest safety by changing the access to a guest room between guests.

L

liability—an economic obligation.

limited service—hotels that do not offer food and beverage outlets as well as meeting space.

local catering—non-group catering.

location types—classified by physical positioning in relation to the customers in the area and to their tangible locale.

lodging management association—the relationship between ownership and management.

M

management contract—is similar to a franchise in that it is supplied with standard operating procedures as well as quality and service level targets. However, these hotels differ in that they are actually operated by the company that supplied those standards.

management fee—fee paid by a hotel owner to a chain or management company in return for operational and management services.

manual posting—occurs when an individual must apply a charge to an account by hand.

market segment—a portion or segment of the actual or potential business mix at any given hotel.

market share—a hotel's occupancy performance in relation to other hotels within a predetermined competitive set.

market tolerance—method of determining average room rates by surveying rates offered by other hotels in the competitive set.

marketing plan—a document put together by a hotel's senior management to chart a course for the next year. It summarizes departmental goals, advertising schedules, financial targets, and market conditions. A marketing plan is sometimes referred to as a budget.

master account—encompasses registration/accounting information for an entire group, not individual attendees.

message report—prints out all the reports that were delivered via the PMS message system in the day. It is a backup document that serves as a permanent record.

mid-market—listed as being part of both the limited- and full-service hotel classifications because these hotels can vary from one place to the other.

minimum length stay (MLS)—a restriction that mandates that all new reservations stay at the hotel for a minimum number of nights.

MOD—manager on duty.

MOD report—a summary of all guest interaction and general hotel conditions during a given shift. This report serves as documentation for the general manager.

MSDS—Material Safety Data Sheet.

Murphy bed—bed that is stored in the wall of a guest room and pulled out when needed.

N

national accounts—preapproved direct billing can be extended to large accounts a hotel chain may do business with. These accounts do not have to go through the billing approval process at each individual hotel they wish to do business with.

needs analysis—the process where hotel owners and senior managers determine the required scope of a potential large purchase.

night audit—a department of the front office that assumes the role of reconciling a hotel's daily activities and transactions.

night audit report—data compiled by the night audit team for management review.

no-show report—This report is also run for the benefit of the accounts receivable department. The verification of who had a guaranteed reservation and did not show up will assist in determining who needs to be billed.

nonaffiliated management companies—organizations with no tie to a chain, but who also offer hotel management and operational expertise in much the same way a chain would.

O

occupancy—is the measurement of how many rooms are sold each night versus how many rooms the hotel has available to sell.

occupancy driven—management philosophy that may forgo a higher average rate for greater occupancy levels.

opportunity cost—Sleeping rooms at a hotel are considered a perishable commodity. Each night, when a room goes unsold, the hotel loses that opportunity to ever sell it again. A hotel cannot regain that opportunity.

out of order rooms report—Any room that cannot be sold must be listed. The reason for the OOO status (e.g., leaky shower, renovation) should be listed and an indication of action taken (notified engineering) should accompany it.

outlet—a food and beverage point of sale.

outlet/ancillary reconciliation report—a report incorporated into the night audit report that must match the total sales reports of each outlet/ancillary venue.

outsourcing—utilizing an outside vendor for products or services.

overselling—a hotel may sell more rooms than are actually in inventory.

owner-managed—consist of hotels where the owner has hired additional (nonfamily) personnel to help run the property.

owner-operated—a hotel that is run by an owner and the owner's family.

owner's equity—the level of ownership the owner has in the operation.

P

paid out slip—debits an account (charges) in return for cash paid out on the guest's behalf.

par—an inventory of supplies.

pass on log—guest information that requires in-depth explanation or other hotel issues that may impact the desk are often communicated via the pass on log.

per diem—typically applies to governmental employees traveling on business. Usually covers hotel, meals, and other out-of-pocket expenses.

perfect sell—reached when every room is occupied and no guest was walked.

petty cash slip—slip used for non–guest-related expenses incurred by the hotel.

pleasure transient—transient market subset comprised of guests traveling for pleasure.

PMS—property management system.

PMS summary-posting report—all the posting activities conducted during the course of business at the front desk is verified against individual bank outs and then included into the night audit report.

PMS hierarchy—the organization of specialized menus within a Property Management System's software.

PMS workstations—Area where a hotel employee or manager can access the Property Management System. Each workstation includes the software, hardware, and monitor.

POS—point of sale.

posting—the act of applying a debit or credit to an account.

pre-key/key pack—check-in system that begins the check-in process before guests arrive. To pre-key is to pre-assign guests a room and issue a key. The actual "key pack" is simply a document to hold the key.

prime selling time—the specific hours during the day when the transient guests are most likely to call in for a reservation.

product types—define a hotel's service level as well as its target market.

profit margin—determined by comparing the sales revenue versus the costs incurred in providing a service or product.

Q

quad occupancy—four occupants in a guest room.

R

rack rate—understood to be the highest published rate a hotel can charge for a specific room.

rate averaging—simply averaging the target rates for any multiple-night reservation.

rate driven—management philosophy that may forgo occupancy levels for higher average rates.

rate restrictions—yield management tools that hotels use by limiting options available to the hotel guest for transient reservations.

rate spread—the difference between the single and double occupancy rates.

rate structure—combination of all the rates offered at a hotel.

rate trigger—a signal programmed into the reservation computer system that instructs it to change the rate based on preset criteria.

readerboard—a listing of meetings taking place at the hotel. Often posted throughout the facility and available on in-room closed-circuit TV channels.

receivables—revenue due to the hotel.

receptive customer—one who is more likely to be interested in a product or service than the general population due to personal interest or need.

referral organization—an association of non-chain affiliated hotels who pool marketing and other resources for mutual benefit.

registration card—a preprinted card that summarizes much of the information contained in the guest registration menu of PMS. It is used to verify the accuracy of the information.

remote check-in—using signage identifying a group, a separate table is set up to accommodate the arrivals and check guests into the hotel; sometimes referred to as satellite check-in.

reservation avenue—a means by which a guest is able to make a reservation at a hotel.

reservation card—a preprinted form that group guests would fill out to make reservations.

reservations map—used to determine what types of rooms are available and when they are available.

resident manager—in charge of all rooms-related functions.

rev-par—revenue per available room.

revenue source—is the result of a product or service a hotel makes available to guests for a price.

rightful market share—reveals how much of the total market potential is made up by its own individual potential.

ROI—return on investment.

room cost—calculation of fixed costs a hotel incurs in preparing a room for sale. Room cost is incurred whether the room is sold or not.

room designation—identifies whether the sleeping room is a smoking or non-smoking room.

room rack—prior to the integration of PMS systems, hotel rooms were laid out behind the front desk in a room rack. The room rack would identify each room type and configuration at a glance.

room rate—the price of hotel accommodation units.

room rate designation—the term used to specify the rate threshold within the overall structure.

room rate posting report—generated for inclusion into the night audit report that verifies the rates for all the rooms within the hotel occupied nightly for management review.

room status code—describes a guest room's readiness for occupancy by combining both occupancy and cleanliness information.

room status reconciliation—ensuring that rooms are properly designated by their current status, and assigned a new status as it changes.

room preferences—defined as the individual guest's choice of room type, configuration, and designation.

room types—based on the intended number of occupants.

rooming a guest—escorting a guest to the room.

rooms controller—reservations employee tasked to block rooms for arriving group and transient guests.

rooms inspector—person assigned to a group of eight housekeepers to inspect the cleanliness of guest rooms at random.

routing—the process where credits/debits incurred by one account are manually or automatically transferred to another account.

run of house (ROH)—another way of describing the standard sleeping room configuration.

S

seasonality—term used to define the time of year when a special attraction is open or at its peak level. (Terms also used to describe seasonality are "in season" and "off-season.")

section—the assignment of rooms to an individual housekeeper.

series groups—groups who book several programs at one time.

service level—is measured by the amount of actual and perceived consideration a guest can reasonably expect to receive.

service mission statement—serves as the rule and/or goal of the guest service philosophy of a hotel.

sign all charges (SAC)—this billing arrangement allows for each member of a group to "sign" all their charges to the group. The group will pay for everything.

sign room and tax (SRT)—this arrangement allows for the group to pay the room and tax charges for the attendees. The guest is responsible for their incidentals.

signature attractions—hotel features that are unique to the property.

single occupancy—one occupant in a guest room.

sleeping room—traditionally the main product for sale at any hotel.

slippage—the term used when analyzing the group room performance. It is the difference between what is contracted and what actually arrives.

SMERF—market segment encompassing the Social, Military, Educational, Religious, and Fraternal markets.

soft goods—easily replaced and relatively inexpensive guest room items, such as bedspreads and draperies.

special attraction—a service or facility that attracts guests for a reason other than the hotel itself.

standard configuration—defined as the room configuration that makes up the majority of the sleeping rooms at a particular hotel.

state of cleanliness—a room status code describing a guest room's cleanliness standing. Those states are (1) Dirty (applies to a room that has not been cleaned by housekeeping); (2) Clean (room has been cleaned but not yet inspected).

state of exception—a room status code describing the reason a guest room is not available for sale. That state is Out of Order (room was removed from inventory for a specific reason such as repairs or renovation).

state of occupancy—a room status code describing a guest room's occupancy standing. Those states are (1) Occupied (applies to a room that has been assigned to a guest and that guest has checked in; (2) Vacant (the guest has checked out

of the room); (3) Ready (room is available for new occupancy).

suburban—a hotel location type identifying non-resort hotels that are not in the downtown or airport areas.

suite configuration—involves a larger room (in terms of square footage) than the standard configuration.

T

target rate—an average rate goal a hotel sets to achieve for a certain day or market segment.

target market—a (combination of) market segment(s) the hotel wants to penetrate.

tariff sheet—document posted on the back of guest room doors that indicates what the rack rate is for that particular room.

10x10 rule—has two parts. The first part states that a guest's perception of the entire stay is, in large measure, instilled in the first 10 minutes upon arrival. The other part states that the front desk must greet a guest 10 feet before he/she approaches the front desk.

total market potential—the total number of available hotel rooms within the competitive set.

transient rooms—rooms that originate from individual reservations.

triple occupancy—three occupants in a guest room.

turn—Housekeeping is said to turn a room when it goes through the act of cleaning and preparing it for resale.

turndown service—the process by which the guest room is made warm and inviting for the evening.

U

upgrades—the process of offering a better room type than initially reserved.

upselling—the ability to move a guest from a lower-priced product to a higher-priced product.

USALI—uniform system of accounts for the lodging industry.

W

walk-in reservations—made by guests arriving unannounced at a hotel looking for rooms.

walked reservation—a guest who must stay at some location other than where they were initially booked to be.

walkouts—those who leave a hotel before properly settling their accounts.

Y

yield management—the pricing strategy managed by a hotel's reservations department. Because a hotel has a group base before the booking cycle starts, the reservations department can charge room rates based on how many rooms are available.

Index

349